ONLY IN
BERLIN

Duncan J. D. Smith

ONLY IN
BERLIN

A Guide to Unique Locations,
Hidden Corners and Unusual Objects

Photographs by
Duncan J. D. Smith

The Urban Explorer

For Roswitha with love and thanks
– and the many friendly Berliners who offered their time and help to
me along the way

Above: Ornate ironwork on the Schlossbrücke, between Unter den Linden and Museum Island

Page 2: Europe's first traffic lights on Potsdamer Platz

Contents

Outer Suburbs – Southwest
(District VI – Steglitz-Zehlendorf, VII – Tempelhof-Schöneberg, & Potsdam)

Inner City – East
(District II – Friedrichshain-Kreuzberg)

Outer Suburbs – Southeast
(District VIII – Neukölln, IX – Treptow-Köpenick)

Outer Suburbs – Northeast
(District III – Pankow, X – Marzahn-Hellersdorf, XI – Lichtenberg)

Appendices

Introduction

"Berlin combines the culture of New York, the traffic system of Tokyo,
the nature of Seattle, and the historical treasures of, well, Berlin."

Hiroshi Motomura, U.S. law professor (2004)

Straddling the Spree and Havel rivers, as well as numerous lakes and
canals, Berlin is one of the most dynamic and fascinating capital cities
in Europe; its tumultuous history over the last century makes it also one
of the most controversial. The spate of guidebooks published since the
fall of the Berlin Wall in 1989 offers the undemanding visitor a broad
and easily accessible array places to visit reflecting the history of the city
from the time of the Hohenzollerns and the Weimar Republic, via the
Third Reich and the Cold War, up to the present day. However, much of
what is proffered tends to bolster the opinion of Kaiser Wilhelm II (1888–
1918)* that "there is nothing in Berlin that can captivate the foreigner,
except for … museums, castles and soldiers". With these words in mind
this new guide has been written, especially for those who want to discover something more of the place for themselves. It only takes a few
minutes of planning, and a glance at a decent street map**, to escape the
crowds and the orchestrated tours and discover a rather different Berlin.

Based on personal experience walking the city's twelve districts
(*Bezirke*) – more correctly boroughs – the author points his fellow explorer in new and unusual directions. This is the Berlin of peaceful former villages, crumbling wartime bunkers and little-known public gardens; traditional breweries and ruined churches; quirky museums and
grand villas; Oriental tea houses and unusual hotels; colourful market
halls and vintage cinemas; not to mention an abandoned pneumatic
postal system and a half-buried Second World War anti-aircraft tower,
both of which can now be visited. Berlin remains, however, a city with a
dark and turbulent past, its myriad memorials to the victims of Nazi and
Soviet aggression, forgotten Jewish cemeteries, battle-scarred buildings,
and Communist-era statuary still bearing grim witness to terrible times.

Several of these uniquely historic locations lie in the city's former
medieval walled town of Berlin-Cölln (today's Museumsinsel and
Nikolaiviertel), as well as in the Baroque 'new towns' of Friedrichstadt,
Friedrichswerder, and Dorotheenstadt, located either side of Unter den
Linden in the historic district known today as Mitte (District I); others
are located in the more workaday Friedrichshain-Kreuzberg (District
II) to the southeast. However, a similar number lie *outside* these long-
established areas of occupation, in the leafy bourgeois suburbs along

the banks of the Havel to the northwest (Districts IV, V and XII), as well as in those to the southwest, around Wannsee and the Teltowkanal (Districts VI and VII). A healthy number are also located in Potsdam, the independent capital city of Brandenburg just outside Berlin.

Despite much of Berlin's urban expansion having been traditionally westwards, the city's industrialised working class suburbs in the east are full of interest too, both beyond the Spree to the northeast (Districts III, X and XI), as well as beyond the former Tempelhof Airport to the southeast (Districts VIII and IX), in what were once predominantly Communist areas behind the Berlin Wall.

Using Berlin's extensive transport network of underground trains (*U-Bahn*), suburban trains (*S-Bahn*), regional trains (*Regionalbahn or RE*), trams (*Straßenbahn/MetroTram*), and buses (*Autobus/MetroBus*), the explorer can quite quickly reach all the places described within the following pages – and that's without detracting from the sense of personal discovery that each of these places has to offer. Indeed, directions have been kept to a minimum so as to leave the visitor free to find their own particular path. Whether searching for remnants of Berlin's medieval town walls, tracking down the building where the atom was split, marvelling at Buddhist treasures from the Silk Road, descending into the crypt of the Hohenzollerns, or exploring the follies of Peacock Island, it is hoped that the visitor will experience a sense of having made the discovery for themselves.

In embarking on these mini-odysseys in search of Berlin's tangible historical legacy the author would only ask that telephones be switched off in places of worship, and due respect be shown at the numerous memorial sites dedicated to those persecuted during the city's short but turbulent history. Other than that, treat Berlin as a giant oyster containing many precious pearls – I just hope you enjoy finding them as much as I did.

Duncan J. D. Smith, Berlin & Vienna

---

* The dates given after the names of Germany's various monarchs are the actual years they reigned for, whereas those given after important non-royal personalities relate to their birth and death.

** Most street maps of Berlin cover the central area and inner suburbs; the excellent Falk Stadtplan Extra map also includes the outer districts, as well as tram, bus, metro and rail routes throughout the city. Please note that the house numbers on many streets in Berlin commence sequentially on one side of the street and then, at end of the street, switch to the other side and run back in the opposite direction.

The Church of St. Nicholas on Nikolaikirchplatz is the oldest church in central Berlin

1 Medieval Berlin

District I (Mitte), a tour of medieval Berlin beginning with the Chapel of the Holy Ghost (Heilig-Geist-Kapelle) at Spandauer Strasse 1
S5, S7, S9, S75 Hackescher Markt

Most guidebooks including this one will tell you that little remains of the medieval town of Berlin-Cölln, which was founded around 1200 on opposing banks of the River Spree (see no. 2). From documentary and archaeological evidence we know that the twin settlement was walled, Cölln occupying the southern part of what is now Museum Island (Museumsinsel), Berlin lying on the eastern bank of the Spree, encompassed by today's elevated S-Bahn railway: the two have remained connected by the Mühlendamm (Mill Dam) ever since.

The densely packed houses of old Cölln were swept away during the 1960s by the authorities of the GDR (German Democratic Republic). By then its medieval structures had long since vanished, the Dominican monastery (Dominikanerkloster) of 1297 having been replaced by the Berlin Cathedral (Berliner Dom), and the early 13th century Church of St. Peter (St. Petrikirche) remembered only by the presence of a later presbytery building on Brüderstrasse (see nos. 5).

Of medieval Berlin there is a little more to see – but only if one knows exactly where to look. An interesting tour of these shadowy remains can be made by entering the old town through what was once the Spandau Gate (Spandauer Tor), at the

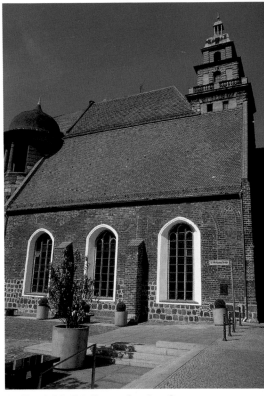

The Chapel of the Holy Ghost on Spandauer Strasse

northern end of Spandauer Strasse, near the Hackescher Markt S-Bahn station.

The first medieval remnant encountered is not only the most interesting but also the least well-known. The little red-brick Chapel of the Holy Ghost (Heilig-Geist-Kapelle) at Spandauer Strasse 1 is the only surviving hospital chapel in Berlin. Built as part of a hospital complex, called variously the Siechenhof ('Invalid Court') or the Armenhof ('Poorhouse') of the Holy Ghost, it first enters the history books in 1272. The city council was responsible for its upkeep and its nurses were Beguines, that is lay sisters sworn to an oath of poverty but who did not take monastic vows. Although rebuilt in the 15th century the hospital was eventually demolished in 1886. The Gothic red-brick chapel, however, was retained and in 1906 it was incorporated into a newly erected business school, now part of the Humboldt University (Humboldt-Universität). The chapel's modest interior features a fine 15th century star-shaped roof vault supported on consoles decorated with the statues of prophets and saints.

The hospital also had its own cemetery, which according to 17th century maps extended westwards down to the banks of the Spree. Excavations south and west of the college have revealed three hundred skeletons orientated east-west in the customary Christian manner. Likely to have been orphans, loners, the poor, and the infirm, the bodies were wrapped simply in sheets and buried in modest wooden coffins.

Moving south along Spandauer Strasse a left turn leads to one of medieval Berlin's two Gothic churches, namely the Church of St. Mary (Marienkirche) at Karl-Liebknecht-Strasse 8. It was founded around 1270 although its distinctive tower was not erected until the 15th century, the neo-Gothic dome being added in 1790 to a design by Carl Gotthard Langhans (1732–1808). The highlight of the interior is a 22-metre-long Gothic wall fresco of 1485 called *Totentanz* ('Dance of Death'), painted on the wall of the tower after an outbreak of plague. Now looking somewhat forlorn the church would originally have been at the centre of a densely built-up neighbourhood called the New Town extension begun around 1250.

Farther along Spandauer Strasse is the so-called Red Town Hall (Rotes Rathaus) at Rathausstrasse 15. Named because it is made of red bricks – and not because it was later the seat of the Communist administration of East Berlin – it stands on the site of a medieval predecessor. Of that 13th century building only its arcaded courthouse survives, having been moved out to Park Babelsberg when the present Red Town Hall was built in 1868 (see no. 47). A replica of the courthouse, known as the Gerichtslaube, was subsequently built in 1969 on a new site at nearby Poststrasse 28. (At Poststrasse 23 is the Knoblauchhaus, the only Baroque building in the area to escape damage during the Second World War. Built in 1760 its neo-Classical façade was added in 1835. The house was once inhabited by Eduard Knoblauch, architect of the New Synagogue (Neue Synagoge) on Oranienburger Strasse.)

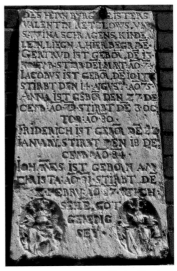

A medieval gravestone outside the Church of St. Mary

Adjacent to the Gerichtslaube stands the Church of St. Nicholas (Nikolaikirche) on Nikolaikirchplatz, Berlin's original parish church and the oldest extant ecclesiastical building in central Berlin. The original structure was erected around 1230, when the town was granted its municipal rights, the oldest visible part being the Romanesque base of the massive front tower built in 1300. The main body of the church is Gothic and was built between 1380 and 1450. Destroyed by bombing during the Second World War it was rebuilt in 1987 (as were its distinctive twin spires from the 1870s) and it now houses a museum of medieval artefacts. An adjoining cemetery containing ninety graves has been excavated by archaeologists.

Like the Church of St. Mary, the Church of St. Nicholas was once surrounded by narrow streets and tightly packed medieval houses. However, the buildings seen here today are mostly reconstructions, the originals having been destroyed during the Second World War. Unlike neighbouring Cölln, the GDR authorities decided to reconstruct the area as part of celebrations marking the 750th anniversary of the founding of the city. Unfortunately, many of the buildings in what is known today as the St. Nicholas Quarter (Nikolaiviertel) are not in their original locations and the resulting architectural pastiche is usually thronged with tourists. For a more authentic taste of Berlin's Old Town (Alt Stadt) it is better to finish this tour amongst the genuinely atmospheric ruins of the Franciscan monastery church (Franziskaner-Klosterkirche), built in the 1250s against the old town wall at what is now Klosterstrasse 74 (see no. 3).

Other places of interest nearby:
2, 3, 4, 5, 6, 7, 8, 14, 15, 16, 17, 18, 19

2 The Other Berlin Walls

District I (Mitte), a tour of Berlin's former city walls beginning with a fragment on Waisenstrasse
U2 Klosterstrasse

For visitors and locals alike there is really only one Berlin Wall, erected in August 1961 and breached in November 1989 (see no. 70). For some it may therefore come as a surprise to learn that Berlin previously had several other walls, fragmentary evidence for which can still be found.

Around 1200 the twin settlements of Berlin and Cölln were founded on opposite banks of the River Spree, Cölln on the southern part of what is now Museum Island (Museumsinsel), and Berlin on the eastern side of the river, encompassed by what is today the elevated S-Bahn railway (see no. 1). During the second half of the 13th century both settlements were surrounded by a water-filled moat and defensive wall, built of fieldstone and brick, and in 1307 they formed a joint government. Although most of the medieval settlement vanished centuries ago, there can still be found a solitary stretch of the original town wall tucked away on Waisenstrasse, not far from the ruins of a contemporary Franciscan Friary Church (Franziskaner-Klosterkirche) (see no. 3). This valuable fragment has survived because it was an integral part of a row of houses that once adjoined the wall. Those that remain are amongst some of Berlin's most ancient and include the city's oldest tavern, Zur letzten Instanz ('Inn of the Last Instance'), dating back to 1621 and so named because it was frequented by the legal profession. (Another fragment of the first wall was revealed recently by archaeologists in Schlossplatz, with the ruins of a Dominican monastery alongside it from c. 1300.)

In 1415 the Holy Roman Emperor Sigismund of the House of Luxembourg (1410–1437) granted the impoverished territory (or 'Mark') of Brandenburg (actually named after an older town to the west) to Burgrave Frederick VI of the southern German family of Hohenzollern, who was known henceforth as Margrave Frederick I (1417–1426) of Brandenburg. Frederick and his heirs also gained the title of Elector of Brandenburg, making them one of only seven people empowered to elect a new Holy Roman Emperor. The twin towns of Berlin-Cölln quickly emerged as the leading commercial centre in the sparsely populated Brandenburg region prompting Elector Frederick II (1440–1470) to dissolve the joint government, revoke many town privileges, and compel Cölln to give up land on its northern edge for the construction of the town's first castle, work on which commenced in 1433. During the reign of Elector Joachim II (1535–1571) the castle was replaced by a Renaissance palace (the Stadtschloss) which became the permanent royal residence of the Hohenzollerns; by this time the townsfolk had become subject to feudal rule.

Despite suffering damage during the Thirty Years War (1618–1648) the Electorate of Brandenburg emerged as one of the most powerful German principalities of the 17th century. The era is defined by the reign of the 'Great Elector', Frederick William (1640–1688), who enlarged his territory by diplomacy and military posturing rather than actual conquest. He sponsored the expansion of Berlin-Cölln (making the

A fragment of Berlin's medieval wall on Waisenstrasse

Stadtschloss the symbolic focal point of both city and state) and in 1658–1683 commissioned new fortification walls, encirling not only the existing town but also a strip of land on the opposite river bank directly west of Cölln, which in 1662 was granted a charter as the town of Friedrichswerder. In 1664 Frederick William issued a bold edict of religious tolerance in order to settle longstanding disputes between Lutherans and Calvinists, which attracted skilled merchants, craftsmen, and farmers in the process, who populated his expanded settlement. He also actively recruited persecuted Protestants, notably French Huguenots, as well as Jews expelled from Vienna. In 1674 he added a further town called Dorotheenstadt, directly north of a tree-lined boulevard leading westwards out of the city, the latter known thereafter as Unter den Linden, which he had added in 1647 in order to connect the palace with the royal game park (Tiergarten).

Of the Great Elector's 17th century walls little survives today. Suffice to say that on the north side of the Spree they continued to follow the line of the old medieval walls; unlike the medieval walls, however, these new defences took the form of a zig-zag series of prismatic bastions, with a gated bridge on what is now Alexanderplatz. South of the Spree the former line of the wall is remembered in the names of Wallstrasse and Niederwallstrasse, which are today followed by the U2 railway. The east end of the wall is marked by a brick-built turret in Köllnischer Park, today the grounds of the Märkisches Museum (see no. 4), whilst the west end stood at Hausvogteiplatz, which still retains the zig-zag line once followed by the bastions. A bridge across the moat at this point was rebuilt in 1787 and embellished with an ornate colonnade (the so-called Mohrenkolonnaden at Mohrenstrasse 37b and 40/41), which is still standing today (see no. 55). The moat was filled long ago and the bridge demolished during the 19th century (see no. 55).

The Great Elector was succeeded by his son Elector Frederick III (1688–1701), who added a fifth town, Friedrichstadt, south of Unter den Linden. The Friedrichswerder wall was accordingly shifted westwards to encompass this new settlement running along what is aptly called Mauerstrasse ('Wall Street'). It was Frederick who took advantage of the fact that Brandenburg had acquired the Duchy of Prussia to the east, outside the borders of the Holy Roman Empire, and curried favour with the emperor. As a result he was granted the right to crown himself Frederick I, King *in* Prussia (1701–1713) but not King *of* Prussia, since part of Prussia lay outside the formal boundaries of the Holy Roman Empire and belonged to the Polish crown. Then, in 1709 King Frederick I officially united the five towns into the single city of Berlin: thus did Berlin become the royal capital of a kingdom named after a territory far to the east.

In 1734, during the reign of King Frederick William I (1713–1740), the 'Soldier King', work began on a brand new town wall, encompassing not only all five former towns but much more besides. Known as the Customs Wall, because it was built to regulate commerce and to prevent soldiers deserting, it ran along Ebertstrasse, north and south of the newly built Brandenburg Gate (Brandenburger Tor), which was given its own drill ground (Pariser Platz) and named after the old town of Brandenburg to which it led. With this further expansion of Friedrichstadt came the creation of Wilhelmstrasse, which quickly became a favoured address for palaces of the nobility.

Southwards the Customs Wall ran to Potsdamer Platz, where the Potsdam Gate (Potsdamer Tor) once stood, inside which was another drill ground, octagonal Leipziger Platz. From here the wall followed Stresemannstrasse southeastwards, where there is a reconstructed wall fragment and information board in the middle of the street, as far as the Halle Gate (Hallesches Tor), again with its own drill ground (now

Mehringplatz). From here the wall ran eastwards along what is today the elevated stretch of the U1 railway, with another gate at Kottbusser Tor.

The Customs Wall reached the Spree at the Silesian Gate (Schlesisches Tor) from where its course is remembered mainly by street names. It ran northwards to the Frankfurt Gate (Frankfurter Tor) and then westwards along Palisadenstrasse and Torstrasse, past the Prenzlauer and Rosenthal Gates as far as the Oranienburg Gate (Oranienburger Tor), from where the wall completed its circuit back at Ebertstrasse. (Linienstrasse, one street to the south of Torstrasse, is named after a timber barrier that preceded the wall, against which an army officers' cemetery (Garnisonfriedhof) was laid out in 1722, at the corner of what is now Gormannstrasse).

Finally, in the 1830s the Customs Wall was further extended, north-westwards along what is now Han-

The Brandenburg Gate (Brandenburger Tor) was once part of the Customs Wall

noversche Strasse, and included another gate remembered in the name Platz vor dem Neuen Tor; a pair of modern red-brick buildings facing each other in the centre of the square today have been designed to remind passers-by of the former gateway's former appearance and location.

In 1788–1791, during the reign of King Frederick William II (1786–1797), a new Brandenburg Gate was erected to a design by Carl Gotthard Langhans (1732–1808), based on the Athenian Propylaeum. It was left standing when the Customs Wall was demolished in the 1860s only to witness the erection of a new wall a century later. The Berlin Wall followed exactly the same line north and south of the Brandenburg Gate as the earlier Customs Wall.

Other places of interest nearby: 1, 3, 4, 5, 6, 7, 66, 67

3　Churches in Ruins

District I (Mitte), the ruined Franciscan Friary Church
(Franziskaner-Klosterkirche) at Klosterstrasse 74
U2 Klosterstrasse

The most famous Second World War ruin in Berlin is undoubtedly the Emperor William Memorial Church (Kaiser-Wilhelm-Gedächtnis-Kirche) on Breitscheidplatz, at the eastern end of Kurfürstendamm (Charlottenburg-Wilmersdorf). The huge Rhenish-Romanesque church was designed by Franz Heinrich Schwechten (1841–1924) and built between 1891 and 1895. It was commissioned by the last emperor, King William II (1888–1918), in memory of his grandfather and namesake Emperor William I (1871–1888). Having been reduced to a smouldering ruin in 1943 the body of the church was cleared away leaving only the spire, at the base of which a *Gedenkhalle* ('Memorial Hall') was created after the war. Here can be found some stunning mosaics from the original building – including one depicting the Hohenzollern royal family – as well as various post-war memorials. They include the Coventry Crucifix made from nails found in the ruins of Coventry Cathedral in England after its destruction during a German bombing raid in 1940. In front of the main entrance to the building a new octagonal church has been built of concrete and blue glass. Designed by Egon Eiermann it was consecrated in 1961 together with a matching hexagonal bell tower on the former site of the original nave.

Berlin has several other ruined churches that are less well-known but no less interesting, for example the Franciscan Friary Church (Franziskaner-Klosterkirche) at Klosterstrasse 74. The friary stood just inside what was once the eastern wall of medieval Berlin, which also contained the Church of St. Nicholas (Nikolaikirche) and the Church of St. Mary (Marienkirche) (see no. 1). The Franciscans arrived in the town during the early 13th century and erected their church between 1250 and 1256. The triple-naved structure, with its elongated choir terminated at the east end by a seven-sided apse, is now considered the oldest and most beautiful early Gothic building in Berlin. After the Reformation, Protestants took over the church and in 1574 converted the friary buildings into the Gymnasium zum Grauen Kloster ('School At the Grey Cloister'), the city's finest grammar school. With its own dynastic family of teachers, the Bellermanns, the school produced such luminaries as royal architect Carl Frederick Schinkel (1781–1841) and

Otto von Bismarck (1815–1898), Chancellor of the German Empire from 1871 to 1890. The friary and church remained essentially unchanged until their destruction by bombing in 1945, after which the friary was demolished and the church preserved as a ruin. In 1992 a group of preservationists founded the Förderverein Klosterruine e.V, an association that uses the ruins for outdoor theatre, concerts, and art exhibitions during the summer months.

After visiting the ruins be sure not to miss the nearby Parochial Church (Parochialkirche) at Klosterstrasse 67, one of Berlin's very few Baroque churches. It too was seriously damaged during the war losing its tower and roof in the process. Today it is still used as a church, its bare brick walls, entirely stripped of their plaster, imbuing the place with a poignant atmosphere.

The ruined Franciscan Friary Church on Klosterstrasse

Another of Berlin's remaining Baroque churches is the Sophien Church (Sophienkirche) at Grosse Hamburger Strasse 29 to the northwest, beyond the old medieval walls. It was founded in 1712 by Queen Sophie Luisa of Mecklenburg, the third wife of King Frederick I (1701–1713), as the first parish church of the newly developed Spandauer Vorstadt area. Although the church survived the Second World War relatively unscathed, its walls remained for many years pockmarked with bullet holes. So as not to forget the conflict that inflicted similar damage on so many of Berlin's other buildings a patch of damaged stucco was preserved when the rest of the church was renovated: it bears the single word 'Pax' (Peace).

Continuing several streets north there stands St. Elisabeth's Church (St. Elisabeth-Kirche) on Elisabethkirchstrasse. Erected in 1830–1834 this elegant neo-Classical church was again the work of Schinkel in his capacity as court architect to King Frederick William III (1797–1840), and was one of four such churches in Berlin's new industrial northern suburbs. Seriously damaged during the fighting in 1945 it has been deconsecrated, its bare brick walls providing a backdrop for temporary exhibitions, concerts and other events. The surrounding churchyard

(Kirchpark der St. Elisabeth-Kirche) is now a small park and contains three bells that once hung in the church.

South of the Spree at Michaelkirchplatz 15, there stands another church partially ruined during the Second World War. St. Michael's Church (Michaelskirche) was built in red-brick between 1851 and 1861 to a design by August Stoller, a pupil of Schinkel, and was one of Berlin's largest Roman Catholic churches. Somewhat Italian in appearance and crowned by a graceful cupola supporting August Kiss's figure of the Archangel Michael, it was hailed by the author Theodor Fontane as the loveliest church in Berlin. Although today the central part of the church remains roofless, services are still held in one of the transepts restored in 1990.

Three final war-damaged churches represent the differing fortunes of Berlin's bomb-damaged buildings. The first, the Bethlehem Church (Bethlehemskirche), once stood in Bethlehemkirchplatz, a couple of streets east of Potsdamer Platz. It was built in the 18th century for Bohemian Protestants fleeing religious persecution. In 1963 the ruins of the church were levelled and marked out at pavement level with different coloured stones. By contrast, the unusual pentagonal German Cathedral (Deutscher Dom), built in 1701 several streets north at Gendarmenmarkt 1, underwent lengthy postwar restoration (between 1983 and 1996), the damage to its internal walls being left deliberately visible. Finally, not far to the east, stands Schinkel's Friedrichswerder Church (Friedrichswerdersche Kirche) on Werderscher Markt, which despite being gutted by fire also underwent restoration in the 1980s. Erected in 1824–1830 the church was Berlin's first neo-Gothic building in brick, reviving a Brandenburg architectural tradition from the Middle Ages.

Near the ruined Franciscan Friary Church on Klosterstrasse lie a pair of large Corinthian-style capitals. They come from Johann Friedrich Eosander von Göthe's early 18th century Baroque extension to the Stadtschloss, the vast Hohenzollern royal palace that for 500 years filled Schlossplatz at the northern end of Museum Island (Museumsinsel). The palace was damaged during the Second World War and demolished in 1950–1951 by the Soviets, in whose sector the building now lay. Under the GDR regime Schlossplatz was renamed Marx-Engels-Platz and in 1976 it became home to the Palast der Republik, which housed the GDR parliament. That too has been demolished and the palace is being rebuilt. Surely a sign of the times!

Other places of interest nearby: 1, 2, 4, 5, 6, 7, 66, 67

4 Fragments of a Bygone City

District I (Mitte), the Märkisches Museum at Am Köllnischen Park 5
S5, S7, S9, S75 Jannowitz Brücke; U2 Märkisches Museum, U8 Jannowitz Brücke

Sometimes overlooked because of its close proximity to the high profile Museum Island (Museumsinsel), the Märkisches Museum across the river at Am Köllnischen Park 5 not only provides a welcome respite from the crowds but also offers an idiosyncratic collection of exhibits from bygone Berlin. The exterior of the museum is itself unusual in that it resembles more a medieval monastery than a museum. It was built between 1901 and 1908 to a design by the architect Ludwig Hoffmann and harks back to the red-brick Gothic style of medieval Brandenburg.

Pseudo-Gothic Brandenburg brickwork at the Märkisches Museum

Inside, the museum chronicles the social and cultural history of Berlin and the Mark Brandenburg – whence the museum derives its name – from prehistoric times, through the Slavic period and the arrival of German settlers, to the foundation of the twin cities of Berlin and Cölln in 1200. From then on the collections illustrate the oft-told tale of how a provincial Hohenzollern garrison town was transformed into the capital of the German Empire. Amongst the thousands of fascinating exhibits on display there is a deer mask dated to 7000BC (the oldest exhibit in the museum), some exquisite Slavic silver jewellery, city models from 1450, 1688 and 1750, a horse's head from the *Quadriga* on top of the Brandenburg Gate (Brandenburger Tor), a sculptural fragment from Carl Frederick Schinkel's celebrated Prussian Architectural Academy (Bauakademie) demolished in 1962, a pair of ornate 18th century tile ovens once common in Berlin, a display of theatre memorabilia, and a collection of mechanical musical instruments, which can be heard each Sunday afternoon at 3pm.

Surrounding the museum is the Köllnischer Park, which is also home to various large-scale fragments of old Berlin. These include a sandstone *Hercules Fighting the Nemean Lion* by the sculptor Johann Gottfried Schadow (1764–1850), a 1740s-era stone vase that formerly adorned the roof of Schloss Sanssouci in Potsdam, the foundation of a windmill that stood here in 1700, and a cylindrical brick-built bastion from the 17th century town wall that once ran along here (see no. 2). Also in the park is a modern bronze statue of the Berlin illustrator Heinrich Zille (1858–1929), whose humorous depictions of Berlin stereotypes are displayed in the museum. Quite unexpected is an enclosure containing a pair of European Brown Bears (*Ursus arctos L.*). Their presence reminds us of the obscure origin of the bear as a symbol for Berlin. The name 'Berlin' is actually of Slavic origin and refers to the marshy ground prevalent across the city in its earliest days. The similarity of the name to the German word for bear (*Bär*) proved an irresistable choice when selecting a city emblem!

After leaving the park it is highly recommended to stroll along nearby Märkisches Ufer, once called Neukölln am Wasser, which is one of the few corners of Berlin where it is still possible to see the town as it must have looked during the 18th and 19th centuries; fortunately, the GDR regime designated the street an "island of tradition" in the 1960s. Of the eight houses preserved along the waterfront number 10 is especially striking. Once the home of Wilhelm Ferdinand Ermeler, who made his fortune trading in tobacco (hence the frieze above the door), the Ermeler House (Ermeler-Haus) was built in 1770 at Breite Strasse 11 in old Cölln (now the southern part of Museum Island). As a result of road widening in 1968 the building was dismantled and moved to Märkisches Ufer, where today it forms the rear of the Art'otel Berlin Mitte, which can be entered at Wallstrasse 70–73.

Other places of interest nearby: 1, 2, 3, 5, 6, 7, 66, 67

5   A Hidden Corner of Museum Island

District I (Mitte), the Nicolai House (Nicolaihaus) at Brüderstrasse 13 (note: the house is not open to the public) U2 Hausvogteiplatz or Spittelmarkt

Tucked away at Brüderstrasse 13, in the southern half of Museum Island (Museumsinsel), there stands a seemingly unassuming building called the Nicolai House (Nicolaihaus). It was built in 1670 in the Baroque style but is named after the writer, critic, publisher and editor Christoph Friedrich Nicolai (1733–1811), who lived and worked here after acquiring it in 1787. A leading light of the Berlin Enlightenment

The Baroque Nicolai House on Museum Island

(*Aufklärung*), Nicolai had the house modified into its present neo-Classical form by the stonemason Carl Frederick Zelter (1758–1832) (who incidentally went on to become a conductor and even taught Felix Mendelssohn).

Despite today being almost entirely hemmed in by modern buildings, many erected during the GDR period when the surrounding area was cleared, the Nicolai House has managed to retain an intimate and charming atmosphere redolent of a bygone age. It is generously proportioned, having more than thirty rooms as well as two elegant staircases: an original made of oak and another brought from the now-demolished Weydinger House (Weydinger-Haus) by way of the Ermeler House (Ermeler-Haus), which was itself dismantled and moved from nearby Breitegasse to Märkisches Ufer 10. It also has a cobbled inner courtyard, quite hidden from the street, around which runs a gallery overlooking a walnut tree.

In its new guise the Nicolai House became a focal point for the city's cultural elite, despite the fact that Nicolai himself was mocked in some quarters as having "failed to recognize Goethe's genius". Visitors to the house during his tenure included dramatist and writer Gotthold Ephraim Lessing (1729–1781), the Jewish philospher and social activist Moses Mendelssohn (1729–1786), architect Carl Frederick Schinkel

(1781–1841), draftsman and etcher Daniel Niklas Chodowiecki (1726–1801), and sculptor Johann Gottfried Schadow (1764–1850), responsible for the *Quadriga of Victory* on the Brandenburg Gate. Recently there has been a resurgence of interest in Nicolai amongst scholars re-evaluating the German Enlightment, and his position in the literary world of 18th century Germany has been reinstated.

It was also here that Nicolai installed a bookshop, as well as the famous publishing house Nicolaische Verlagsbuchhandlung, founded in 1713 by his father Christoph Gottlieb Nicolai. After Nicolai's death in 1811 the bookshop passed into the hands of his son-in-law, the bibliographer Gustav Parthey. The house continued to be a literary magnet, attracting the poet and soldier Theodor Körner (1791–1813), who lived here briefly during the Napoleonic wars, and the writer Charlotte Elisabeth (Elise) Konstantin von der Recke (1756–1833), who took up residence in 1814. Elise was the sister of the reigning Duchess of Courland (as Latvia was known at the time) and had been one of the last female acquaintances of the legendary Casanova, who died in 1798.

In 1892 the bookshop was moved to Dorotheenstrasse and in 1925 a new branch (Nicolaische Buchhandlung) was opened at Rheinstrasse 65 (Tempelhof-Schöneberg), where it remains to this day. The shop specialises in Berlin-related literature, including many titles published by Nicolaische Verlagsbuchhandlung, which after nearly three centuries remains one of Germany's leading quality publishers.

Next door but one to the Nicolai House is the Galgenhaus ('Gallows House') at number 10, where according to legend a maid was hanged for stealing a silver spoon, found later to have been trodden into the sand by a goat! Remodelled in 1805 in the neo-Classical style the house was built originally in the 1680s as a presbytery for the now vanished medieval Church of St. Peter (St. Petrikirche) (see no. 1).

The Danzig-born Baroque sculptor and architect Andreas Schlüter (1660–1714) also once lived on Brüderstrasse. He was responsible for the Baroque reworking of Berlin's Renaissance royal palace (Stadtschloss) during the 1690s, the bronze Equestrian Monument to the Great Elector (Reiterdenkmal des Grossen Kurfürsten) on Luisenplatz in front of Schloss Charlottenburg, the sculptures adorning the Zeughaus on Unter den Linden, and the legendary lost Amber Room *(Bernsteinzimmer)*, given as a gift by Frederick William I (1713–1740) to Tsar Peter the Great in 1716.

After leaving Brüderstrasse walk down either Sperlingsgasse or Scharrenstrasse to see Berlin's oldest bridge, the Jungfernbrücke, a Dutch-style drawbridge from 1798.

Other places of interest nearby: 1, 2, 3, 4, 6, 7, 8, 16, 17

6 The Crypt of the Hohenzollerns

District I (Mitte), the Hohenzollern Crypt (Hohenzollerngruft) in the Berlin Cathedral (Berliner Dom) on Am Lustgarten
S5, S7, S9, S75 Hackescher Markt

With the death in 1320 of Henry II (1317–1320), the last ruler of the House of the Ascanians, the Margraviate of Brandenburg became the object of a long and bloody feud between the House of Wittelsbach (1322–1373) and the House of Luxemburg (1373–1417). In 1411 the desperate townspeople appealed for help to the Holy Roman Emperor Sigismund (1410–1437), in response to which he sent Burgrave Frederick VI of Nuremberg, a member of the southern German family of Hohenzollern, as special protector. Frederick fought against the rebellious nobility and brought a measure of security, as a result of which Sigismund made him Margrave Frederick I (1417–1426), as well as Prince Elector of the Holy Roman Empire, a powerful privilege granted to Brandenburg by Golden Bull in 1356.

Under the Hohenzollern monarchy Brandenburg grew in power, especially during the 17th century when it inherited the Duchy of Prussia. As such, Brandenburg-Prussia was the predecessor to the Kingdom of Prussia, which was created in 1701. It in turn became a leading German state during the 18th century, although despite its name the Hohenzollern power base remained Brandenburg, with its two royal capitals of Berlin and Potsdam.

Although the Margraviate

Berlin's cathedral, the Berliner Dom

of Brandenburg was abolished in 1806 with the dissolution of the Holy Roman Empire, in 1815 it was superseded by the Prussian Province of Brandenburg. By 1871 the Hohenzollerns had become not only the most important family in Germany but had also been instrumental in the military revival of Prussia, the unification of Germany, and the creation of the German Empire, with Berlin as its imperial capital: they would remain in power until the abolition of the monarchy at the end of the First World War.

For an unusual glimpse of the Hohenzollern family that is far removed from their glittering palaces and military academies a visit to the Berlin Cathedral (Berliner Dom) on Museum Island (Museumsinsel) is highly recommended. Here can be found the fascinating Hohenzollern family crypt (Hohenzollerngruft), which contains nearly one hundred coffins and sarcophagi dating from the late 16th century up until the early 20th century. From the plain to the sumptuous, and made of stone, metal and wood, the tombs are an art lesson in themselves, demonstrating both Renaissance and Baroque styles.

The beginnings of the crypt date back to 1536 and the time of the Protestant Reformation, when the newly converted Elector Joachim II (1535–1571) decided that a late 13th century Dominican monastery church (Dominikanerkloster), south of the Hohenzollern palace inside what had been medieval Cölln, should become not only the court church but also the burial site for his family. A crypt was excavated and the remains of Electors John Cicero (1486–1499) and Joachim I (1499–1535) were placed here. Excluding George William (1619–1640), all subsequent Hohenzollern monarchs down to King Frederick I (1701–1713) were buried here too, the latter in an elaborate Baroque coffin designed by the sculptor Andreas Schlüter (1660–1714).

In 1747 King Frederick II, 'the Great' (1740–1786) commissioned a new Baroque cathedral to replace the old church and constructed a new crypt in the process, with King Frederick William II (1786–1797) the last monarch to be interred here. By this time the presence of groundwater and a risk of flooding prompted subsequent monarchs to have themselves buried in either Potsdam or at Schloss Charlottenburg. Although the cathedral was remodelled in 1821 by Carl Frederick Schinkel (1781–1841) it was eventually torn down and replaced during the reign of King and Emperor William II (1888–1918) (a few of the old columns can be found inside the Technical University (Technische Universität) at Strasse des 17. Juni 135). The new cathedral, designed by Julius Raschdorff (1823–1914) in the Italian High Renaissance style and built between 1894 and 1905 on Am

The sarcophagus of John Cicero of Brandenburg in the Hohenzollern Crypt

Lustgarten, was given a towering central dome in an attempt to make it a Protestant equivalent to St. Peter's Basilica in Rome. To emphasise the building's Hohenzollern connections a memorial chapel was added on the ground floor in which six important Hohenzollern sarcophagi were placed (Elector John Cicero, Frederick William 'the Great Elector' and his second wife Dorothea, King Frederick I and his wife Sophie Charlotte, and King Frederick III); the rest being installed in a new crypt below. (The only additional Hohenzollern to be laid to rest here *after* the construction of the new crypt was the Emperor's granddaughter, who died in 1915.)

On 24th May 1944 the cathedral received a direct hit during an Allied bombing raid causing extensive damage to the crypt and memorial chapel (the latter was subsequently demolished). The building was given a makeshift roof to keep out the elements and was effectively abandoned until reconstruction began in 1975. Not until 1993 was the restored cathedral reopened and the six sarcophagi from the memorial chapel put on display. In 1999 the crypt was opened up too, having never before been accessible to the public. It is an atmospheric and sombre place, its many coffins and sarcophagi partially concealed in permanent reverential gloom.

Other places of interest nearby: 1, 2, 3, 4, 5, 6, 7, 8, 14, 15, 16, 17, 18

7 Wonders ex oriente

District I (Mitte), the Pergamon Museum (Peramonmuseum)
on Am Kupfergraben
S5, S7, S9, S75 Hackescher Markt; S1, S2, S25 Friedrichstrasse;
U6 Friedrichstrasse; Tram 2, 4, 5, 12, M1, M2, M4, M5

Berlin's museum holdings of art and artefacts from the Near, Middle and Far East, an area known collectively by Western travellers as 'the Orient', are quite exceptional and feature many unusual objects. They include the Museum of Asian Art (Museum für Asiatische Kunst) and the Ethnological Museum (Ethnologisches Museum), both part of the Dahlem museum complex (Museen Dahlem) (see no. 40). They also include the Museum of Pre- and Early History (Museum für Vor- und Frühgeschichte), in the New Museum (Neues Museum) on Museum Island (Museumsinsel), containing the so-called 'Treasure of Priam', excavated by Heinrich Schliemann at ancient Troy. The civilisation of the Nile is represented by the Egyptian Museum and Papyrus Collection (Ägyptisches Museum und Papyrussammlung), also located in the New Museum. Undoubtedly the most famous object here is the mesmerising head of Queen Nefertiti, uncovered at Tell el-Amarna in 1912. On Museum Island too, in the Bode Museum (Bode-Museum) at Monbijoubrücke, is the Museum of Byzantine Art (Museum für Byzantinische Kunst), with its stunning mosaic icons from Constantinople, and the Numismatic Collection (Münzkabinett), displaying the world's first coins, from Asia Minor dating back to the 7th century BC (modern Turkey-in-Asia).

Adjacent to the Bode Museum stands the Pergamon Museum (Pergamonmuseum), built between 1912 and 1930 in order to house large-scale archaeological finds acquired during German expeditions to the Near and Middle East in the late 19th and early 20th centuries. It actually contains three distinct collections including the Museum of Near Eastern Antiquities (Vorderasiatisches Museum), featuring the reconstructed Gate of the Goddess Ishtar from Babylon and examples of man's earliest writing in the form of inscribed clay tablets from Uruk, and the Collection of Greek and Roman Antiquities (Antikensammlung) (a part of which is also displayed in the nearby Old Museum) containing the famous Pergamon Altar from Hellenistic-era Turkey.

The Pergamon Museum's third collection is the Museum of Islamic Art (Museum für Islamische Kunst). Three unusual exhibits warrant special attention, not only for their great beauty but also the excellence of their craftsmanship. The first is the 33-metre-long, ornately carved limestone façade of a desert palace from Mushatta, south of Amman in present-day Jordan. It was constructed in 744 AD during the Umayyad period as part of a series of defence fortresses for the Caliph al-Walid II (743–744 AD). The palace was deserted after al-Walid's murder and was later toppled by an earthquake, the ruins being used as a winter camp ('Mushatta' in Arabic) by Bedouin herdsmen. In 1903 the remains were given as a gift to the last German Emperor, King William II (1888–1918) by the Ottoman Sultan 'Abd al-Hamid II.

The Ishtar Gate from Babylon now stands in the Pergamon Museum

The second exhibit is a brilliantly-glazed, blue and gold *Mihrab*, a prayer niche built into the wall of a mosque to indicate the direction of Mecca (the *qibla*). This particular example, which is some four metres high, originally adorned a mosque erected in 1226 in the Iranian town of Kāšān. The town was renowned for its ceramics, its name being derived from the Persian word for 'tile'.

The final exhibit is the so-called Aleppo Room (*Aleppo-Zimmer*), an Ottoman reception hall built of painted wooden panels, which dates to the early 17th century and formed part of a Christian merchant's house in the Syrian city of the same name. The house itself is now the Beit Wakil hotel, its owners having sold the panelling to the Pergamon Museum in order to finance renovation work.

Other places of interest nearby:
1, 2, 3, 4, 5, 6, 8, 9, 10, 11, 14, 15, 16, 18, 19

8 Lenin's Head

District I (Mitte), the Lenin window in the Old Library
(Alte Bibliothek) on Bebelplatz
S1, S2, S25 Brandenburger Tor; U6 Französische Strasse

Visitors in search of the former East Berlin may well be disappointed to find so few fragments of the famous wall that once defined it (see no. 70). However, the area still contains plenty of other remnants from GDR times, mainly in the form of public sculpture, murals, and mosaics.

Like all cities once under the sway of the Soviet Union, East Berlin has its fair share of monuments in the so-called Socialist Realism style, the Stalinist art form and propaganda tool that emphasised heroic fighters, mourning mothers, militant politicians and happy workers. The most prominent examples are the three Soviet War Memorials (Sowjetisches Ehrenmal) unveiled between 1945 and 1949 in Treptower Park (Treptow-Köpenick), Volkspark Schönholzer Heide (Pankow), and on the Strasse des 17. Juni (Mitte) respectively (although the latter soon found itself in what became West Berlin). The three memorials act as the last resting place for more than 20000 Red Army soldiers, who lost their lives during the Battle for Berlin.

Another highly visible example is the oversized bronze bust of Ernst Thälmann on Greifswalder Strasse (Pankow), chairman of the German Communist Party from 1925, who was murdered in Buchenwald concentration camp in 1944. Fifteen metres wide and almost as tall it was commissioned in the 1980s by GDR leader Erich Honecker (1971–1989), Thälmann having been made into an anti-Fascist icon for the working classes, many of whom lived in the surround-

The Lenin window in the Old Library on Bebelplatz

ing pre-fabricated concrete apartment blocks of Prenzlauer Berg.

Two other prominent examples of Socialist Realism sculpture have not fared so well. The first, a huge statue of Communist Party General Secretary Joseph Stalin (1878–1953), once stood on Strausberger Platz at the entrance to Stalinallee, East Berlin's showpiece Socialist boulevard constructed in the 1950s (see no. 67). The statue was pulled down unceremoniously in 1961, after the Stalinist regime had been discredited by Nikita Kruschev, and the street re-named Karl-Marx-Allee.

A detail of the Lenin window

The second was Nikolai Tomsky's nineteen metre high statue of the Russian revolutionary and Communist politician Vladimir Ilyich Lenin (1870–1924), who became the first head of the Soviet Union in 1917. Hewn from Ukrainian red granite and unveiled in 1970 on Lenin's hundredth birthday by the GDR leader Walter Ulbricht (1950–1971) it was the focal point of a huge apartment complex designed by Hermann Henselmann on Landsberger Allee, which at the time was called Leninallee. Following German reunification the statue was taken down amidst tight security, cut into pieces and buried secretively in a gravel pit (the square on which it stood, called Leninplatz, was then renamed Platz der Vereinten Nationen). As was the case when it came to changing many of East Berlin's street names back to their pre-1933 forms, many former East Berliners ('Ossis') took offence, not only at losing what had become a familiar part of their urban landscape but also at being assimilated forcibly by the 'Wessis' into the ways of West German society; some critics suggested that Berlin's reorganised Communist party, the Party of Democratic Socialism, exploited this discontent.

Eventually, the hidden grave of Lenin's statue was discovered and souvenir hunters began chiselling pieces off as souvenirs. Attempts to further conceal it failed and it was proposed that the statue be ground down for building material. However, by this time it had achieved a sort of celebrity status, especially after the statue's three and a half ton head was seen being airlifted away by helicopter in the 2003 film *Goodbye Lenin!* Left-wing city councillors intervened to save what they called an "important part of the city's cultural heritage". In 2014 Lenin's head was put on public display in the Zitadelle Spandau at Am Juliusturm 64 (Spandau), and again opinions were divided. Understandably, some of those fighting to preserve what remains of the Berlin Wall as an important reminder of the divided city see the head's reappearance as an unwarranted glorification of a brutal era.

Elsewhere in the former East Berlin comrade Lenin retains a less controversial presence, for example in a surprising stained glass window entitled *Lenin in Deutschland* in the law faculty library of the Humboldt University (Humboldt-Universität), on the 2nd floor of the Old Library (Alte Bibliothek) on Bebelplatz. It commemorates the fact that Lenin studied here in 1895. Not far away at Unter den Linden 63–65 stands the Russian Embassy (Russische Botschaft), built of white marble between 1948 and 1953 in the prevailing neo-Classical style of Stalin's Soviet Union (typically it is adorned with working class heroes rather than Greek and Roman gods). Although a bust of Lenin in the garden vanished after the fall of the Soviet Union, his image is still very much in evidence on the façade of the embassy's brick-built former swimming pool, just around the corner on Behrenstrasse.

Most of East Berlin's other examples of Socialist Realism art are more modest works, emphasising the vital role played by the anonymous masses. Examples include the relief of a 'rubble woman', on a building by Hermann Henselmann facing the Weberwiese Park on Marchlewskistrasse (Friedrichshain-Kreuzberg), and the statues of a man and woman facing the Rotes Rathaus on Spandauer Strasse (Mitte), all three busy with rebuilding the war-damaged city. Not far away is the vast open space of Alexanderplatz, which features Henselmann's twelve-storey Teachers' Building erected in 1964 and adorned with a huge mural entitled *The Victory of the Human Being in Socialism*. On the western side of the square is the Marx-Engels-Forum, the focal point of which is a statue of the creators of 'Scientific Socialism', Karl Marx (1818–1883) and Friedrich Engels (1820–1895); erected in 1986 the absence of militant monumentality was supposed to convey a peaceful and secure East Germany. Other examples of late Socialist Realism include Werner Stötzer's *Reading Worker* (1961) in the forecourt of the Old State Library (Alte Staatsbibliothek) at Unter den Linden 8, and a glass mural depicting scenes from the workers' movement by Walter Womacka inside the former Staatsratgebäude on Schlossplatz.

Lenin's head on a former GDR swimming pool on Behrenstrasse

Our final example is probably the most telling about the erection of memorials in post-war Berlin. The massive former Reich Air Ministry (Reichsluftfahrtministerium) of Reichsmarschall Hermann Göring (1893–1946) at Wilhelmstrasse 97 (Mitte) has nothing on it to recall its significant wartime role. However, inside the pillared pavement loggia on the corner with Leipziger Strasse a mural from 1950 recalls the founding of the GDR, which was officially established here in 1949; not surprisingly it depicts happy workers in the Socialist Realism style. On 17th June 1953, 12000 East German workers gathered here to demand better working conditions, free elections and German reunification. Soviet tanks were used to crush the uprising leaving many dead. In 2000 a water feature commemorating the uprising was installed in the pavement in front of the mural, providing a deliberate contrast to the official version of the German workers' state and a tacit connection to the brutality of the previous Nazi regime.

For an idea of what is was like to live in East Berlin during the GDR regime visit the DDR Museum Berlin at Karl-Liebknecht-Strasse 1 (Mitte), where visitors can sit in a Trabant car and relax in the living room of a typical prefabricated apartment block.

Other places of interest nearby: 1, 2, 3, 6, 7, 9, 10, 11, 14, 15, 16

9 An Appointment with Hitler

District I (Mitte), the former site of Hitler's New Reich
Chancellery (Neue Reichskanzlei) at the corner of
Wilhelmstrasse and Vossstrasse
S1, S2, S25 Potsdamer Platz; U2 Mohrenstrasse, U2 Potsdamer
Platz

Of the numerous buildings erected by the Nazi regime during the Third
Reich, discounting the many unrealised ones drawn up as part of a
proposed rebuilding of Berlin as the world capital *Germania*, Adolf
Hitler's favourite was undoubtedly the New Reich Chancellery (Neue
Reichskanzlei) on Vossstrasse, designed for him by his preferred archi-
tect Albert Speer (1905–1981).

Far from becoming what Hitler claimed would be a "structure that
will outlast the centuries and will speak to posterity of our times" the
war-damaged New Reich Chancellery was levelled by Soviet authorities
in 1948, its subterranean cellars and air raid shelters mostly back-filled
as part of the construction of a series of huge GDR apartment blocks
in the 1980s. However, with a little imagination a walk taken along
Vossstrasse today can still evoke strong memories, helping visitors not
only to understand the way in which Hitler used the building to intimi-
date visitors but also to reflect on the colossal loss of life brought about
by some of the decisions that were made here. Thus, the former site of
the New Reich Chancellery can act both as an important reminder of
where the perpetrators of some of the greatest war criminals spent their
days, and as an invisible monument to their many victims.

The Second World War was the single deadliest conflict in world
history causing the death of approximately 72 million people (47 million civilians and 25 million soldiers). As we follow in the footsteps of
those visitors to the New Reich Chancellery more than seventy years
ago, from the main entrance on Wilhelmstrasse all the way to the Führer's office itself, it is sobering to bear in mind that *each* of the 200 or
so paces necessary represents more than 350 000 lives lost in a conflict
provoked by Nazi Germany.

The starting point for this virtual visit begins at the corner of Wilhelmstrasse and Vossstrasse, where once stood the Borsig Palace, one
of numerous nobles' palaces built here after the town of Friedrichstadt
was expanded in the early 19th century (see nos. 2). In 1934 Hitler
evicted Vice Chancellor Franz von Papen (1879–1969) from his offices

here and converted the building into the headquarters of the brownshirted pro-Nazi paramilitary organisation, the SA (*Sturmabteilung*), or 'Storm Division'. Attached to the north side of the palace, at what was once Wilhelmstrasse 78, was the so-called Siedler Building, an extension added in 1928–1930 to the south side of the Old Reich Chancellery (Alte Reichskanzlei) farther north at Wilhelmstrasse 77, which had housed Prussian Chancellor Otto von Bismarck (1815–1898) and his successors. In 1938–39 both the Borsig Palace and the Siedler Building were cleverly incorporated by Albert Speer into Hitler's New Reich Chancellery, the main façade of which ran the full length of Vossstrasse. It seems that the sole aim of the new building,

The former site of Hitler's New Reich Chancellery on Vossstrasse

with its series of oppressively long galleries, unnecessary steps, and oversized doors, was to belittle visiting diplomats room-by-room, whilst at the same time enhancing the stature of the Führer. As Hitler said himself, his New Reich Chancellery would give the visitor "a taste of the power and grandeur of the German Reich".

The New Reich Chancellery was entered by a great double doorway, cut by Speer through the façade of the Siedler Building, which had previously been described by Hitler as fit only for a soap company. The doorway, with vehicular access, stood some 30 paces north of where we are standing (near to where, coincidentally, a modern double entrance now stands at Wilhelmstrasse 93). However, since much of the site is now occupied by apartment blocks our entrance into the New Reich Chancellery must be replicated by walking 15 paces westwards along Vossstrasse itself.

At a point parallel to where we now stand the visitor would have entered the open-air Courtyard of Honour (*Ehrenhof*), an idea of its size being gained by walking a further 60 paces along Vossstrasse. A further 5 paces forward mimics entry into a stepped portico that lay at the far end of the courtyard, flanked by two bronze sculptures by official Nazi sculptor Arno Breker (1900–1991) representing the party (*Partei*) and the armed forces (*Wehrmacht*) (Breker's studio can still be found at Käuzchensteig 10 (Charlottenburg-Wilmersdorf)). We now enter the Chancellery proper.

Beyond the portico lay an ante-room (*Vorhalle*), represented by walking another 10 paces onwards (to check your pacing at this point, ensure that the former Reich Transport Ministry building at Vossstrasse 33–35, the only extant building from the time of the New Reich Chancellery, is directly across the road). The ante-room gave onto the Hall of Mosaics (*Mosaiksaal*) by means of a double doorway over five metres high. This hall was faced with red marble and its size can be gained by walking along Vossstrasse a further 40 paces. Hitler is said to have been delighted at the prospect of visitors slipping on the highly polished marble floor and refused to allow the use of carpets: "diplomats should have practice in moving on a slippery surface", he said.

Beyond the Hall of Mosaics and up some further steps lay the Round Salon (*Runder Saal*), some 15 paces in diameter. The salon's function was to alter the building's axis imperceptibly in order to navigate a bend in Vossstrasse (the bend can still be detected farther back along the road, the U-shaped ground plan of the apartment block at the corner of Wilhelmstrasse and Vossstrasse being broken slightly open to accommodate it; the salon itself lay between it and the adjacent apartment block on what is now Gertrud-Kolmar-Strasse).

Finally, and continuing westwards along Vossstrasse for a further 120 paces, we can imagine Speer's *pièce de résistance*: his 146-metre-long Marble Gallery (*Marmorgalerie*) (its eastern third would have fitted snugly within the inside corner of today's second apartment block). Fitted out with paintings, tapestries, candelabra, and fine furniture, the Marble Gallery greatly pleased Hitler since it was twice the length of the Hall of Mirrors at Versailles.

Half way along the Marble Gallery, reached by walking 60 paces from the Round Salon, there stood a marble-framed double doorway reaching almost to the ceiling. Above it were inscribed the initials "A.H." leaving the visitor in no doubt as to whose room it was. Located where there is now a car park for two modern government buildings on the south side of In den Ministergärten (some 45 paces north from Vossstrasse), Hitler's study (Arbeitzimmer des Führers) was 390 square metres in size and contained his marble map table, a huge metal globe, Franz von Lenbach's portrait of Bismarck, and a desk inlaid with a mask of Mars, a sword, and a lance. "That should make visiting diplomats shiver and shake", Hitler said of the desk, which can be seen today in the German Historical Museum (Deutsches Historisches Museum) in the former Arsenal (Zeughaus) at Unter den Linden 2. Above the doorway on the inside of the room was a stylised martial eagle clutching a swastika, one of several in the Chancellery building, which were removed as spoils after the building was stormed by Red Army troops on 30th April 1945 (see no. 10). Directly beneath the study was a large air raid shelter with a ceiling 1.7 metres thick, either side of which ran a series of normal cellars along the length of the Marble Gallery. Not deemed strong enough for Hitler, who later moved into the so-called Führer Bunker nearby, the shelter would be used by civilians and as a military hospital from January 1945 onwards.

Although Speer's New Reich Chancellery is long gone, an idea of its proportions can be gained from the Ehrenhalle of the Messegelände on Hammarskjöldplatz (Charlottenburg-Wilmersdorf), which displays the same pared-down and repetitive neo-Classicism so typical of Third Reich public architecture. The Chancellery's former opulence can also be glimpsed since its red marble was reused in the construction of the Soviet War Memorial (Sowjetisches Ehrenmal) in Treptower Park and the rebuilding of the nearby Mohrenstrasse U-Bahn station.

Another vanished but still potent Nazi site can be found a couple of roads south of the New Reich Chancellery on what was once Prinz-Albrecht-Strasse (now Niederkirchner-strasse). Number 8 was once home to the Reich Security Main Office (Reichssicherheits-hauptamt) under Heinrich Himmler (1900–1945), which included both the Security Police (Secret State Police *(Gestapo)* and Criminal Police), and the Security Service *(Sicherheitsdienst)* of the SS *(Schutzstaffel)*. Excavations at this once-feared address have revealed the cells in which the Gestapo interrogated their prisoners. The site is now preserved as the Topography of Terror (Topographie des Terrors).

Other places of interest nearby: 8, 10, 12, 63, 64

10 The Facts about the Führer Bunker

District I (Mitte), the former site of Hitler's last command
shelter (Führerbunker) at the junction of In den Ministergärten
and Gertrud-Kolmar-Strasse
S1, S2, S25 Potsdamer Platz; U2 Mohrenstrasse

It is not really surprising that the highest concentration of Second
World War air raid shelters in Berlin existed below the Nazi regime's
government quarter (*Regierungsviertel*), bounded by Wilhelm-, Voss-,
and Ebertstrasse (the latter known at the time as Hermann-Göring-
Strasse). Many of the ministries, party offices and other administrative bodies hereabouts were fitted with their own personal shelters,
most famous of which was Hitler's last personal command shelter, the
much-storied Führer Bunker (*Führerbunker*).

There has probably been more written about this inaccessible and
largely destroyed underground structure than any other subterranean
location in the world, primarily because it was here on the afternoon
of 30th April 1945, with a vengeful Red Army scarcely 100 metres away,
that Adolf Hitler and his newly-wed bride Eva Braun took their own
lives. Since then many books have been written about the increasingly
desperate events leading up to and following the suicides: the comings
and goings of Führer's ever-diminishing circle of loyal supporters, his
futile attempts at commanding armies that no longer existed, his self-
pitying rants, his last birthday, the double suicide of Joseph and Magda
Goebbels after they had murdered their six children, and the post-war
visit by a triumphant Winston Churchill. Such tales have exerted a
ghoulish fascination over many readers to the extent that the relatively
mundane constructional (and deconstructional) history of the Führer
Bunker itself has often been either ignored or inaccurately related. Only
now, sixty years after it was abandoned, have the true facts finally
emerged from the depths.

The Führer Bunker actually comprised two distinct shelters. The
first was constructed in 1935–1936, directly beneath a banqueting hall
commissioned by Hitler in the Ministry Gardens, to the rear of Bismarck's Old Reich Chancellery (Alte Reichskanzlei) at Wilhelmstrasse
77 and a Foreign Office building at Wilhelmstrasse 76. Following air
raids made on Berlin by the Royal Air Force in January 1943 Hitler
ordered that a deeper and stronger westward extension be made to

An information board today marks the site of the Führer Bunker

this shelter, which was made habitable in mid-January 1945. Referred to as the Main Bunker – the earlier shelter being known henceforth as the Front Bunker (*Vorbunker*) – it is here that Hitler moved permanently sometime in late February or early March and where he spent the remaining days of his life.

Compared with Hitler's personal 390-metre-square office in his New Reich Chancellery (Neue Reichskanzlei) on Vossstrasse, which he had now abandoned, the concrete Führer Bunker complex provided dank, cramped but secure accommodation, its two shelters each affording approximately 250 square metres of useable space, in which 20 people had to live and work.

Surviving construction plans of the Front Bunker show that it had 19 rooms, with walls 1.2 metres thick and a ceiling 1.6 metres thick. (It is interesting to note that the word *Bunker* does not appear on these plans since it only entered Third Reich parlance in Autumn 1940.)

Of the Main Bunker no blueprint has ever come to light and its structural statistics have long been disputed, both by eyewitnesses and commentators. Regarding its depth Hitler's architect Albert Speer (1905–1981) probably came closest to the truth when he recalled it having a concrete base plate 2.5 metres thick, rooms that were 3.4

metres high, a massive steel-reinforced concrete ceiling up to 5 metres thick, and a 2-metre-thick layer of earth on top of that. Also subject to dispute are numerous claims about tunnels connecting the Führer Bunker to other government buildings in the neighbourhood, such as the neighbouring Foreign Ministry, Goebbels' Propaganda Ministry across the road, the Reichstag, the nearby north-south S-Bahn line, and even Tempelhof Airport. During the early 1970s a Stasi-led survey, prompted by concerns that spies as well as normal citizens might be using such tunnels to move unseen between East and West Berlin, provided no evidence whatsoever for the tunnels' existence.

In December 1947, in an effort to prevent the Führer Bunker becoming a grisly tourist attraction, Red Army engineers attempted to destroy the Main Bunker with explosives but succeeded only in demolishing its half-metre-thick partition walls and toppling the garden exit and its pair of ventilation shafts. Then in 1949 both chancelleries were torn down by the Soviets, so determined were they that nothing remain of the Nazi leader's former seat of power. The East German authorities made further efforts to destroy the bunkers in June 1959 amidst talk of converting the site into a people's park: holes were drilled into the ceiling of the Front Bunker (and probably also the Main Bunker) in which explosive charges were placed but again the operation failed. This time it was decided to conceal the entrance to the Main Bunker with an earthen mound.

With the erection of the Berlin Wall in 1961 the bunker site fell just inside the inner (or 'Hinterland') wall of the so-called 'Death Strip' (see no. 70). Visible from a viewing platform in West Berlin the mound above the bunker temporarily became an object of curiosity in its own right. Eventually in 1988 construction began on a series of huge, pre-fabricated apartment blocks along Wilhelmstrasse and part way along Vossstrasse for members of the GDR elite (to maximise the building space the 'Hinterland' wall had been moved westwards at this point). As a result the Front Bunker was removed entirely and at the same time the Main Bunker (as well as the easternmost 'small bunker' beneath the New Reich Chancellery's Mosaic Hall) had its ceiling and the tops of its side walls removed and the cavities below filled in. The Chancellery's 'large bunker' beneath Hitler's study was only partially cleared since it lay alongside the new line of the 'Hinterland' wall.

With the collapse of the GDR regime in November 1989 the Führer Bunker and Chancellery areas became accessible once again. Public knowledge of the Führer Bunker was negligible since discussion about the structure during GDR times had been taboo. This explains the spurious "re-discoveries" of the Führer Bunker in the popular press during the early 1990s – and at least one serious plan to open it up as a memorial despite it having been all but destroyed in 1988! Subsequent geomagnetic surveys have revealed that only the floor plate and the 3.5 metre-thick side walls to a height of 1.6 metres remain of the rubble-filled Main Bunker today.

On 8th June 2006, the site now considered sufficiently neutralised, a permanent information board was erected over the former site of the Führer Bunker (today a car park at the junction of In den Ministergärten and Gertrud-Kolmar-Strasse) in a ceremony attended by Rochus Misch, the last living person from those present in the Führer Bunker at the time of Hitler's suicide. The motive behind the board, which was financed not by the government but by a private initiative called the Berlin Underworlds Association (Berliner Unterwelten e.V.), is less about remembering the victims of the Nazi regime and more about not forgetting one of the key sites associated with the perpetrators of such terrible crimes.

Elsewhere on what still remains one of Berlin's most controversial pieces of real estate, other underground shelters remain partially or completely intact. These include the so-called *Fahrerbunker* ('drivers' shelter'), a part of the New Reich Chancellery's underground car park, which was unearthed in 1990 at the corner of Ebertstrasse and Vossstrasse. Found to contain amateurish wall paintings depicting SS soldiers protecting Germany's women it remains sealed and unmarked whilst the land above it has been redeveloped. Even more controversial was the discovery of the personal command shelter of Propaganda Minister Joseph Goebbels (1897–1945), during the construction of the new Holocaust Memorial on Ebertstrasse (see no. 11). Occupying what was once the cellar of his town villa it today lies forever hidden beneath a monument to the memory of the people his regime attempted to eradicate.

Other places of interest nearby: 8, 9, 12, 63, 64

11 Holocaust Memorials

District I (Mitte), the Holocaust Memorial (Holocaust Mahnmal)
on Ebertstrasse
S1, S2, S25 Brandenburger Tor; U2 Potsdamer Platz

In 2003 the construction of an official memorial for the five to seven million European Jews killed under the Nazi regime between 1933 and 1945 began. It was unveiled on 10th May 2005 at a cost of 27 million Euros and was visited by 3.5 million people in its first year. Still attracting 2000 visitors daily Berlin's Memorial to the Murdered Jews of Europe (Denkmal für die ermordeten Juden Europas) on Ebertstrasse can hardly be considered one of the city's hidden corners, but it is certainly one of the most unusual.

Known more commonly as the Holocaust Memorial (Holocaust Mahnmal) it was designed by the American architect Peter Eisenman and consists of 2711 steel-grey concrete blocks of slightly varying heights (called 'stelae'), which are spread across an undulating area of 20 000 square metres. Visitors are able to access the monument at any point and walk between the tomb-shaped blocks, the overall effect being akin to walking along the serried ranks of graves in a cemetery. But Eisenman's blocks are uninscribed: they are cenotaphs to those who have no grave. The blocks are tall too, which combined with the narrow paths between them, creates a deliberately claustrophobic and disorienting feeling of a once ordered system that has broken down. The experience remains with the visitor long afterwards.

However, far from being a vast *ersatz* necropolis to the nameless, the concrete blocks represent only a part of the memorial: below ground there is an information hall that holds the names of all known Jewish victims of the Holocaust, obtained from the Yad Vashem museum in Jerusalem. Taken together, the two parts represent a bold and original attempt not only at memorialising the Jewish victims of Nazi aggression but also at coming to terms with the fact that the crime was perpetrated by Germans living and working nearby. The latter is hard to escape when one is reminded that the memorial occupies the former Ministry Gardens of the Nazi government quarter along Wilhelmstrasse, where high ranking officials once strolled. Indeed, preliminary work on the memorial uncovered the personal command bunker of Propaganda Minister Joseph Goebbels (1897–1945) in the northeast corner of the site, beneath what had been his town residence; it is today sealed and unmarked.

A part of the Holocaust memorial on Ebertstrasse

Needless to say, the memorial courted controversy from the start, not least when it was discovered that the company enlisted to produce an anti-graffiti coating for the memorial allegedly had links to a company that produced Zyklon B gas during the Second World War, which was used in the Nazi death camps. Criticism has also been levelled at the exclusive dedication of the monument to the Jews: some commentators are of the opinion that the term 'holocaust' – from the Greek *holokauston* meaning 'that which is completely burnt', itself a translation of the Hebrew *ōlâ* meaning 'that which goes up (in smoke)' – should refer to the total Nazi extermination programme, victims of which also included Roma, Jehovah's Witnesses, homosexuals, Russians, Poles, and many other minorities, bringing the total number of victims to between 10–14 million. It is interesting to note that the Hebrew word *shoah* (meaning 'catastrophe') was originally used to describe the Jewish genocide, only becoming 'holocaust' in the late 1950s, and eventually '*The* Holocaust" by the 1970s.

Until recently the non-Jewish victims of the Nazi regime were remembered only by modest memorials in the suburbs, for example one to homosexuals in Nollendorfplatz (Tempelhof-Schöneberg) and another to Roma and Sinti inside the entrance to the Marzahn Cemetery (Marzahn Städtischer Friedhof) at Wiesenberger Weg 10 (Marzahn-Hellersdorf) (during the Second World War a notorious 'gypsy camp' was located north of the cemetery in which many died). However, in 2008 a memorial to the Nazis' gay victims was unveiled opposite the Jewish Holocaust Memorial, consisting of a bunker-like block with a peephole through which a video-clip of two men kissing can be seen. And in 2012 a memorial to as many as half a million Roma and Sinti was unveiled near the Reichstag. It consists of a circular pool with a plinth in the middle on which a fresh flower is placed daily, acknowledging that anti-Roma sentiment is every bit as unacceptable as anti-Semitism.

Berlin's earliest memorials to the victims of the Holocaust take a variety of forms. They include a pair of wall plaques erected in the 1960s on Wittenbergplatz (Charlottenburg-Wilmersdorf) and Kaiser-Wilhelm-Platz (Tempelhof-Schöneberg), inscribed with an arbitrary list of concentration camps that have nothing to do with their specific surroundings. Another memorial on Steinplatz (Mitte), erected in the 1950s, is hewn out of stone salvaged from the ruins of the Fasanenstrasse synagogue (see no. 54). It is made all the more interesting by being deliberately sited next to a memorial to the victims of Stalinism, representing the postwar belief that the West was threatened by totalitarianism in general and not just either Fascism or Communism specifically.

The most unlikely Holocaust memorial is a bus shelter in front of a modern hotel at Kurfürstenstrasse 115–116 (Mitte). It marks the former site of the anonymously-titled Bureau IV B4, in reality a part of the Reich Central Office for Jewish Emigration and Relocation, from where Adolf Eichmann (1906–1962) organised the deportation of Jews from all over Europe to the death camps. By contrast, another unusual Holocaust memorial, on Rosenstrasse (Mitte), marks a unique victory for the city's Jews. In February 1943 the SS chose a Jewish community building here, next to Berlin's oldest synagogue, as a collection point for several hundred Jewish armaments workers not yet deported because they had 'Aryan' wives. When word spread of the arrests the wives gathered here in protest and the men were eventually released, albeit back into forced labour camps. This rare episode of open and successful defiance of the Nazis is remembered today by Eva Hunzinger's affecting sculpture depicting women and imprisoned men.

Most Holocaust memorials, however, are unremittingly grim and none more so than the one at the S-Bahnhof Grunewald (Charlottenburg-Wilmersdorf): it was from this otherwise picturesque railway station that many of Berlin's Jews were deported to death camps from 1941 onwards. A plaque put up in 1973 and a concrete memorial sculpture erected in 1991 have now been supplemented by a series of steel plates embedded in Platform 17 (Mahnmal Gleis 17), each engraved with the date, number of passengers, and destination of the trainloads of Jews that left from here never to return.

Other places of interest nearby: 8, 9, 10, 14, 15, 64

12 The End of the Stauffenberg Plot

District I (Mitte), the Memorial to the German Resistance (Gedenkstätte Deutscher Widerstand) at Stauffenberg-strasse 13–14
U2 Mendelssohn-Bartholdy-Park

The difficult and painful process by which Berliners have acknowledged their part in supporting Adolf Hitler's Nazi regime, whilst at the same time memorialising the few who opposed it, is perhaps best reflected in a group of anonymous-looking buildings at Stauffenbergstrasse 13–14, occupied today by the Federal Ministry of Defence. The oldest building on the site, a pedimented structure facing the canal, was built in 1911–1914 as headquarters for the imperial navy. During the Weimar Republic (1919–1933) the building served additionally as the seat of the *Reichswehr*, Germany's modest national defence force, severely limited in size under the terms of the Versailles Treaty of 1919. In 1935, however, as part of Hitler's re-arming of Nazi Germany, the *Reichswehr* was re-branded the *Wehrmacht* ('defence force') and the old canalside building was extended back

The statue of a shackled man stands where Stauffenberg was shot

along Stauffenbergstrasse (then called Bendlerstrasse) to provide headquarters for its High Command. It was here, in the so-called Bendlerblock, that a group of likeminded army officers, united in the belief that Hitler's military ambitions would eventually destroy Germany, planned their abortive attempt to overthrow the Nazi regime.

The group was led by Infantry General Friedrich Olbricht (1888–1944), head of the General Army Office (*Allgemeinen Heeresamtes*) at High Command. In October 1943 he requested that Claus Schenk Graf von Stauffenberg (1907–1944), a Lieutenant-Colonel injured in North Africa, come to work for him as Chief of Staff. Stauffenberg was a conservative aristocrat and a staunch Catholic, who whilst not opposed to

German nationalism was vehemently opposed to the Nazis' treatment of the Jews and the suppression of religion. He was deeply shocked at reports of mass murder accompanying Germany's invasion of Russia. Working for Olbricht legitimised Stauffenberg's access to military briefings at the *Wolfsschanze*, or 'Wolf's Lair', Hitler's East Prussian headquarters during the Russian offensive, and Stauffenberg volunteered to eliminate Hitler there with a briefcase bomb. A coup would be staged thereafter in Berlin and the Nazi government toppled.

On the day of the attempt, 20th July 1944, Olbricht and Colonel Albrecht Ritter Mertz von Quirnheim (1905–1944) initiated Operation Valkyrie, thereby mobilising the Wehrmacht's Reserve Army (*Ersatz-heer*). Valkyrie had originally been conceived as a contingency plan to assume control of the Reich in the event of an unexpected uprising from within Germany. Meanwhile, after detonating his bomb, Stauffenberg flew back to Berlin to take part in the planned coup. It soon became clear, however, that Hitler had miraculously survived the blast and the conspirators were quickly rounded up. A courtmartial was hastily arranged later the same day under Colonel-General Friedrich Fromm, Commander of the Reserve Army, who had prior knowledge of the plot but now betrayed its leaders. Immediately afterwards Olbricht, von Stauffenberg, von Quirnheim and von Haeften were led out into the courtyard of the Bendlerblock and shot.

To assuage his guilt, Fromm ordered that the dead officers be given an honourable burial in the Old St. Matthew's Cemetery (Alter-St.-Matthäus-Kirchhof) on Grossgörschenstrasse although the bodies were exhumed the next day by the SS, stripped of their medals and cremated. A fifth co-conspirator, General Ludwig Beck (1880–1944), who had resigned in opposition to Hitler's annexation of the Sudetenland in 1938, was forced to shoot himself in his office. It is estimated that subsequent Nazi retributions in the wake of the July plot claimed the lives of a further 5000 people, as a result of which no further serious attempt was made on Hitler's life for the rest of the war.

In 1953 a bronze statue by Richard Scheibe depicting a shackled young man was unveiled in the courtyard of the Bendlerblock. It was the first attempt at memorialising the plotters, although not until 1967 was the site designated as a Memorial to the German Resistance (Gedenkstätte Deutscher Widerstand). The West German regime used the memorial to illustrate the democratic ideals of the Federal Republic, the conspirators being held up as proof that there were Germans during the Nazi regime, albeit a tiny minority, willing to risk everything for a moral post-war republic.

By contrast, Communist resistance to the Nazis formed the cornerstone of the GDR's identity as the anti-Fascist German state. When an exhibition in the Bendlerblock documenting the history of German anti-Nazi resistance was expanded in 1989 to include other groups that resisted Hitler, conservatives denounced it for devoting space to Communists, the founders of what some termed 'the second German dictatorship'. Leftists replied that at least the Communists had resisted Hitler from the start, whereas Stauffenberg and his aristocratic fellow-officers had at first welcomed the Nazis, only later plotting against them when Germany started losing the war. Either way, Germans in search of heroes had to acknowledge that *both* Communists *and* aristocrats were among the few to openly resist Hitler, and that both had operated before the Berlin Wall created further divisions in public opinion. Today's visitors to the Bendlerblock are left to draw their own conclusions about the motives of those who opposed Hitler's Third Reich.

Such soul searching is unnecessary at another site associated with the failed Stauffenberg Plot, namely the Plötzensee Memorial Centre (Gedenkstätte Plötzensee) on Hüttigpfad (Charlottenburg-Wilmersdorf). From 1933 until 1945 this prison was the primary place of execution for political opponents of the Third Reich, including several of Stauffenberg's co-conspirators. The latter suffered a humiliating trial in the Volksgerichthof chaired by the notorious Nazi judge Roland Freisler and were then suffocated slowly with piano wire nooses (see no. 55). Others executed at Plötzensee included members of the Communist resistance group *Rote Kapelle*, and those of the *Kreisauer Kreis*, dedicated to creating a peacetime government for Germany as an alternative to the Nazi regime. A memorial wall built against the execution shed was unveiled in 1952.

An interesting example of the different ways in which the regimes of East and West Berlin have memorialised victims of Nazi aggression can be found in Platz des 23. April in Köpenick. The square, named after the Red Army's liberation of the district in 1945, contains a 1970 memorial to Köpenicker Blutwoche ('Köpenick Blood Week'), the period in June 1933 when SA *(Sturmabteilung)* brownshirts rounded up and murdered many of their Communist and Socialist opponents. Unlike the subdued Bendlerblock memorial, this one takes the form of a raised and clenched fist, a symbol of proletarian militancy reminding the onlooker of the role of anti-Fascism in the foundation of the GDR.

Other places of interest nearby: 13, 55, 63

13 The Victory Column and Other Highpoints

District I (Mitte), the Victory Column (Siegessäule) at the
Grosser Stern on Strasse des 17. Juni
S5, S7, S75 Bellevue; U9 Hansaplatz

In a city such as Berlin, which is built predominantly on flat terrain, it is helpful every now and then to orientate oneself from a tall structure in order to gain an overview of the surrounding area. Berlin is fortunate in having a good number of such structures, both ancient and modern, which not only offer good vantage points but are also accessible to the public.

Probably the most centrally located is the 67 metre-high Victory Column (Siegessäule) in the middle of the Tiergarten. An observation terrace at the top of the column, reached by means of an internal staircase, looks out along the Strasse des 17. Juni towards the German Parliament (Reichstag) and the skyscrapers of Potsdamer Platz in the east and the towers of the Hansa Quarter to the west. Standing at the top of the column today it is difficult to imagine that it has not always stood here.

In reality the Victory Column was unveiled in 1873 on Königsplatz (now Platz der Republik) before the Reichstag was even built. It was designed by Johann Heinrich Strack (1805–1880) to commemorate victory in the Prusso-Danish War of 1864. After further Prussian military victories against Austria (1866) and France (1871) a gilded figure representing Victory by Frederick Drake (known as the *Goldelse*) was added to the top. The surface of the column is faced with the gilded barrels of captured cannon, whilst the base of the column is decorated with bas-reliefs commemorating the battles themselves. Higher up the column there is a mosaic frieze depicting the founding of the new German Empire in 1871, which resulted from these victories. To the south of the column ran the Victory Avenue (Siegesallee), a wide boulevard lined with marble statues of the historic rulers of Brandenburg (see no. 63).

Both column and avenue remained in place until 1938, when Hitler authorised their wholesale relocation to the Tiergarten. He did this to clear the way for the planned North-South Axis of his new capital of *Germania*, which would run from Tempelhof Airport northwards to the Spree Bend (Spreebogen), where a colossal new government quarter was planned (see no.57). Hitler would not tolerate the presence of a paean to the military glory of Bismarck's Second Empire amidst the new architectural glories of his Third.

In its new location the Victory Column became the focal point of the so-called Great Star (Grosser Stern), an intersection of paths radiating out into the Tiergarten. The main path was widened to become part of the so-called East-West Axis of *Germania*, as was the Star itself. At its outer edges were built four ceremonial guardhouses giving access to the column by means of tunnels under the road: still standing they are notable for being the only extant Berlin buildings of Hitler's architect, Albert Speer (1905–1981). During the last weeks of the war the column was used as a radio control tower in order to guide aircraft that were using the Axis as a makeshift runway.

Although the column survived the war the Victory Avenue, which had been rebuilt on a radial path renamed the Neue Siegesal-

Goldelse stands on the top of the Victory Column

lee (now the Grosse Sternallee) to the southeast of the column, was afterwards unceremoniously dismantled and taken away. Calls for the toppling of the column itself, because of its imperialist origins and glorification of war, were eventually ignored, although the reliefs around its base were removed to Paris as war spoils. Here they remained until their eventual return in 1987 to mark the 750th anniversary of the founding of Berlin.

Dotted around Berlin are numerous other highpoints, each offering a different vista of the city. South-west of the Victory Column, for example, is the 90 metre-high Panorama Floor of the Europa-Center at Tauentzienstrasse 9–12, offering a broad vista of western Berlin (as well as a cinema screening of an aerial jouney over the former Berlin Wall). Farther to the west is the 150 metre-high Radio Tower (Funkturm) on Hammarskjöldplatz (Charlottenburg-Wilmersdorf), erected in 1926 and resembling the Eiffel Tower; its observation terrace affords stunning views both eastwards towards the city centre and westwards across the Grunewald forest. Half its size is the 77 metre-high bell tower at the Olympic Stadium (Glockenturm am Olympiastadion), reached by express lift and offering vistas towards Spandau and Potsdam (see no. 30). Small by comparison, the 56 metre-high Grunewald Tower (Grunewaldturm) on Havelchaussee to the southwest, is a neo-Gothic red-brick *belvedere* designed by Franz Heinrich Schwechten (1841–1924), architect of the Emperor William Memorial Church (Kaiser-Wilhelm-Gedächtnis-Kirche), and erected in 1899 to commemorate the centenary of the birth of King and Emperor William I (1861–1888) (of a similar height is another *belvedere* called the Flatow Tower (Flatowturm) in Park Babelsberg in Potsdam (see no. 47)).

Directly south of the Victory Column, in John-F.-Kennedy-Platz, stands the Schöneberg Rathaus, the seat of West Berlin's Cold War government under Willy Brandt, which has a 70 metre-high tower offering a rare view of Berlin's southern districts (it was here that the American president gave his now famous "Ich bin ein Berliner" speech on 26th June 1963).

Moving east of the Victory Column, another striking overview of Berlin can be gained by taking Europe's fastest lift to the 96 metre-high Panorama Point (Panorama Punkt) in Hans Kollhoff's skyscraper at Potsdamer Platz 1 (Mitte), which marks the entrance to the Quartier Daimler. One of the many visible landmarks is the Reichstag, which itself contains a rooftop restaurant (Käfer im Bundestag) offering extensive vistas. Less well-known is the view from the Solar bar on the 16th floor of a tower block at Stresemannstrasse 76, reached by a glass lift.

The best viewpoint in the former East Berlin is undoubtedly the unmistakeable Television Tower (Fernsehturm) on Panoramastrasse (Mitte), built in 1969 and at 365 metres high Germany's tallest structure. In the silver sphere near the top there is a viewing platform, offering vistas stetching 40 kilometres away on a clear day, and a rotating café that takes half an hour to turn 360°. If there are long queues for the lifts why not try the less well-known view of the tower itself from the foyer of the CineStar Cubix cinema at Rathausstrasse 1 on nearby Alexanderplatz, or the 50 metre-high gallery around the dome of the Berlin Cathedral (Berliner Dom) on Museum Island, with its panoramic views over the historical centre of Berlin.

This roundup of Berlin's highpoints concludes at the Müggelturm in the woods south of Köpenick far to the southeast, an 80 metre-high concrete tower erected in 1960 to replace an earlier one that burned down.

14 Remembering Mori Ōgai

District I (Mitte), the Mori Ōgai Memorial (Mori Ōgai-Gedenk-
stätte) at Luisenstrasse 39
S1, S2, S5, S7, S25, S75 Friedrichstrasse; U6 Friedrichstrasse

On the morning of 24th August 1884, a French liner set sail from the Japanese port of Yokohama. It was carrying a young student called Mori Rintarō (1862–1922), who together with several other compatriots was on his way to Europe to further his education. The 22-year-old Mori was the son of a doctor and the youngest medical student to graduate from Tokyo University. Now a first lieutenant in the Japanese Medical Corps it was the intention of the ruling Meiji government (1867–1912) that he study military hygiene.

Running parallel to Mori's interest in medicine was a strong literary bent. Always a voracious reader, and no doubt urged on by his disciplinarian mother, he had mastered Confucian and Japanese classics at an early age and would translate Japanese and Western classics into Chinese for his own entertainment; he celebrated his arrival in Germany by composing two poems in Chinese.

Mori stayed in Germany for fours years, in Leipzig, Dresden, Munich and Berlin. During his stay in Berlin he initially occupied lodgings at the corner of Luisenstrasse 39 and Marienstrasse 32, whilst studying at the Hygiene Institute on Klosterstrasse under the renowned bacteriologist Robert Koch (see no. 15). Two months later he re-located to Klosterstrasse itself and then to Grosse Präsidentenstrasse. At the same time he immersed himself in European literature and philosophy thereby gaining a deep awareness of the gulf between European and Japanese culture.

Upon his return to Japan in 1888 Mori was appointed instructor at the Army Medical School in Tokyo. Wishing to modernise both Japanese medicine and Japanese literature he began lecturing and writing about hygiene, as well as his experiences in Germany. He wrote three novellas based on his experiences abroad including *Maihime* (*The Dancing Girl*), published in 1890 under the literary name MoriŌgai, the story of a love affair between a Japanese man and a German girl. Such works are now considered as having signalled the birth of modern Japanese literature. A year earlier in 1889 he published a collection of translated poetry called *Omokage* (*Vestiges*), the first Japanese anthology to convey the aesthetics of Western poetry.

A memorial room
for Mori Ōgai on
Luisenstrasse

As a physician Mori specialised in the treatment of beriberi, an acute ailment now known to be caused by a dietary deficiency of Vitamin B1 (Thiamine). Unfortunately, Mori's assertion of the commonly-held belief that beriberi was an infectious disease meant that many Japanese soldiers succumbed unnecessarily to the illness during the Russo-Japanese War (1904–1905). Despite this, following Japan's bloody defeat of Russia, Mori was promoted to army surgeon general, the highest ranking medical officer in the Japanese army.

Mori produced his most popular novel, *Gan* (*The Wild Goose*), in 1911 and completed the first translation of both parts of Goethe's *Faust* into Japanese in 1913. Following his retirement from the army in 1916 he became Director of the Imperial Museum and President of the Imperial Academy of Arts, amongst other official duties, indulging his literary interests in his leisure time: it is said that he only slept 2–3 hours each night. His later works, in the wake of the death of Emperor Meiji in 1912, were often fictionalised accounts of historical incidents and personages, stressing the virtues of patriotism and self-sacrifice: a uniquely Prussian-Japanese set of values! Mori himself died in 1922 in Tokyo from tuberculosis. By this time he had translated 130 works of German and European literature into Japanese, including Schiller, Lessing, Kleist and Heine, and had introduced modern literary criticism into Japan.

Although a wall plaque had been erected to Mori Ōgai as early as 1966, it was not until 1984, exactly a century after his arrival in Germany, that a Mori Ōgai memorial room was opened at Luisenstrasse 39, in a ceremony attended by members of his family. Under the guidance of the renowned *Gründerzeit* specialist Charlotte von Mahlsdorf, the room was painstakingly furnished in the late 19th century style that would have been famliar to Ōgai (see no. 80). Following a visit by the Prime Minister of Japan in 1987 the East German Ministry of Higher Education sanctioned and financed the extension of the room into the Mori Ōgai Memorial (Mori-Ōgai-Gedenkstätte), its library of Ōgai's works and attendant exhibition rooms providing visitors with an insight into the world of this extraordinary man, who on the threshold of the 20th century was able to view his native land through European eyes and vice-versa. In doing so he exposed Japan to German literature, culture and medicine, achieving a unique cultural synthesis in the process.

The Mori Ōgai Memorial is today part of the Centre of Japanese Language and Culture of the Humboldt University (Humboldt-Universität), which uses the premises to host lectures, exhibitions, literary evenings, traditional tea ceremonies, and courses in calligraphy and Japanese flower arranging (*Ikebana*).

Other places of interest nearby: 6, 7, 8, 9, 10, 15, 16, 19, 20

15 The Anatomical Theatre

District I (Mitte), the Veterinary School's Anatomical
Theatre (Anatomisches Theater der Tierarzneischule)
at Luisenstrasse 56
U6 Oranienburger Tor

Langhan's Anatomical Theatre is an architectural gem

A street in central Berlin long associated with medical research is Luisenstrasse, the northern extension of Wilhelmstrasse beyond the River Spree. In 1710, King Frederick I (1701–1713) founded a plague and military hospital here, on land that lay outside the city walls. Called the Haus Charité it was Germany's first medical training institute.

The oldest surviving buildings of the hospital stand on the east side of the street, including an imposing neo-Classical building at Luisenstrasse 56, erected in 1840 as a veterinary school and now part of the surrounding Humboldt University (Humboldt-Universität) campus. Hidden behind it is a neglected park, designed by the 19th century landscape designer Peter Joseph Lenné (1789–1866), through which runs the tiny River Panke (the park can be entered either through the gate at the northern end of the school or else via Philippstrasse). Amongst the forlorn buildings and forgotten monuments in this hidden corner of Berlin can be found one of the city's architectural gems, namely the Veterinary School's Anatomical Theatre (Anatomisches Theater der Tierarzneischule). This simple neo-Classical building was erected in 1789–1790 to a design by Carl Gotthard Langhans (1732–1808), a pioneer of the German Classicist movement and architect of the famous Brandenburg Gate (Brandenburger Tor). The theatre was part of the Berlin Royal Veterinary School (Königliche Tierarzneischule zu Berlin), founded in 1787 by King Frederick William II (1786–1797), at a time when the Prussian army urgently required healthy horses. This explains the presence of a former blacksmith's workshop around the corner at Philippstrasse 13.

Langhans' Anatomical Theatre, known also as the Langhansbau, was based on the world's first anatomical theatre, the Teatro Anatomico, built in 1594 in Padua, Italy. It is a two-storey building with a cross-shaped ground plan, at the centre of which is a low cupola covering the circular theatre itself. Inside the theatre three rows of wooden benches with intricately carved backs climb steeply upwards, with a balcony for those standing at the top, somewhat reminiscent of a miniature Roman amphitheatre. On a table in the centre of the theatre surgical dissections would be carried out for the edification of students and academics. In this respect the sculpted animal skulls on the building's façade seem quite apt.

After a century of use, Langhans' Anatomical Theatre changed usage and became the lecture hall for the newly-founded Berlin Hygiene Institute, which explains why one of the building's four pavilions is still marked 'Institute for Meat Hygiene' ('Institut für Fleischhygiene'). A key figure at the institute was physician and bacteriologist Robert Koch (1843–1910), who in 1882 identified the bacillus that causes tuberculosis, and a little later the cholera bacillus, too. A wall plaque at Luisenstrasse 57 commemorates this fact and there is a marble monument of Koch, who was awarded the Nobel Prize for medicine in 1905, in Robert-Koch-Platz at the northern end of Luisenstrasse.

Despite suffering considerable neglect between 1949 and 1990, when the area was a part of East Germany, Langhans' Anatomical Theatre is still standing and has recently been restored. It serves today as a lecture hall and events venue.

The area around Luisenstrasse contains many memorials to those who made medical history here. They include one to pioneering ophthalmologist Albrecht von Graefe (1828–1870) on the corner of Luisenstrasse and Schumannstrasse, and another to pathologist Rudolf Virchow (1821–1902) on nearby Karlplatz. It was Virchow who founded the Museum of Pathology, now the Berlin Medical History Museum (Berliner Medizinhistorisches Museum), at Schumannstrasse 20–21 containing both medical instruments and specimens.

Other places of interest nearby: 1, 6, 7, 8, 9, 10, 15, 16, 19, 20

16 A Pneumatic Postal Dispatch System

District I (Mitte), the pneumatic postal system in the former
Central Telegraph Office at Monbijoustrasse 1
S1, S2, S25 Oranienburger Strasse; Tram M1, M6

It was the ancient Greek scientist, Hero of Alexandria (c. 70–10 BC), who first described machines powered by air, water and steam pressure, in his book *Pneumatica*. One of the many applications this new technology would find for itself over the following two millennia was pneumatic post, that is a system of delivering letters in capsules through pressurized air tubes. The pneumatic postal system was invented by the Scottish engineer William Murdoch in the 1800s and was later developed by the London Pneumatic Dispatch Company, the first system being installed in 1853 to convey telegrams between the London Stock Exchange and the city's main telegraph office. This localised use of pneumatic post can still be found today in many banks and large retailers, where it is used to dispatch money and documents away from the shop floor.

Throughout the second half of the 19th century, extensive pneumatic postal systems were constructed in many large cities, including Paris in 1866, Vienna in 1875, and Prague in 1887, as well as Hamburg, Munich, Rome, Chicago, New York and Rio de Janeiro. Such networks, punctuated regularly by pneumatic post stations, linked post offices, banks, stock exchanges and ministries. In Germany, France, Italy and Austria special postal stationery was issued exclusively for pneumatic use. During the 20th century, however, with the advent of computers and fax machines, the pneumatic systems were largely abandoned, beginning with Vienna in 1956, Paris in 1984 and finally Prague in 2002, prompted by the city's extensive flooding.

After Paris the world's most extensive pneumatic postal system was in Berlin, running 400 kilometres in length at its height. Having witnessed the successful introduction of a pneumatic postal system in London in 1861, construction of the Berlin system commenced in 1865. Undertaken by the company Siemens & Halske the first line ran between the Main Post Office and the Stock Exchange. In 1876 the system was made available to the public, at which time it gained the popular name *Rohrpost*, literally 'Tube Post'. By 1939 there were ninety stations on the network delivering eight millions pieces of post annually at a speed of 16 metres per second. By 1945, however, many of the sub-pavement tubes had been destroyed by bombing. Rudimentary repairs were undertaken but with the start of the Cold War all pneumatic postal links between East and West Berlin were severed, never to be reconnected. For a while West Berlin's pneumatic postal system was even extended but by 1963 it was clear it would soon become technologically redundant and was taken out of commission; a

The remains of the pneumatic postal sytem on Monbijoustrasse

few further deliveries were made until the system was dismantled in 1972. The East Berlin system continued regular dispatch until 1976 and was decommissioned fully in the 1980s.

Today, very little remains of Berlin's all-but-forgotten pneumatic postal dispatch system, and what is left (for example a station in a former post office on Mauerstrasse and pipework below the Olympic stadium, installed to relay news of Nazi sporting victories) cannot be seen by the public. However, a rare glimpse can be had by joining a fascinating guided tour hosted by the Berlin Underworlds Association (Berliner Unterwelten e.V.), which visits one of the last intact pneumatic post stations in the basement of what was once the city's Central Telegraph Office, erected in 1913 at Monbijoustrasse 1. A little farther along Oranienburger Strasse, at the corner with Tucholskystrasse, stands a neo-Renaissance building from 1875, which was once a postal despatch office (*Postfuhramt*). Used also as stables for the horses that delivered the post the building has a ceramic-clad façade depicting messenger boys clutching post horns, parcels and letters.

For a full postal history of Berlin visit the Museum of Telecommunications (Museum für Kommunikation) at Leipziger Strasse 16 (Mitte), the oldest museum of its kind in Europe.

Other places of interest nearby: 1, 5, 6, 7, 14, 15, 16, 18, 19

17 The World's Biggest Model Railway

District I (Mitte), Loxx on Alexanderplatz Miniature
World Berlin (Loxx am Alex Miniatur Welten Berlin) in the
Alexa-Center off Alexanderplatz
S5, S7, S75 Alexanderplatz; U2, U5, U8 Alexanderplatz

Berlin is home to the world's largest digitally-controlled model railway. Opened in 2004 and covering an area of 3000 square metres, the Loxx model railway boasts over 4000 metres of track and cost almost three million Euros to construct. The model's full name is Loxx on Alexanderplatz Miniature World Berlin, reflecting the fact that its 400 locomotives (or *Loks* for short, hence the name) run through a miniaturised version of Berlin itself.

The Brandenburg Gate is one of many famous Berlin buildings featured in the LOXX am Alex model railway

The Loxx model railway is built at a scale of 1:87, which is known to railway modellers as the HO scale. The most popular scale for modellers throughout Continental Europe and North America, the name HO is derived from the German 'Halb-null', meaning 'half zero'. This is because 1:87 is approximately half that of O scale, which was introduced by the German toy manufacturer Märklin in 1900. By the time of the Second World War, O scale model railways had declined in popularity as the demand for smaller scale trains increased, enabling serious modellers to incorporate more scale miles and more details into the same space. Thus, the 1:48 ratio of the old O scale – a convenient scale for those using the Imperial sytem of measurement in which a quarter inch represented one scale foot – was replaced in popularity by the HO ratio of 1:87 (modellers in Britain, incidentally, settled for their own slightly larger OO scale of 1:76). The seemingly awkward ratio of 1:87, in which 3.5mm represents one scale foot, means that model rails are spaced 16.5mm apart in order to mimick the actual standard railway gauge of four feet eight and a half inches.

It took some seventy professional modellers to create the Loxx model railway, with all its moving features being controlled digitally by 34 computers. Needless to say, the modellers have made every effort to represent all the city's many types of trains, from municipal S-Bahn and regional trains to long-distance trains and the high speed Intercity Express (ICE). Even without the trains the model is alive with 10000 cars, buses, trams and trucks, not to mention aircraft taking off and landing at the make-believe Loxx City Airport. The layout is especially magical when night falls, as it does every 20 minutes, and 18000 tiny lights on vehicles and inside buildings are switched on.

The actual physical landscape of the Loxx model railway is fascinating for the Berlin visitor in that many of the city's famous buildings and other landmarks are represented. These include the Reichstag, the Brandenburg Gate, Hackescher Markt, the Zoologischer Garten, with its tiny animals, and the television tower (Fernsehturm) in Alexanderplatz. The newest additions include a model of Berlin's new Main Station (Berlin Hauptbahnhof), as well as the Alexa-Center just off Alexanderplatz to where the model was re-located in 2007. There are also occasional historical scenes included for good measure, such as the Nazis' burning of books in 1933 in Bebelplatz (see no. 77). Most fascinating to visitors are all the tiny details of day-to-day living in Berlin, including outdoor summer cafés, games of tennis, mourners tending graves, and even sunbathing naturists. As well as being landscaped with 45000 trees it is said that this scaled-down version of Berlin is currently populated by an estimated 50000 figures!

For those visitors wishing to construct a miniature railway of their own, HO scale locomotives, rolling stock, buildings and scenery are readily available from the model railway stockist Michas Bahnhof at Nürnberger Strasse 24 (Charlottenburg-Wilmersdorf).

Other places of interest nearby: 1, 2, 3, 4, 5, 6, 7, 18, 67

18 Silver Screen Berlin

District I (Mitte), some historic Berlin cinemas including the
Babylon Cinema (Filmkunsthaus Babylon) at Rosa-Luxemburg-
Strasse 30
U2 Rosa-Luxemburg-Platz; Tram M8

By the 1920s Berlin rivalled Hollywood as one of the most innovative and prolific centres of cinema. It was focussed around the fabled
Babelsberg Film Studios, the UFA film production company, and legendary stars such as Marlene Dietrich (see nos. 51 & 53). By 1936 the
city boasted 5253 cinema houses: more than in any other country in
Europe.

Berlin's first cinemas were clustered around bustling Kurfürstendamm in Charlottenburg, for example the Union-Palast at number 26
and the Marmorhaus at number 236, both of which were opened in
1913. The cinema would remain one of Ku'damm's greatest attractions
right up until the arrival of the modern multiplexes, rendering both of
these venerable examples obsolete.

Fortunately, of the many cinemas erected in Berlin during the
1920s, a surprising number are still extant, and several of them have
managed to retain not only their audiences but also something of their
original atmosphere. A prime example is the Babylon Cinema (Filmkunsthaus Babylon) at Rosa-Luxemburg-Strasse 30, which was built
between 1927 and 1929 as part of a housing development to replace
a notorious slum known as the *Scheunenviertel*, or 'Barn Quarter'
(see no. 54). Designed by the architect Hans Poelzig (1869–1936) the
cinema had 1200 seats and a large balcony, and was considered one of
the best cinemas in Berlin. By the 1990s, however, the main auditorium
had become so dilapidated that films could only be shown in the foyer!
The cinema has since undergone an extensive programme of refurbishment and, although the interior is now quite different, the exterior still
sports the bold horizontal lines and curving corners so typical of 1920s
Modernism.

Built at the same as the Babylon and suffering a similar fate was
the Universum Cinema (Universum-Kino) on Lehniner Platz, just
off the upper Ku'damm. Constructed in 1927 it is important for being the most important extant Berlin building of Modernist architect
Erich Mendelsohn (1887–1953). Quite unlike previous cinema buildings, the Universum's curving low frontage and high-rise auditorium

behind demonstrated Mendelsohn's preoccupation with the dynamism of modern times, which was often reflected in the films being shown. Burned down in the last days of the war the cinema was rebuilt in 1981 by the Berlin Schaubühne theatre company leaving only the façade intact.

Other preserved cinemas from the 1920s include the Art Deco style Astor Film Lounge at Ku'damm 225, the FSK designed by the Modernist architect Bruno Taut at Segitzdamm 2 (Friedrichshain-Kreuzberg), the Colosseum at Schönhauser Allee 123 (Prenzlauer Berg), and the towering Titania Palast built in 1927 at Gutsmuthsstrasse 27–28 (Steglitz-Zehlendorf). Having survived the war it hosted the first postwar concerts by the Berlin Philharmonic Orchestra, as well as the first Berlin Film Festival.

From the 1940s comes the elegant Delphi Filmpalast at Kantstrasse 12a (Charlottenburg-Wilmersdorf), opened in 1949 on the bombed-out remains of a 1920s-era dance hall. Such cinemas filled an important niche in post-war West Berlin's cultural scene. Meanwhile, the 1950s witnessed a resurgence in cinema construction in West Berlin, for example the Odeon at Hauptstrasse 116 (Tempelhof-Schöneberg) and the Eva at Blissestrasse 18 (Charlottenburg-Wilmersdorf). Of particular interest was the opening in 1957 of the Zoo Palast at Hardenbergstrasse 29a, again in Charlottenburg, its nine screens under the same roof making it one of the very first multiplexes.

During the 1960s it was the turn of the GDR regime in East Berlin to leave its mark on the city's cinema landscape, with the construction of a pair of cinemas on its showcase boulevard, the

Bold Modernist curves identify the Babylon Cinema on Rosa-Luxemburg-Strasse

Soviet Functionalism at the Kino International on Karl-Marx-Allee

Karl-Marx-Allee (see no. 67). In 1962 the Kosmos 1000, so named because that is how many it seated, was opened at number 131 (it is now a club and restaurant). Its architects Josef Kaiser and Herbert Aust were also responsible for the Kino International at number 33, a perfect example of extravagant Soviet-style Functionalism, erected directly opposite the Café Moskau. Built between 1961 and 1964 it has twin staircases, a grand first-floor foyer, and even a silver sequinned curtain!

The commercial focus of Berlin's cinema industry today is undoubtedly Potsdamer Strasse. Modern high-tech cinemas abound, such as the Arsenal cinema within the Deutsche Kinemathek at number 2 (the house cinema of the Friends of the German Film Archive), the 8-screened CineStar Original and the 360° IMAX in the Sony Center at number 4, and the 19-screened CinemaxX at number 5, the latter being the main venue for the Berlin Film Festival (Berlinale – Internationale Filmfestspiele) held in the second and third week of February.

Set into the pavement at the corner of Kastanienallee and Schönhauser Allee (Pankow) is the name 'Skladanowsky'. It was here in 1892 that Max Skladanowsky carried out experiments in film projection before premiering the world's first film presentation in Berlin on 1st November 1895, some two months before the Lumière Brothers. Skladanowsky's original projector is displayed in the Filmmuseum Potsdam, which also contains a working cinema organ from the days of silent film. To hear such an organ visit the Musical Instrument Museum (Musikinstrumentenmuseum) at Tiergartenstrasse 1 (Mitte), where a mighty Wurlitzer is demonstrated every Saturday.

Other places of interest nearby: 1, 2, 6, 7, 16, 17, 18, 19, 83, 84

19 The Last of the Old Market Halls

District I (Mitte), the Ackerhalle Market Hall at Ackerstrasse 23–26/ Invalidenstrasse 158
S1, S2 Nordbahnhof; U8 Rosenthaler Platz; Tram M8

An easily overlooked aspect of Berlin's 19th century architecture are its market halls (*Markthallen*) of which fourteen were built between 1883 and 1892. Designed by the municipal architect Hermann Blanckenstein and identified by Roman numerals they were an attempt to provide more organised and sanitary selling conditions to those offered by the city's twenty or so weekly open-air markets. Typically they were of red-brick construction and occupied the full depth of a residential block. A cost-cutting exercise, this meant that only two narrow facades containing the entrances from the street needed to be built. The facades themselves featured arched windows, statuary and terracotta ornament depicting the produce sold within. Inside the hall was a high central aisle with clerestory windows flanked by lower transverse aisles illuminated by skylights. The roof was supported by steel trusses resting on cast iron girders and columns.

The market hall that best retains its original exterior is Markthalle

Terracotta ornament on the Ackerhalle, an old market hall on Ackerstrasse

VI, known as the Ackerhalle, built in 1888 within a tenement block between Ackerstrasse 23–26 and Invalidenstrasse 158. The building's beautiful façade still retains its terracotta roundels depicting fish, vegetables, poultry and fruit. Unfortunately, a supermarket occupies much of the building today leaving little room for any sense of an old-fashioned bustling market hall.

For a more authentic market hall experience visit Markthalle X, the Arminiushalle, farther west across the Spandauer Schifffahrtskanal. Unusually, it occupies an entire block at the corner of Bremer Strasse, Arminiusstrasse and Jonasstrasse. Known also as the Moabiter Markthalle it still contains plenty of colourful market stalls selling locally-sourced meat, vegetables, fruit and dairy produce.

Berlin's two other remaining market halls are both to be found in Friedrichshain-Kreuzberg, namely Markthalle IX (the Eisenbahnhalle) at Eisenbahnstrasse 42–43/Pücklerstrasse 43–44, and Markthalle XI (the Marheinekehalle), south of the Landwehrkanal at Zossener Strasse/Bergmannstrasse, near Marheinekeplatz. The latter was completely rebuilt in the early 1950s after being wrecked at the end of the Second World War.

With the advent of the department store in the early 20th century market halls declined somewhat in popularity and were sometimes adapted to other uses. Markthalle IV at Dorotheenstrasse 29, for example, became a postal sorting office in 1914. Its blocked-off tunnel, once used to convey goods directly from the River Spree, can still be seen at Reichstagufer 12. A more recent conversion is Markthalle VII at Dresdener Strasse 27/Legiendamm 32, which still retains its richly ornamented terracotta façade but now contains apartments and a restaurant. Another was Markthalle III (the Zimmerhalle) at Zimmerstrasse 90–91, which was converted in 1910 to the Konzerthaus Clou, Berlin's largest dance hall (for an intact 1920s ballroom visit the glittering Clärchens Ballhaus at Auguststrasse 24 (Mitte)). By the late 1920s the building was being rented by the nascent Nazi Party for mass meetings and on May Day 1927, with Socialists and Communists demonstrating nearby, Hitler gave his first-ever Berlin speech here, introduced by the recently appointed city *Gauleiter* ('regional leader'), Joseph Goebbels (1897–1945). In February 1943 the building was used as an assembly point for hundreds of Jewish forced labourers rounded up for deportation to the concentration camps. It was destroyed shortly afterwards although its brick and terracotta doorway has since been restored.

Two other market halls destroyed during the Second World War were Markthalle II at Lindenstrasse/Friedrichstrasse and Markthalle

V on Magdeburger Platz. Another victim, and once the largest of all Berlin's market halls, was Markthalle I, the Central Market Hall on Alexanderplatz (Zentralmarkthalle am Alexanderplatz), which the East German authorities deemed unworthy of being rebuilt.

For many Berliners the old market halls are now the place not only to pick up a few items on the way home, such as pickles, sausages and Pumpernickel, but also those regional specialities not readily available in the big supermarkets.

Ironically, the open-air markets that the halls were meant to replace are now thriving once more, notably the Winterfeldmarkt on Winterfeldtplatz and the Wochenmarkt Wittenbergplatz (both in Tempelhof-Schöneberg), the latter transformed into a farmers' market (Bauernmarkt Wittenbergplatz) each Thursday. Typical of the regional produce available here are Spreewald pickled cucumbers (*Salzgurken*), sweet aromatic local strawberries, wild mushrooms such as *Steinpilze* and *Pfifferlinge*, and asparagus (*Spargel*) hand-picked from April to June in Beelitz, south-west of Berlin. Other bustling venues are the wholesale produce market at the end of Beusselstrasse (Mitte) adjacent to the Westhafen, and the Turkish Market on Maybachufer (Türken Markt am Maybachufer) (Kreuzberg-Friedrichshain) (see no. 71). Those who prefer their produce to be completely organic should visit the Biolüske bio-supermarket in a converted 1950s cinema at Drakestrasse 50 (Steglitz-Zehlendorf), and the bio-market and café at the Galerie Mutter Fourage at Chausseestrasse 15a on Wannsee Island.

The successor to the old market halls (and the precursor to modern shopping malls) was the department store *(Kaufhaus)*, and Berlin was at the forefront of its development. One of the first was the Kaufhaus Wertheim on Leipziger Strasse opened in 1905 by a Jewish family of the same name. A landmark of commercial architecture it was lost in the war. A new Wertheim store (now owned by Karstadt) opened subsequently at Kurfürstendamm 231 (Charlottenburg-Wilmersdorf) not far from which is the Kaufhaus des Westens (KaDeWe) at Tauentzienstrasse 21–24 (Tempelhof-Schöneberg), now Berlin's most famous department store.

Other places of interest nearby: 1, 6, 7, 14, 15, 16, 18, 21, 22, 83

20 Home of the Berlin Archaeopteryx

District I (Mitte), the Natural History Museum
(Museum für Naturkunde), at Invalidenstrasse 43
U6 Naturkunde Museum; Tram M8

The Natural History Museum on
Invalidenstrasse

Berlin's Natural History Museum (Museum für Naturkunde) is one of the largest in the world and contains 25 million specimens. As well as displaying the world's largest mounted dinosaur skeleton (a *Brachiosaurus brancai* discovered in 1909 by German fossil hunters in Tanzania), the largest piece of amber known to man, and important geological specimens from the collection of scientist and explorer Alexander von Humboldt (1769–1859), it is also home to innumerable smaller but no less interesting historical specimens, which are easily overlooked.

Typical is a trio of stuffed birds to be found in an antique cabinet illustrating historical taxidermy (Historische Präparate). The first is a stuffed White-throated Kingfisher (Braunliest) (*Halcyon smyrnensis*) from Pondicherry in India, which comes from the collection of French natural historian, Baron Georges Cuvier (1769–1832). Author of the popular book *The Animal Kingdom*, Cuvier was a pioneer in the comparison of living creatures with fossils and was the first to suggest that many fossilised creatures died in a catastrophe-induced mass extinction. Alongside is a Starling (Star) (*Sturnus vulgaris*) from the collection of Christian Ludwig Brehm (1787–1864), the so-called "bird pastor from Renthendorf", a village south of Leipzig. During his five decades as pastor, Brehm wrote several books on German birds, in which he described them in the minutest of detail. He also accumulated 15000 bird skins, two thirds of which eventually found their way to the American Museum of Natural History in New York (via the Walter Rothschild Zoological Museum in Tring, England)

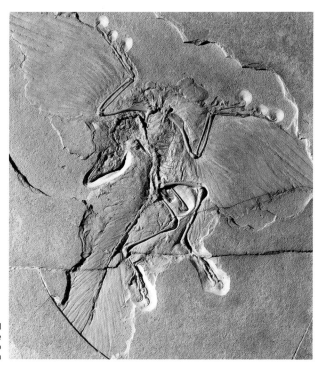

Berlin's fossilised Archaeopteryx, the oldest bird known to man

and the rest now reside in Bonn. The third bird is the wonderfully-named Purple Swamphen (Purpurhahn) (*Porphyrio porphyrio*), the only bird so revered by the ancient Romans that they did not eat it! This specimen found in Madagascar comes from the collection of William Bullock (1773–1849), a London-based goldsmith and owner of the largest private natural history museum of the early 19th century. When the collection was auctioned in 1819 the Swamphen was bought by the Natural History Museum in Berlin.

At the same auction a tiny Ou bird (pronounced *oh-uh*), brought back from Hawaii during one of Captain James Cook's expeditions, was also purchased. It is the original sample used when the species was named – a so-called 'type specimen' – and as such will probably never be displayed publicly because of its inestimable value to the scientific community.

Even rarer than the Ou, and certainly long extinct, is the Natural History Museum's fossilised *Archaeopteryx lithographica*, one of the most controversial fossils in the world. From the Greek *archaios* meaning 'ancient' and *pteryx* meaning 'wing', *Archaeopteryx* dates to the

Late Jurassic period (155–150 million years ago) and is considered to be the earliest and most primitive bird known to man. It was similar in shape and size to a Magpie, with broad, rounded wings and a long tail. However, where *Archaeopteryx* differed from modern birds was that it had several dinosaur-like features, namely jaws lined with sharp teeth, three 'fingers' ending in curved claws on its wings, and a long, bony, lizard-like tail. As such, *Archaeopteryx* is a so-called transitional fossil, in this case providing compelling, though as yet incomplete evidence that many of today's birds evolved to a greater or lesser degree from dinosaurs. Certainly there is evidence that *Archaeopteryx* itself was related to the dinosaurs, as demonstrated by similarities with bipedal carnivorous Dromaeosaurids, known popularly as *Raptors*, from the ensuing Cretaceous period (made famous by the film *Jurassic Park*). The role of *Archaeopteryx* in the development of flight, however, remains a moot point, its feathers perhaps only being used to regulate body temperature. The bird's rather flat breastbone, or sternum, to which flight muscles would be attached suggest it was not a strong flier.

The description of the first intact *Archaeopteryx* fossil in the early 1860s, coming hard on the heels of the publication of Charles Darwin's *The Origin of Species*, triggered a vigorous debate about the role of transitional fossils in evolution that continues to this day. The Berlin *Archaeopteryx* remains the most complete of only ten such specimens found so far, all of which have hailed from the Solnhofen Limestone of Southern Germany. It was discovered by one Jakob Niemeyer sometime in 1876–77 on the Blumenberg, near the Bavarian town of Eichstätt. Niemeyer famously sold the fossil to Johann Dörr in exchange for a cow, after which it was properly described by Wilhelm Danes in 1884.

Berlin's Natural History Museum finds its origins in the 'Cabinets of Arts and Marvels' (*Wunderkammern*) assembled by aristocrats and travellers during the Renaissance and Baroque periods. A modern example of such a cabinet has been created at the ME (Moving Energies) Collectors Room (Stiftung Olbricht) at Auguststrasse 68 (Mitte). Objects such as a narwhal's tusk, an amber mirror, and a seventeenth century anatomical model are deliberately juxtaposed so as to stress the connection between art, nature and science.

Other places of interest nearby: 1, 7, 14, 15, 16, 19, 21

21 Concealed Courtyards

District I (Mitte), a tour of old Berlin tenements beginning
at Hussitenstrasse 4–5
S1, S2, S25 Nordbahnhof; U8 Bernauer Strasse

In 1859–1862, in response to an enormous influx of new workers
into Berlin due to the Industrial Revolution, planning officer James
Hobrecht (1825–1902) drafted a development plan for the controlled
extension of the city. Systematic but inconspicuous development of
bourgeois suburbs, such as Wilmersdorf around Hohenzollerndamm
and Friedrich-Wilhelm-Stadt around Oranienburger Strasse, was
already underway. The Hobrecht Plan, on the other hand, envisaged a
complete transformation of the areas north, northeast and southeast of
Mitte, which would become the new working class suburbs. Enormous
tenement blocks were to be constructed along a generous grid of right-
angled streets, punctuated by a large number of city squares (although
many were never built) giving this part of Berlin an urban planning
framework that would be influential for decades.

Hobrecht hoped that his bold plan would prevent wild speculative
development. In reality, however, because the city council had to bear
the cost of new road construction, it actively encouraged the erection
of tenement blocks that were not only long (200–400 metres) but also
deep (150–200 metres). With no planning laws restricting the internal
layout of the blocks, except for a law of 1853 prescribing that an inner
courtyard (*Innenhof*) must be at least 5.30 metres square to enable a
firefighting hose to turn (increased in 1887 to 60 metres square), speculative property developers built as densely as possible. In so doing, the
Hobrecht Plan unwittingly initiated the transformation of Berlin into
"the largest tenement complex in the world".

The typical Berlin tenement block is little more than a huge,
brick-built box, its outer walls masked by a layer of plaster heavily
laden with moulded historicist ornament. It is entered through a large
doorway directly off the street, wide enough to take a horse and cart,
beyond which lies a passageway running through the thickness of the
building. This usually leads into a dark inner courtyard, sometimes
made brighter by the use of glazed white brickwork or white-painted
plaster. Larger, and so more expensive, rooms tended to face the street,
being light and airy, whilst cheaper and smaller ones overlooked the
courtyard. Toilets and washing facilities were usually communal affairs

in halls and stairwells. The longest tenement blocks often contained a series of linked courtyards running their entire length, known as *Hinterhäuser*, and it is little wonder that these vast edifices were sometimes dubbed *Mietskasernen*, or 'rental barracks'.

Many of Berlin's late 19th and early 20th century tenement blocks were destroyed during the Second World War; others fell victim to urban renewal, as well as the East German regime's clearances for the so-called 'Death Strip' (*Todesstreifen*) along the east side of the Berlin Wall (see no. 70). Many still remain, however, with some in more affluent neighbourhoods being subsequently restored and even enhanced by the incorporation of studios, cafés and designer boutiques. Three such examples in Mitte, north of the Spree, are the Heckmann-Höfe, on the corner of Oranienburger Strasse and Tucholsky Strasse, the Kunsthof at Oranienburger Strasse 27, and the Hackesche Höfe, running between Rosenthaler Strasse 40–41 and Sophienstrasse. The latter was constructed in 1906 to a design by Kurt Berendt and August Endell, leading exponents of the German *Art Nouveau* (next door at Rosenthaler Strasse 39, in an extremely modest courtyard by comparison, can be found Museum Otto Weidt's Workshop for the Blind (Museum Blindenwerkstatt Otto Weidt), a former brush workshop in which proprietor Otto Weidt employed blind Jews in an ultimately futile attempt to save them from the death camps: in February 1943 all Jews were removed from their place of work and deported as part of 'Operation Factory').

For a more authentic and atmospheric taste of Berlin's original tenements a tour must be made around the city's backstreets, peering through doorways, which may or may not be locked, and exploring concealed courtyards beyond. Our journey begins at Hussitenstrasse 4–5, just north of Invalidenstrasse, where there is an enormous tenement complex built in 1904 that once housed a thousand people. A most unusual feature was its series of six courtyards, stretching all the way back to Strelitzer Strasse, each of which was built in a different architectural style, designed to illustrate the architectural development of Berlin itself. Unfortunately, of the original Romanesque, Gothic, Nuremberg, Renaissance, Baroque and Wilhelmine style courtyards, only the Gothic and Nuremberg ones remain today (the latter a hybrid Gothic-Renaissance style, known as German Renaissance, which was popular in Nuremberg in the 15th century).

Several streets to the east, at Kastanienallee 12, there is a good example of the more usual type of dark, deep courtyard tenement building, which provided a relentlessly gloomy outlook for many Berlin citizens, enlivened only by an occasional call from a passing pedlar or organ grinder, or a visit to the public bath house around the corner on Oderberger Strasse (worth a glance too are the traditional courtyards at Kastanienallee 32 and 40).

A little more elegant are the yellow- and red-brick courtyards to the south along Linienstrasse, for example numbers 98 and 155, the former comprising a series of courtyards extending through the block to Torstrasse 164. At Torstrasse 85 and 87 are two simple façades behind which are apartments without courtyards, marking the earliest attempts at tenement reform.

South of Torstrasse there is an especially ornate, red-brick courtyard at Sophienstrasse 18 that was built in 1905 to house an artisans' association, the name of which in moulded terracotta still adorns the entrance. A series of courtyards at number 21 – the Sophie-Gips-Höfe – was once home to a sewing machine factory, and there is another decorative courtyard at number 22a. Nearby Neue Schönhauser Strasse 13 offers a variant on the usual courtyard in the form of a Volkskaffeehaus, providing coffee and cheap meals to workers, with men entering through an arch on the right and women on the left.

Looking into the courtyards of Hussitenstrasse 4-5

We travel to Friedrichshain-Kreuzberg for the second leg of this tour, where many old tenement blocks are still wholly or partially extant (wartime destruction has opened up many of the previously hidden courtyards), some of which still retain the metal tracks once used to guide wagons from the street into the building. These were used to service small industrial workshops and lofts, as was the case at Oranienstrasse 24–26 and 183–187.

Running at right angles to Oranienstrasse is Leuschnerdamm, where an apartment building erected in 1904 at number 13 was once all but blocked off by the Berlin Wall; on the other side is Erkelenzdamm, where at number 59–61 stands the sprawling Elisabethhof built in 1898 and still home to a typical Kreuzberg mixture of residential and commercial usages. A couple of streets to the east, on Mariannen-

An ornate courtyard entrance at Sophienstrasse 18

platz, are some of Berlin's first tenement blocks to be deliberately restored, their ornate stuccoed façades stripped away to give them a more modern feel.

After calling in at Wilhelmstrasse 9, where a fine apartment building has been torn open by Second World War bomb damage to reveal its splendidly stuccoed inner courtyard enhanced by the Tommy Weissbecker work collective, our journey finishes with a final group of courtyards south of the Landwehr-kanal, around Gneisenaustrasse and Yorckstrasse, which were part of Hobrecht's original grid street plan (although the extension of nearby railyards meant once-straight Yorckstrasse later developed a kink). A warren of mixed-use courtyards can be explored in the Mehringhof at Gneisenaustrasse 2, whilst a series of traditional courtyards can be glimpsed fleetingly along Hagelberger Strasse, whenever the doors in the typical neo-Classical facades from the 1870s are left open.

During the 1920s an alternative to tenement living was provided by the construction of spacious yet affordable housing estates, most notably the Horseshoe Estate (Hufeisen-siedlung) in Britz. Based on the Garden City ideal it was designed by Modernist architect Bruno Taut. Other examples include the Waldsiedlung Zehlendorf and the White City (Weisse Stadt) in Reinickendorf. With so many houses lost during the Second World War even more estates were erected, including the Otto-Suhr-Siedlung on Oranienstrasse (Friedrichshain-Kreuzberg), which was imitated in East Berlin by pre-fabricated, slab-built apartment complexes, which at the time were a welcome change to Berlin's crumbling 19th century buildings.

Other places of interest nearby: 15, 16, 20, 22

22   Descent into a Flak Tower

District I (Mitte), the Humboldthain anti-aircraft tower
(*Flakturm*) in the Volkspark Humboldthain
S1, S2, S25, S41, S42 Gesundbrunnen; U8 Gesundbrunnen

In September 1940, Adolf Hitler ordered that Berlin, Hamburg and
Vienna be protected by a series of colossal anti-aircraft towers (*Flak-türme*) (an acronym from *Fliegerabwehrkanonen*, meaning anti-aircraft
guns). Each installation would comprise a pair of towers, namely an
attack tower (*Gefechtsturm*) and a smaller control tower (*Leitturm*).
Designed by the architect Friedrich Tamms and constructed of steel-reinforced concrete 2.5 metres thick, each tower was erected in six
months using slave labour. The finished towers were manned by Hitler
Youth *Luftwaffenhilfer* under the command of experienced Luftwaffe
officers and NCOs of the *Turmflak-Abteilung*. Needless to say, follow-ing Germany's unconditional surrender, the towers were deemed of-fensive instruments of war and were rendered inoperable after serving
briefly as hostels for Germany's many homeless.

Attack towers were up to 42 metres high and formidably armed,
with four, twin-barrelled 128mm anti-aircraft guns on the roof, each
with a range of 14 800 metres. They were fed by shell hoists that reached
down inside the tower, which were themselves protected by a 70-ton
steel rooftop bunker. On the projecting balconies below were various
20–37mm guns. Having their own water and power supplies meant
that attack towers could also be used as civilian air raid shelters and
field hospitals, with 22 000 people able to shelter on the lower floors of
a single tower, and almost double that if needed. Each attack tower re-ceived its instructions from a nearby, more lightly armed control tower,
some 30 metres high and equipped with retractable radar equipment
and aerials for direction finding and ranging purposes. If necessary,
each control tower could hold 8000 civilians during an air raid.

Six pairs of towers were planned for Berlin of which three were
completed by the end of the war, located in parks forming a defen-sive triangle around the city centre. Berlin's *Flak* Tower I, known also
as the Zoo Tower, stood in the Zoologischer Garten (Mitte). Building
work commenced in October 1940 and the completed tower provided
support as far afield as the Gatow airfield in the west. It was also
used to safeguard many priceless exhibits from Berlin's museums (in-cluding the famous head of Egyptian Queen Nefertiti) and remained

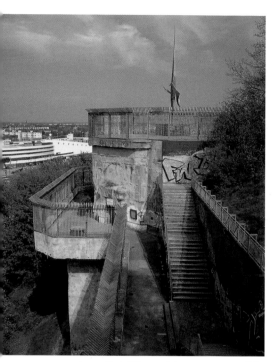

One of the remaining corner turrets of the Humboldthain anti-aircraft tower

a stubborn focus of German resistance during the Battle for Berlin in Spring 1945. The nearby control tower was especially important because it provided the communications link between Hitler's personal command shelter – the Führer Bunker (*Führerbunker*) – and troops defending the city during the last days of the war (see no. 10). After the war the Zoo Tower found itself in the British sector and Royal Engineers successfully demolished the control tower by sealing its openings and blowing it outwards using ammonal explosive. However, not enough ammonal was available to destroy the huge attack tower and so twenty tons of TNT were used instead: it failed, as did further charges placed around one of the corners. Eventually a thermic lance was used to burn 435 holes into the structure inside which more explosives were set and after 4 months of preparation the attack tower fell in June 1948. All traces of the tower were removed in 1958 to make way for an extension to the U-Bahn network.

Flak Tower II was erected in the Volkspark Friedrichshain (Friedrichshain-Kreuzberg), with construction commencing in April 1941. After the war it lay inside the Soviet sector and was reduced in height by blowing out its lower storeys. War debris was then heaped around the remains forming an artificial hill known as the *Grosse Bunkerberg*. Under the GDR government of East Germany a stairway was built leading up to a viewing area on the top of the mound, where parts of the tower's roof can still be made out. It is said that the uppermost layers of debris came from the controversial demolition of Berlin's royal palace (Stadtschloss) in 1950–51 and that the steps up the hill were carved from palace stone. The nearby control tower was also concealed in rubble and dubbed the *Kleine Bunkerberg*.

Looking down inside the Humboldthain anti-aircraft tower

Berlin's third tower, *Flak* Tower III, stood in Humboldthain Park (Mitte). Its construction began in October 1941 and was undertaken by Italian 'volunteers', Soviet POWs and other forced labourers. Falling inside the French sector after the war its attack tower was only partially demolished in 1948–51 because of its close proximity to the S-Bahn railway. Consequently, its two north-facing gun platforms are still extant, jutting out defiantly from an estimated 1.6 million cubic metres of bomb debris deliberately piled up around it forming another artificial hill. An exciting descent into the tower from the top of the hill (now marked on maps as *Humboldthain Höhe*) can be made on a guided tour with the Berlin Underworlds Association (Berliner Unterwelten e.V.), during which the top two of the tower's seven storeys can be explored. The Humboldthain control tower, in which captured British radar equipment was once tested, was also buried in rubble by the French, again leaving fragments of its upper walls visible.

Other places of interest nearby: 19, 20, 21

23 Some Unusual Museums

District I (Mitte), a tour of unusual museums beginning
with the Anti-War Museum (Anti-Kriegs-Museum) at
Brüsseler Strasse 21
U6 Seestrasse, U9 Amrumer Strasse

Considering the fact that there are approximately 280 museums and galleries in Berlin it is inevitable that a few of them are devoted to specialised, unusual and uniquely Berlin-related subjects.

Typical is the modest yet perennially relevant Anti-War Museum (Anti-Kriegs-Museum) at Brüsseler Strasse 21. The first museum of its type in the world it was founded in 1923 at Parochialstrasse 1–3 (Mitte) by the pacifist Ernst Friedrich (1894–1967). He was well-known in Berlin at the time for his book *War Against War!* Not surprisingly, in 1933 the museum was closed down by Hitler's brown-shirts, the SA *(Sturmabteilung)*, and the building converted into a torture centre. After spending a year in prison for his activities Friedrich emigrated to Belgium, where he opened a second Antiwar Museum; he also created a peace centre near Paris. Fifteen years after his death, Friedrich's Berlin museum was reopened at its current address, where his grandson, Tommy Spree, and a group of likeminded volunteers run it as a non-profit organisation. The museum includes photographs, documents and objects from both World Wars, as well as a large map indicating present day wars and conflicts.

A fascinating collection of objects thrown up by the very conflict the Anti-War Museum hoped to prevent can be found in the museum of the Berlin Underworlds Association (Berliner Unterwelten e.V.), which can be found inside the Gesundbrunnen U-Bahn station at Brunnenstrasse 105 (Mitte) (the entrance is suitably marked by a pair of concrete sentry boxes). The museum is the result of the association's ongoing exploration of subterranean Berlin, including air raid shelters, brewing cellars, and drainage systems, and can be visited as part of the association's guided tour of the Gesundbrunnen Second World War air raid shelter (see no. 65). Not surprisingly, the destruction wrought by the Second World War also features in the equally enlightening Fire Brigade Museum (Feuerwehrmuseum Berlin) at Berliner Strasse 16 (Reinickendorf).

Moving south from the Anti-War Museum into the Tiergarten is the most recent of Berlin's unusual museums, namely the outdoor museum of street lamps (Gaslaternen-Freilichtmuseum Berlin), stretching from the Strasse des 17. Juni at Klopstockstrasse down to the Landwehrkanal. No less than 90 different lamps are on display representing more than 20 German cities and 11 other European countries, including England, Ireland, Denmark and Switzerland. Each lamp is labelled with its age and provenance, and the whole makes for a romantic evening stroll.

A plaque marks the site of the world's first Anti-War Museum

Directly eastwards, in the rebuilt St. Nicholas Quarter (Nikolaiviertel) on the eastern bank of the Spree, is the tiny Hemp Museum (Hanfmuseum) at Mühlendamm 5 (Mitte). It illustrates the many uses – including fabrics, rope and cannabis – to which the tough fibres of the bushy Hemp plant have been put over hundreds of years. Loosely connected, in so much as cannabis is a technically legal drug in Germany (but not possession), is the former pharmacy of the Bethanien Hospital at Mariannenplatz 2 (Friedrichshain-Kreuzberg), which contains a collection of 19th century medicine bottles. One of the pharmacists that worked here was Theodor Fontane (1819–1898), who found fame later in life as a novelist.

Moving westwards, Berlin's relaxed attitude towards sexual freedom is reflected in the Schwules Museum at Mehringdamm 61 (Friedrichshain-Kreuzberg), the world's only museum to extensively document Gay culture and thinking. Farther west again, at Joachimstaler Strasse 4 (Charlottenburg-Wilmersdorf), is the Beate Uhse Erotik-Museum, founded in 1996 by a former German stunt pilot. Beate Uhse (1919–2001) had flown her son and nanny single-handedly out of Berlin in April 1945 and surrendered to the Allies. Unable to earn an income because of her connection with the Luftwaffe, and realising the poor quality of sex education amongst German women, she instead founded the world's first sex shop out of which grew a hugely successful chain of stores. Her museum contains five thousand exhibits from around the world and claims to be the largest of its type.

The most westerly of Berlin's unusual museums is the little-known

Berlin U-Bahn Museum (Berliner U-Bahn-Museum), occupying a railway workshop at the Olympia-Stadion U-Bahn station on the U2 line; it contains everything from tickets and uniforms to real rolling stock.

This tour of unusual museums finishes just outside Berlin in Potsdam, where the Dutch-style Historic Windmill (Historische Mühle) just north of Sanssouci Park contains a collection of mechanical windmills. Built originally in the early 18th century, rebuilt in 1790 and destroyed in 1945, the building seen today is a replica erected in 1993. It is said that King Frederick II, 'the Great' (1740–1786) was defeated in court in an attempt to get the mill dismantled because of its noise!

A special display illustrating the importance of Berlin in the story of sugar can be found in the German Technical Museum (Deutsches Technikmuseum Berlin) at Trebbiner Strasse 9 (Friedrichshain-Kreuzberg). In 1747 a renowned Berlin pharmacist and chemist, Andreas Sigismund Marggraf (1709–1782), was the first to identify high concentrations of sucrose in the root of the sugar beet plant *(Mangelwurzel) (Beta vulgaris L.)*. In 1798 his successor, Franz Carl Achard, produced the first ever beet sugar and presented it to King Frederick William III (1797–1840). With the king's financial support the world's first beet sugar factory was established in Silesia, at that time part of Prussia (now Poland). Such home-grown production not only saved the king the expense of importing cane sugar from the colonies but was also important during the French blockade of Napoleonic Europe in 1806. The same technique is still used today to produce a third of the world's sugar.

24 The Real Metropolis

District I (Mitte), the former AEG Turbine Factory
(AEG-Turbinenfabrik) at the corner of Huttenstrasse
and Berlichingenstrasse
U9 Turmstrasse

Undoubtedly one of the most memorable silent-era films to come out of Berlin's famous Babelsberg Film Studio was Fritz Lang's 1927 science fiction classic *Metropolis*, with its soaring skyscrapers and machine-filled factories (see no. 51). It is interesting to note that the architectural backdrop for this stirring vision of a dystopian future was inspired by early 20th century Modernism, with its rejection of traditional artistic and architectural ideas in favour of unadorned, pared-down, industrial forms. When interviewed about his influences Lang claimed that a visit to New York City had made a great impression on him, however it should not be forgotten that Berlin too had made important inroads into architectural Modernism. The city's greatest practitioner was the artist and architect Peter Behrens (1868–1940)

The former AEG turbine factory on Huttenstrasse

and it makes for an unusual tour to track down some of his industrial buildings and reflect on just how modern they must have appeared when first built.

Starting out as an illustrator and bookbinder Behrens joined an artists' colony in Darmstadt in 1899, where he built his own house and designed everything inside from the furniture down to the towels. In 1907 he was invited to join the German Work Federation (Deutsche Werkbund) in Munich, an association of forward-thinking artists, manufacturers and architects founded by Hermann Muthesius (1861–1927). Less of an artistic movement and more a state-sponsored effort to combine traditional crafts with industrial mass-production techniques, the Werkbund's motto "Vom Sofakissen zum Städtebau"

("From sofa cushions to city-building") indicates its broad range of interests.

In the same year Behrens was offered the extraordinary position of design consultant for the German General Electric Company (Allgemeine Elektricitäts-Gesellschaft), which together with Siemens led Europe in the new electrical industry. His brief was to oversee everything built, used or manufactured by the corporation, including factory and office buildings and their furnishings, industrial and household products, and even the official AEG stationery! Behrens had unwittingly created the modern notion of design-led corporate identity.

The earliest and most outstanding building to result from this new alliance between architect-designer and modern industry was the AEG Turbine Factory (AEG-Turbinenfabrik), constructed in 1909 at the corner of Huttenstrasse and Berlichingenstrasse, in the Berlin district of Moabit (Mitte). Structurally the building consists of a row of triple-hinged steel arches, similar to those used in 19th century railway stations and exhibition halls. However, whereas in the 19th century those buildings would have resembled either an iron and glass latticework cage, or else been concealed behind a plastered brickwork façade, Behrens transformed his simple arched factory shed into a new architectural form, with just a hint of the Classical temple about it. He achieved this by recessing the high slanting windows down the long sides of the building so that the vertical supports stand out like a colonnade; similarly, the corner supports emerge like massive pylons supporting a pediment-style gable that closes off the roof space above. Most striking of all is the huge yet delicate glazed curtain wall, hanging in front of the pylons from the projecting pediment above; it is a futuristic *tour de force* that sits well amongst the more traditional elements of a building hailed as the first masterwork of modern industrial architecture. To appreciate quite how original Behren's building was at the time it should be compared to a neo-Classical factory built for the Loewe machinery company in 1917 at the nearby junction of Huttenstrasse and Wiebestrasse.

Over the following years Behrens worked on a larger AEG complex spread out between Ackerstrasse and Brunnenstrasse in Wedding (Mitte). The first buildings erected here date from the 1890s to designs by Franz Heinrich Schwechten (1841–1924), architect of the Anhalt railway station (Anhalter Bahnhof) and the Kaiser Wilhelm Memorial Church (Kaiser-Wilhelm-Gedächtnis-Kirche). Typically 19th century in style, being of red-brick construction with arched windows and terracotta decoration, Schwechten's work can best be seen in the block

Peter Behrens' factory hall on Hussitenstrasse

opposite the church on Gartenplatz and in the ornate entrance used by white-collar workers at Brunnenstrasse 111 (although much of his work was demolished after AEG ceased production on the site in 1978). Behren's work, by contrast, appears noble but austere. At the corner of Hussitenstrasse and Voltastrasse stands his large factory hall from 1911–1913, in a style similar to his Moabit turbine factory. Behind it and accessible from Voltastrasse is his high-voltage factory of 1910, almost devoid of ornament but recalling Egyptian motifs. Also on Voltastrasse is his huge small-motor factory (1911–1913), a model of stripped back Greek neo-Classicism, with a seven-story façade of glazed brick and glass.

During the time he was working for AEG, Behrens employed numerous students and assistants, including Ludwig Mies van der Rohe (1886–1969), Charles-Edouard Jean-neret (better known as Le Corbusier) (1887–1965), and Walter Gropius (1883–1969), all of whom would become highly successful in their own right, incorporating many of Behren's new ideas into what became known as the International Style (Gropius would found the Bauhaus movement in 1919, the archive of which is at Klingelhöferstrasse 14 (Mitte)). Behrens himself finished his days as director of the architecture department at Berlin's Prussian Academy of Art.

25 The Old Villages of Berlin

District XII (Reinickendorf), a tour of former villages
including Alt-Lübars
S1 Waidmannslust, then Bus 222 Alt-Lübars

Until as recently as 1920 the city of Berlin consisted only of the central districts of Mitte, Tiergarten, Wedding, Prenzlauer Berg, Friedrichshain and Kreuzberg: beyond lay numerous old towns and villages, which had evolved independently. The establishment of Greater Berlin in 1920 swallowed up seven of these towns, together with twenty seven country estates, and fifty nine villages. Berlin was thus transformed into an entirely new city of 3.8 million inhabitants, occupying an area of 900 square kilometres.

Over the course of the last century, most of the old villages of Berlin, some of which predate the founding in 1200 of medieval Berlin-Cölln itself, have been completely absorbed into the urban fabric, as modern housing developments and industrial centres have sprawled across what were once green fields. It makes for an interesting journey, therefore, to identify what remains of these former medieval settlements.

Fortunately for the explorer, more than 40 old village churches are still standing, invariably located on streets prefixed conveniently by the word '*Alt-*' (old) – and occasionally still surrounded by their original village greens. Some of the best-preserved can be found in southern Berlin, on land settled in the 13th century by the Christian military order known as the Knights Templar. They were responsible not only for the largest of Berlin's village churches, on Reinhardtplatz near Alt-Tempelhof (Tempelhof-Schöneberg), with its 18th century half-timbered tower rebuilt after the Second World War, but also the oldest, on Alt-Marienfelde. The latter is a typically sturdy, granite-built structure with a squat tower, situated on a leafy village green surrounded by converted farmhouses; replete with a village pond it appears much as it did in the early years of the 20th century. Other village churches in the same district include Alt-Mariendorf and Alt-Lichtenrade, whilst neighbouring Neukölln to the east contains Alt-Buckow and Alt-Britz. Moving northwards, Alt-Stralau (Friedrichshain-Kreuzberg), at the end of a peninsula jutting into the River Spree, also retains its old church and contains Berlin's only remaining piece of late Gothic stained glass. Other village churches can be found at Alt-Blankenburg and Alt-Karow

(Pankow), and Alt-Reinickendorf (Reinickendorf).

One of the few medieval village churches that still retains something of its original rural setting is the Church of St. Anne (St.-Annen-Kirche) in Dahlem (Steglitz-Zehlendof), on the corner of Königin-Luise-Strasse and Pacelliallee. Surrounded by a leafy cemetery the church was built in the 14th century to which a tower was added in the 18th century. Inside there are still original medieval wall paintings depicting the life of St. Anna, as well as Gothic sculptures of the saints. The rustic charm is reinforced by the presence next door of the Domäne Dahlem, a Baroque

Where the country meets the city: the village of Alt-Lubärs

manor house and farming estate created in 1680 that is now a working museum of traditional village agriculture. . The picture is completed by Dahlem's U-Bahn station, which was thatched by royal decree to make it look like a peasant's house – only in Berlin! (Another reconstructed farming community on the remains of an abandoned 13th century village is the Museumsdorf Düppel at Clauertstrasse 11)

Museums and reconstructions aside, in order to explore the only remaining example of a truly unspoilt Berlin village, a visit should be made to the little-known suburb of Lübars, on the city's northern edge. Around the village green of Alt-Lübars, with its venerable oak and chestnut trees and cobblestoned road, stands a picture postcard ensemble of Baroque church (1793), village inn, schoolhouse, and old water pump. Originally a farming community, Alt-Lübars is now known for its equestrian facilities, which account for the presence of its numerous stables and blacksmiths. At the end of a waymarked track leading north-west from the entrance to the village green is the Tegeler Fliess, an Ice Age drainage channel that flows gently into the Tegeler See to the west: the surrounding peaceful water meadows could not be further removed from the bustle of modern Berlin.

26 Europe's Oldest Buddhist Site

District XII (Reinickendorf), the Buddhist House
(Buddhistisches Haus) at Edelhofdamm 54
S1 Frohnau

Buddhism is practised today by 300 million people living mostly in Asia. It is based on the teachings of Siddhārtha Gautama, known today as Buddha, who lived in India 2500 years ago. He refuted the idea that man had an immortal soul nor did he believe in a supreme deity, rather he taught that man should seek freedom from greed, hatred and delusion, and thereby gain enlightenment (*Nirvana*) through the Four Noble Truths (acknowledging, understanding and destroying suffering, and pursuing the Eightfold Path to correct understanding, behaviour and meditation). Buddhism gradually spread from India to East Asia and in the process split into two distinct camps. In China, Japan, Korea and Vietnam, *Mahayana* Buddhism (the 'Great Way') became prevalent, with its emphasis on collective salvation. By contrast, in Ceylon (now Sri Lanka), Burma (now Myanmar), Thailand, Laos and Cambodia, *Theravāda* Buddhism (the 'Way of the Elders') prevailed, with its emphasis on personal salvation.

The study and practice of Buddhism in Germany stretches back a mere two centuries. One of the first Germans to be influenced by Buddhism was the philosopher Arthur Schopenhauer (1788–1860), whose writings influenced other fledgling Buddhists and Orientalists such as Friedrich Zimmermann, who in 1888 published the *Buddhist Catechism*. In 1903 the first German Buddhist organisation was founded in Leipzig by the Indologist Karl Seidenstücker, and in 1904 Anton Walther Florus Gueth became the first German *Theravāda* Buddhist monk, Nyanatiloka. Around the same time the scholar Karl Eugen Neumann translated some important Pāli texts into German (Pāli being the language in which the Theravāda scriptures had been first written in Sri Lanka in the 1st century BC) and in 1922 Hermann Hesse published his famous novel *Siddhartha*.

Against this backdrop one man did more than anyone else to establish a centre for Buddhism in Berlin: the homeopathic doctor and writer Paul Dahlke (1865–1928). Born in East Prussia to parents of modest means, Dahlke realised early on that homeopathic medicine was a profession that suited him. After moving to Berlin his reputa-

Entrance to the Buddhist House in Reinickendorf

tion grew, whilst at the same time he began pursuing interests outside medicine, notably Buddhism. In 1898 he embarked on a journey to the islands of the South Pacific, inspired by the writings of the botanist Adelbert von Chamisso (see no. 62). Two years later he set out again, this time to Ceylon, where he received his first official Buddhist teachings (*Dhamma*). Further journeys followed together with a growing belief that the solution to the problems of the West lay in a fuller understanding of Buddhism. With this in mind, Dahlke embarked on a series of groundbreaking German translations of *Theravāda* Buddhist texts and founded a quarterly periodical, *New Buddhist Journal*. Most significantly he proposed the construction of Germany's first Buddhist meeting house where likeminded people, no longer in accord with their inherited, materialistic religion, could meet.

So it was that shortly after the First World War Dahlke acquired several acres of woodland in Frohnau, a suburb in the far north of Berlin. Despite raging inflation construction began and in August 1924 he and several colleagues moved into the so-called Buddhist House (Buddhistische Haus) at Edelhofdamm 54, identified today by its gateway crowned with sculpted elephants. Designed in Ceylonese style by the architect Max Meyer, the house with its library and meeting hall sits on top of a hillock and is reached by a steep staircase, the number of steps

The Buddhist House on its symbolic hill

and landings being dictated by Buddhist teaching. Conceived as a place of inner purification through meditation, contemplation and study, the house stands as one of the boldest attempts to introduce Buddhist principles into a secular world.

After Dahlke's death in 1928 the house fell into disrepair and was all but abandoned during the Nazi period. Fortunately, in 1957 the then recently-founded German Dharmaduta Society (originally the Lanka Dhammaduta Society), dedicated to spreading the Buddhist message in Europe, purchased the house. They converted it into a temple (*Vihāra*) and sent Sri Lankan monks to run it. Today, it is again a centre for the spread of *Theravāda* Buddhism in Europe and the German authorities have designated it both the oldest Buddhist site in Europe and a national heritage site.

27 From Russia with Love

District XII (Reinickendorf), the Russian Orthodox Church of Sts. Constantine and Helen (Russische-orthodoxe Hl. Konstantin- und Helena-Kirche) at Wittestrasse 37
U6 Holzhauserstrasse

The part played by Russia in Berlin's liberation from the Nazis at the end of the Second World War is obvious from its three Soviet War Memorials (Sowjetisches Ehrenmal), erected in the Tiergarten, Treptower Park, and the Volkspark Schönholzer Heide (see no. 8). The human cost of that conflict is felt, perhaps even more sharply, in small Red Army cemeteries like the one behind the Church of Sts. Peter and Paul in Bassinplatz (Potsdam); such burial grounds are to be found in almost every town in the former GDR.

However, the influence of Russia on Berlin goes back much farther than the Second World War and it has left some unusual physical remains that are well worth exploring. The name Alexanderplatz, for example, is in commemoration of a visit to Berlin by Tsar Alexander I (1801–1825) in 1805. The period was dominated by Napoleon's ongoing military campaigns in Europe, in the face of which Prussia wanted to remain neutral and Russia hoped to eventually make an alliance with France. The tsar displayed a chivalric loyalty to Prussia's King Frederick William III (1797–1840), parts of Prussia having already been already occupied by French forces. Napoleon defeated the Prussian army at the Battle of Jena in 1806, causing the Prussian royal family to flee to East Prussia and seek protection from the tsar. The Russians were themselves defeated at Friedland in 1807, after which a formal alliance between Russia and France was signed at Tilsit. Relations inevitably soured, however, once the tsar realised that Napoleon was simply trying to buy time with Russia, whilst setting about the conquest of Central Europe – and eventually even Russia itself.

By the time of Napoleon's defeat at the Battle of Waterloo (1815) Prussia had long since turned against France and had signed an alliance with Russia. This was cemented in 1817 when the Prussian king's daughter, Charlotte, married the tsar's son, later Tsar Nicholas I (1825–1855). As a wedding gift the king commissioned the construction of the Blockhaus Nikolskoe, at the northern end of Nikolskoer Weg on Wannsee Island (Steglitz-Zehlendorf). Erected in 1819 and rebuilt after a fire in 1985 it is based on a Russian log-built country house (*dacha*), which the king and his daughter had seen on their way to the wedding. The house is today a restaurant said to date back to when the king's Russian coachman supplemented his income here by selling refreshments to visitors. The king also insisted that the nearby Church of Sts. Peter and Paul, completed in 1837 to a neo-Romanesque design by Frederick August Stüler (1800–1865), have a Russian-style onion dome, although Eastern Orthodoxy is not observed here.

Frederick William III continued his Russian theme across the Heiliger See from Wannsee, where he commissioned the oldest of the Berlin area's three *genuine* Russian Orthodox churches. Built in 1829 and dedicated to Saint Alexander Nevsky it stands on the Kapellenberg ('Chapel Hill'). The church was designed at the tsar's court and built under the supervision of the architect Carl Frederick Schinkel (1781–1841); the icons were painted in Russia. The church is in actual fact a visual complement to an entire Russian-style village, laid out to the south at the junction of Russische Kolonie Allee and Puschkinallee. The king decreed the creation of the village in 1826, calling it Alexandrowka in memory of his recently deceased ally Tsar Alexander I. The village was created for the singers of a Russian choir, recruited in 1812 from a group of Russian prisoners of war, who had fought with Napoleon. When Prussia and Russia joined forces the choir was retained by the king and eventually installed in the village. The royal landscape gardener Peter Joseph Lenné (1789–1866) laid out the central oval space, in imitation of 18th century Russian army villages. Two main streets were constructed within the oval, along which a dozen log-built houses were constructed, each finished off with traditional carved overhanging gables.

Berlin's second Russian Orthodox church can be found on Hoffmann-von-Fallersleben-Platz, off Berliner Strasse (Charlottenburg-Wilmersdorf), adjacent to Germany's oldest mosque (see no. 38). On its roof can be seen the distinctive Russian Orthodox cross, made up of two horizontal bars and one diagonal, crossing a vertical shaft. The upper bar represents the inscription 'INRI' ("Jesus of Nazareth, King of the Jews"), the mocking title bestowed on Christ by the Romans in the New Testament account of the Crucifixion. The lower, diagonal bar is a stylised foot rest although later folklore holds that one end points down to hell (the destiny of the unrepentant thief Gestas) and the other up to heaven (the destiny of the repentant thief Dismas).

Berlin's third Russian Orthodox church stands within a Russian cemetery established in 1894 at Wittestrasse 37 (Reinickendorf); indeed, it is the only Russian Orthodox church in Germany that has its

The Russian Orthodox
Church of Sts.
Constantine and Helen

own burial ground. The cemetery is entered through an ornate gateway
with a finely carved roof housing nine cemetery bells. Beyond there is
an avenue of lime trees leading to the brick-built church itself, which is
dedicated to Sts. Constantine and Helen (Russische-orthodoxe Hl. Kons-
tantin- und Helena-Kirche). It still serves the local Russian Orthodox
community today. The delightful building is topped off with five blue
cupolas and Russian Orthodox crosses. Inside the church are a pair of
icons of the Virgin Mary donated by two Eastern Orthodox monasteries
from Mount Athos in Greece. The surrounding cemetery contains many
graves marked with Russian Orthodox crosses, as well as several memorial stones to the likes of opera composer Mikhail Ivanovich Glinka

(1804–1857), who died in Berlin and is buried in St. Petersburg, Latvian architect Mikhail Ossipovich Eisenstein (1867–1921), father of the famous film director Sergei Mikhailovich Eisenstein (1898–1948), and Alexander Alexandrovich Rimsky-Korsakov, a nephew of the famous composer Nikolai. Along the western wall of the cemetery are mass graves for the children of Russian forced armaments labourers, who succumbed to starvation and disease during the Second World War.

When the cemetery was first laid out, Tsar Alexander III (1881–1894) sent 4000 tons of soil by train to Berlin, to be scattered over the site so that his subjects could be buried in Russian earth. This nationalistic act reflects the political tensions of the day. During the reign of his father Tsar Alexander II (1855–1881), who had strong German sympathies and even spoke German, the *tsarevich* disliked Prussian influence and dreamt of a homogenous Russia with a single language, religion, and administration. During the Franco-Prussian War (1870–1871), when Alexander II supported Berlin, the *tsarevich* did little to conceal his sympathies with the French. His fears were eventually confirmed at the Congress of Berlin in 1878, when German Chancellor Otto von Bismarck (1815–1898) failed to reward Russian support and instead contracted an alliance with Austria, specifically to counteract Russian designs in Eastern Europe. After becoming tsar in 1881, Alexander III avoided conflict with Prussia despite remaining indignant at Bismarck's actions. Instead, he believed that the best means of averting war was to be well prepared for it, and so he set about reorganising the Russian army and navy. It would be a problem that would haunt both nations well into the second half of the 20th century.

For a real taste of Russia try the Pasternak restaurant at Knaackstrasse 22-24 (Pankow), named after Boris Leonidovich Pasternak (1890-1960), the author of *Dr. Zhivago*. This convivial restaurant is popular with both Russian expatriates and German students, who come here for traditional beetroot (*Borscht*), and sausage and cabbage (*Soljanka*), soups, as well as Russian-style pancakes (*blinis*), and Beef Stroganoff. The latter is named after a St. Petersburg family called Stroganov, whose personal chef won a cooking competition with the dish in the 1890s. For the more affluent visitor, vodka and caviar is available for brunch!

28 No Longer a Famous Prison

District V (Spandau), the former site of Spandau Prison
on Wilhelmstrasse
S5 Berlin Spandau or U7 Rathaus Spandau,
then Bus 134 Melanchthonplatz

Spandau is one of the oldest towns in Berlin, the distinctive '-*au*' name ending identifying it as a place formerly occupied by Slavic tribes. They were called the Havolane (or Heveller in German), since they lived around the river Havel, and they built a fortress here in the 8th century. During the mid-12th century, however, they came into conflict with the Duke of Saxony, who wanted to take control of the Brandenburg area, and they were forced out (see no. 31). Consequently, around 1200 the German conquerors built their own fortress here, at the strategically important confluence of the Havel and the Spree, near to which emerged a town that was chartered in 1232.

All that remains of Spandau Prison

Spared serious damage during the Second World War, the town of Spandau still retains its medieval street plan, as well as the fine late Gothic Church of St. Nicholas (St-Nikolai-Kirche), fragments of its 14th century town walls (on Hoher Steig), and several timber-framed houses. Most striking of all though is the late 16th century moated fortress called Zitadelle Spandau, its 36-metre high crenellated Julius Tower (Juliusturm) a part of the original 13th century castle. Not surprisingly a prison was included within its ramparts. However, it is a more recent prison, standing some distance away to the south at the junction of Wilhelmstrasse and Gatower Strasse that is today most associated with the name 'Spandau'.

The military prison of Spandau was opened in 1876 with the capacity to hold six hundred prisoners. It later became a civil prison but under Hitler it was again used for military prisoners awaiting trial, as well as for political prisoners in transit to concentration camps. Requisitioned in 1946 by the Allies, on 18th July 1947 it took on a new role, when seven Nazi war criminals sentenced at the Nuremberg trials arrived: they were *Gauleiter* ('regional leader') of Vienna Baldur von Schirach (1907–1974), Grossadmiral Karl Dönitz (1891–1980), one-time Reischsprotektor of Bohemia and Moravia Konstantin Freiherr von Neurath (1873–1956), Grossadmiral Dr. Erich Raeder (1876–1960), Reichsbank President Walther Funk (1890–1960), Armaments Minister Albert Speer (1905–1981), and Hitler's former deputy Rudolf Hess (1894–1987), who had flown to Scotland in a much-storied attempt to create an Anglo-German alliance against Russia.

The sturdy red-brick prison, which was surrounded by a perimeter wall punctuated by nine watch towers and a floodlit electric fence, was operated under rotating four-power control. Watched over by 32 soldiers, 18 warders and various ancillary staff, the prisoners were outnumbered 10 to 1. After 1966, when Speer and von Schirach were released, Rudolf Hess remained the sole inmate. Bizarrely, the entire prison continued to operate as before until 93-year old Hess's suicide in August 1987, almost exactly forty years since his incarceration. Needless to say, the Russians had been insistent that Hess's life sentence be just that.

The Four Powers had long agreed that when the last prisoner died the prison should be demolished to avoid it becoming a shrine to Nazism. Consequently, on the day Hess died it was announced that the Allied Prison Administration would be terminated and demolition would start immediately. There is nothing left of Spandau prison today except for four red-brick ancillary buildings, which actually stood *outside* the perimeter wall that ran along Wilhelmstrasse. The original entrance to the prison stood between the middle two buildings, still marked today by a pair of mature trees. Either side of the old entrance the former line of the perimeter wall is marked by an access road encirclng what is now a new shopping and leisure centre. Directly ahead once stood the main prison block on the far side of which, amidst a clump of trees, is the former exercise garden used by Rudolf Hess during his final years.

29 A Most Beautiful Cemetery

District IV (Charlottenburg-Wilmersdorf), the Heerstrasse
Cemetery (Friedhof Heerstrasse) at Trakehner Allee 1
S5 Olympia-Stadion; U2 Olympia-Stadion (Ost)

Berlin's cemetery statistics are staggering: at the last count the city had more than 200 burial grounds! Of these, the majority are Protestant, a minority Catholic or other faiths (including Jewish, Muslim, Russian Orthodox, and British), and the rest open to all religions. In an ever-changing city such as Berlin many of these cemeteries have offered not only tranquillity but also continuity against a turbulent historical backdrop.

Probably the most beautiful is the Heerstrasse Cemetery (Friedhof Heerstrasse), created in 1921–1924 and attributed to the influential landscape gardener Erwin Barth (1880–1933). The cemetery actually stands on Trakehner Allee, its misleading name referring to an

exclusive villa colony (Villenkolonie Heerstrasse) established contemporaneously on nearby Heerstrasse, for whose inhabitants the cemetery was provided (a good example of a villa stands at Heerstrasse 107, built in 1924 to a design by the Modernist architect Erich Mendelsohn (1887–1953)).

The Heerstrasse Cemetery is noteworthy because it is laid out as a 'forest cemetery' (*Waldfriedhof*) on an undulating site that was originally part of the Grunewald Forest. At its heart is the Sausuhlensee, or 'Wild Boar's Lake', lying some 20 metres below the level of the surrounding streets. South-west of the lake there is a large circular plant-

The beautiful Heerstrasse Forest Cemetery

ing of trees and hedges, from where paths radiate outwards forming a star shape along which the graves themselves are located.

In 1936 Berlin's huge Olympic Stadium (Olympiastadion) was inaugurated on land immediately adjacent to the burial ground. Adolf Hitler took considerable offence to the cemetery's red-brick chapel, which had been built originally in an Oriental style and was visible from the stadium: he ordered its tower be lowered! Badly damaged during the Second World War the chapel was eventually remodelled in 1948. Around the same time the cemetery was extended eastwards beyond the lake, although this section, which can be reached by a series of peaceful wooded paths, remains informal and largely unused.

The Heerstrasse Cemetery's prominent position in affluent Charlottenburg accounts for the large number of famous German actors, writers, artists, and musicians who are buried here, a long list of their names being displayed at the cemetery gates. They include the actor Alfred Abel (1879–1937), who appeared in Fritz Lang's *Dr. Mabuse* (1922) (although his grave is now lost), the Expressionist artist George Grosz (1893–1959) (16 B-19), a prominent member of the Berlin Dada group renowned for his savage caricatures of Weimar life in the 1920s, Oskar Sala (1910–2002) (II Ur3-224), a pioneer of electronic music, who played an early version of a synthesizer called a Trautonium and composed the non-musical soundtrack to Alfred Hitchcock's film *The Birds* (1963), the renowned German sculptor Georg Kolbe (1877–1947) (2D 4), whose work is displayed in the nearby Georg Kolbe Museum at Sensburger Allee 25, and the actress Tilla Durieux (1880–1971) (5C 3–4), famed for working with the theatre director Max Reinhardt (1873–1943). Also buried in the Heerstrasse Cemetery is the satirical author and artist Joachim Ringelnatz (1883–1947) (12 D-21), who was banned by the Nazis as a "degenerate artist". By contrast, the grave of the Ullstein Family (8D 7–10) is by Josef Thorak (1889–1952), an official sculptor to the Third Reich, whose penchant for muscular neo-Classical nudes earned him the nickname 'Professor Thorax'!

Landscape gardener Erwin Barth moved to the affluent and rapidly developing district of Charlottenburg in 1912, where he was Director of Gardens until 1926. His largest project was the creation of the Volkspark Jungfernheide (Charlottenburg-Wilmersdorf); his most prolific the creation of public squares such as Brixplatz not far from the Heerstrasse Cemetery.

Other places of interest nearby: 30, 32

30 The Olympic Bell Tower

District IV (Charlottenburg-Wilmersdorf), the bell tower at the Olympic Stadium (Glockenturm am Olympiastadion) on Passenheimer Strasse
S5 Pichelsberg

On 9th July 2006 more than 74 000 football fans took their seats in Berlin's Olympic Stadium (Olympiastadion) for the final of the eighteenth World Cup. Although the stadium had previously been used to host the 1974 World Cup it was decided in 1998 to extensively refurbish it in time for the 2006 event at a cost of 242 million Euros. In doing so one of Berlin's most controversial historic buildings, in which the Nazi regime hosted the XIth Olympiad in August 1936, was transformed into a state-of-the-art sports venue for the 21st century.

Football aside, Berlin's Olympic Stadium still holds several secrets. Most will already know that Adolf Hitler, who originally derided the Olympic movement, eventually hijacked the games as a propaganda tool for his Third Reich. Fewer may be aware that an earlier stadium (Kaiser Wilhelm Stadion) was built here for the 1916 Olympics, which were postponed because of the First World War. This stadium was sunk into the middle of the pre-existing Grunewald racecourse (Grunewald-Rennbahn), so as not to be too intrusive; after the collapse of the monarchy in 1918 it was re-named the Grunewald Stadion. Prior to Hitler's rise to power preparations had been made to modify the stadium, whilst maintaining its low profile. Hitler, on the other hand, envisaged his Berlin games as bigger and more impressive than any in history, and for that he needed a stadium to match. Consequently, both racecourse and stadium (by this time re-named the Deutsche Stadion) were obliterated and a colossal oval-shaped stadium capable of holding 100 000 spectators built in their place. Even the Oriental-looking tower of a chapel in the nearby Heerstrasse Cemetery was lowered on Hitler's orders for fear it might contaminate his purely Germanic vision of the games (see no. 29). (Curiously, the distinctly non-monumental entrance of the old stadium, with its quaint red-tiled roofs, was left standing and can still be seen on what is today Jesse-Owens-Allee, named after the brilliant African-American sprinter, who beat Hitler's sportsmen to four gold medals in 1936).

For the Nazis, Berlin's Olympic Stadium was much more than just a sports arena: it was a powerful symbol for the world of German national revival and a potent reminder to the German people of their racial origins. The long, eastern approach to the stadium, down an avenue lined with pillars representing Germanic tribes, was designed to impress and overawe, the statues of muscular Classical figures by official Third Reich sculptors Arno Breker (1900–1991) and Josef Thorak (1889–1952) emphasising the spurious Nazi notion of Aryan supremacy traced back to the ancient Greeks. A gap in the west end of the stadium continued the main axis across the so-called Maifeld ('May Field'), an open space covering an area of 112 000 square metres for polo and dressage events; since it could hold 250 000 people it was earmarked for use after the games to stage not only May Day celebrations but more importantly Nazi rallies (it was here that Hitler and Mussolini jointly addressed the masses in 1937).

The eye finally settles at the western edge of the May Field and a tiered grandstand capable of holding a further 60 000 spectators. Below it is the so-called Langemarck Hall (Langemarck-Halle), a memorial to 2000 young German troops who died on 10th November 1914 after launching a futile attack against superior British riflemen at the Battle of Langemarck in Belgium. Nazi propaganda glorified the 'Langemarck Attack' as an example of supposedly willing self-sacrifice, adding that the soldiers were singing what became the German national anthem as they fell.

Above the grandstand is a 77 metre-high tower containing Berlin's Olympic bell. From its summit the other elements of the *Reichssportfeld*, as the stadium complex was known originally, can be made out, including the House of German Sports (Haus des Deutschen Sports) to the northeast, containing swimming, boxing and training facilities, and the Dietrich-Eckart-Freilichtbühne to the northwest, an open-air performance area based on the ancient Greek theatre at Epidaurus, in which gymnastic events were staged before an audience of 20 000. Now called the Waldbühne ('Forest Stage') it was named originally after the anti-Semitic poet responsible for the slogan "Deutschland Erwache!" (Wake up Germany!).

Throughout the Berlin Olympics the tower housed the observation stands of the games' organisers, as well as the media, police, and medical services. During the war the service tunnels beneath the stadium were used to house an armaments factory and the grandstand either side of the tower was used to store the film archives of the Third Reich (see no. 65). After the Red Army entered Berlin in April 1945 the stadium became the scene of fierce fighting as members of a Hitler Youth unit made a futile last stand against Red Army machine gunners leaving 2000 of them dead. It was around this time that the film archives caught fire, the hollow bell tower above acting like a chimney. The steel framework of the tower was so badly damaged by the heat that in 1947 it had to be demolished by British engineers. The bell cracked as it fell. It then lay buried until 1956, when it was exhumed and placed on a podium outside the House of German Sports, which had been the post-war headquarters of the British Military Government in Berlin. On its surface are representations of the Brandenburg Gate, a martial eagle clutching the Olympic rings, and a partially-erased swastika, together with the following inscription: "Ich rufe die Jugend der Welt" ("I summon the youth of the world"). Also visible is a neat hole made by an artillery shell whilst the bell was still hanging, fired in error by a schoolboy drafted in to man nearby anti-aircraft guns in the closing stages of the war.

Looking out from the Olympic bell tower, with the stadium on the right

Remarkably, between 1960 and 1962 the bell tower was rebuilt, using the original plans; a new bell was cast by the same firm that cast the original and a viewing platform added at the top. Today the tower contains an express lift enabling visitors to take in vistas of both the Olympic Stadium and of the surrounding Brandenburg countryside.

Other places of interest nearby: 29, 32

31 The Schildhorn Column

Berlin is watered by the Spree and Havel rivers, the former being a tributary that traverses the city from east to west, joining the Havel at Spandau. By contrast, the Havel flows north to south down the western flank of the city. Rising near Neustrelitz in Mecklenburg-Western Pomerania, this 325 kilometre-long river eventually joins the River Elbe near Havelberg in Saxony-Anhalt.

Of the 30 kilometres that the River Havel spends within the city boundaries of Berlin it is said that its most beautiful stretches are around Schildhorn, Lindwerder, Schwanenwerder and Pfaueninsel, a series of promontories and islands west of the Grunewald Forest (see no. 43). The area is popular with those in search of fresh air and nature. However, during the late 18th and early 19th centuries this area was also a favourite of the Prussian kings, who embellished the landscape with a series of castles, follies and architectural whimsies, which are well worth exploring today (see nos. 27, 46 & 47).

The northern extremity of this royal landscape is punctuated by the so-called Schildhorn Column, which stands at the end of a small peninsula stretching northwards into the Havel. It is reached by means of the Havelchaussee and the Strasse am Schildhorn, which passes the historic Schildhorn Inn (Wirtshaus Schildhorn). Close to the riverbank a flight of steps leads up to the sandstone column itself, set high above the river and surrounded by pine trees. King Frederick William IV (1840–61) commissioned the architect Frederick August Stüler (1800–1865), best known for designing the Old National Gallery (Alte Nationalgalerie) at Bodestrasse 1–3 on Museum Island (Museumsinsel), to have the column built in 1845 using the king's own sketches. Together with Stüler's Church of Sts. Peter and Paul (1837) at Nikolskoe on Wannsee Island, and Ludwig Persius's (1803–1845) Church of the Redeemer (Heilandskirche) (1841) in Sacrow on the opposite shore, the column is part of a religious landscape that gave expression to the Hohnzollern's romantic ideas about the redeeming power of Christianity and their wish to glorify it.

The Schildhorn Column, destroyed in 1945 and restored in 1954, depicts a stylized tree crowned by a cross, from which a carved shield, sword and horn once hung (only the shield remains today). As such it illustrates a legend concerning the Slav Duke Jaczo (Jaksa), who in 1157 was forced to flee from Albert I, Margrave of Brandenburg (1157–1170) following military defeat at Spandau. While attempting to escape he came to the River Havel, whereupon he drove his horse into the water, swearing that he would convert to Christianity if God saved him. Upon safely reaching the far bank, he hung his weapons and horn from the branches of a tree and fulfilled his promise; the name of the column taking the name Schildhorn ('shield-horn') as a result.

The Jaczo legend reflects an interesting chapter in the early history of Brandenburg. The mid-12th century saw Albert, then Duke of Saxony (1138–42), expanding his inherited estates, establishing bishoprics under his protection, and encouraging German migration from the Rhine valley as he went along. At the same time he launched a cru-

The Schildhorn Column on the banks of the Havel

sade against pagan Slavs, whom he encountered between the Rivers Oder and Elbe, in an effort to Christianise them. One of these was Duke Jaczo, a Slavic tribal ruler from the Łaba river region in the northern Caucasus, who was waging a war against Albert for control of the Brandenburg region (since the 8th century Slavs had occupied strategically-located forts in what are now the Berlin suburbs of Spandau and Köpenick). Albert's military success enabled him in 1157 to found the March, or Margraviate (*Mark, Markgrafschaft*), of Brandenburg – that is the governorship of a medieval border province – which would later become the nucleus of the Kingdom of Prussia. His heirs, the Ascanians, held the Margraviate until the line died out in 1320, after which it was taken over by the Houses of Wittelsbach, Luxembourg, and eventually Hohenzollern (see no. 6). Being one of the seven electors able to decide on the next emperor, the Margraviate of Brandenburg soon became one of the most powerful titles in the Holy Roman Empire.

Back on Havelchaussee it's not far to Schildhornweg and the Grunewald Forest Cemetery (Friedhof Grunewald Forst), where Nico of the American rock Band The Velvet Underground is buried.

32 Curious Devil's Mountain

District IV (Charlottenburg-Wilmersdorf), the Teufelsberg
on Teufelsseechaussee
S5 Heerstrasse; U2 Theodor-Heuss-Platz

The city of Berlin and the state of Brandenburg are both located on what is called the North German Plain, itself a part of a geomorphological region known as the North European Lowlands. With an elevation less than 100 metres above sea level the horizon of Berlin is predominantly flat, broken only by a few unimposing hills such as the Kreuzberg and the Prenzlauer Berg. This makes it all the more curious to discover a 120 metre-high hill standing in complete isolation in the northeastern corner of the Grunewald. Known as the Teufelsberg it is Berlin's highest hill and noteworthy for being almost entirely artificial!

By May 1945 it is estimated that 612 000 homes and a fifth of all buildings in Berlin had been either totally destroyed or else seriously damaged, leaving over a million people homeless. The destruction is thought to have generated between 60 and 70 millon cubic metres of rubble. Whilst some was re-used as construction material, the sheer volume was overwhelming. The solution was to dump it at selected locations around the city and in so doing to create rubble mountains (*Trümmerberge*), which could later be landscaped.

The largest of these manmade mountains is the Teufelsberg, or 'Devil's Mountain', so-named because of the nearby Teufelssee, although the epithet seems most apt considering the events that led to its construction. During the 1930s the site had been earmarked by Hitler for a new university campus, to be located astride Heerstrasse at the western extremity of the so-called East-West Axis (Ost-West Achse), part of his proposed rebuilding of Berlin as the new capital *Germania* (see no. 57). Work commenced on only one of the buildings, namely the Faculty of Military Technology (Wehrtechnischen Fakultät), to a design by Hitler's architect Albert Speer (1905–1981). Hitler himself laid the foundation stone in 1937 although building was halted once the war began. After the Allied victory of 1945, Britain considered using the building, which had an air raid shelter capable of holding 5000 people, as its Berlin headquarters, but the idea was dropped. When the Allies had difficulty in demolishing the building due to its sturdy construction they instead earmarked the site for the dumping of war debris. Consequently Hitler's faculty disappeared beneath thirteen

A disused Cold War listening station crowns the Teufelsberg

million tons of brick and stone, creating a 120 metre high rubble mountain.

During the Cold War the US military installed a listening station on top of the Teufelsberg, as part of NATO attempts to monitor radio communications in the GDR. A recently-discovered 300-metre-long tunnel could be used as an escape route by Allied soldiers in the event of a sudden Russian attack. Of the numerous urban myths that inevitably surrounded this secretive installation the only one ever proven concerned the improved signal reception reported during the annual German-American Festival on nearby Hüttenweg: the reason was the temporary erection of a Ferris wheel, which acted as a giant receiver! The facility was eventually closed in 1992 and the site is still awaiting redevelopment, its distinctive spherical 'radomes' once used to protect its antennae still visible for miles around. Meanwhile, the surrounding hillsides – actually two hills – are used for winter sports. The highest is considered Berlin's own *bona fide* ski resort and has even hosted a world championship competition.

The task of sifting through Berlin's rubble fell initially to women, since by the end of the war the city's population had been reduced from 4.3 million to 2.3 million, two-thirds of whom were female. Sixty thousand of them between the age of 15 and 65 were conscripted as 'Rubble Women' (*Trümmerfrauen*) to salvage bricks, timbers and girders for reuse. A common sight on the city's streets up until 1957 they were at first paid with little more than handfuls of potatoes but eventually received food rations. The women's work had started as early as 1st May, with the clearing of Tempelhof Airport, resulting in Berlin's first rubble mountain in the Volkspark Hasenheide on Columbiadamm, where a statue of a rubble woman by Katharina Singer stands today. An example of the narrow gauge railways used by the women to transport the rubble has been reconstructed in one of the locomotive sheds at the German Technical Museum (Deutsches Technnikmuseum Berlin) at Trebbiner Strasse 9 (Friedrichshain-Kreuzberg).

Berlin's sixteen rubble mountains also include Der Insulaner on Munsterdamm (Steglitz-Zehlendorf), named after a memorial set up there in 1972 to Günter Neumann, the star of a radio comedy show called *Die Insulaner*; the hill is now home to an astronomical observatory and a planetarium constructed in the 1960s (see no. 72). Others were built up around the remains of the city's partially demolished anti-aircraft towers (*Flaktürme*) in Volkspark Humboldthain and Volkspark Friedrichshain (see no. 22).

Other places of interest nearby: 29, 30

33 Death and Glory on the AVUS Race Track

District IV (Charlottenburg-Wilmersdorf), the former AVUS
racetrack near Messe Damm
S41, S42, S46 Messe-Nord; U2 Kaiserdamm

The AVUS, a time-saving acronym for *Automobilverkehrs- und Übungs-strasse*, was a motor racing circuit constructed on the southwest out-skirts of Berlin. Consisting of two long straights in the form of a dual carriageway, with a tight, anti-clockwise turning curve at each end, it ran through the Grunewald forest between Charlottenburg and Nikolassee. The circuit was devised in 1907 by the Automobile Club of Germany, both as a motor-sport venue and a testing track for the motor industry, although lack of finances delayed the start of construction un-til 1913. During the First World War Russian prisoners were employed on the project but the track still remained unfinished by 1918; its com-pletion was eventually financed by the businessman Hugo Stinnes.

The 19 kilometre-long AVUS circuit finally opened in September 1921 and in 1926 it played host to the first ever German Grand Prix. It was won by Rudolf Caracciola in a Mercedes-Benz travelling at 129 km/hour before an audience of 500 000. A year later the Nürburgring

A racing car sweeps around the the north curve of the Berlin AVUS in 1936

circuit opened in the Eifel Mountains providing competion for the AVUS race track. Thus, in an effort to make the AVUS the world's fastest race track, its north turning curve (*Nordschleife*) was raised up 43° on a steep, brick-built bank enabling drivers to take the bend at higher speeds. Mercedes-Benz and their opponents Auto Union raced their streamlined racing cars – dubbed 'Silver Arrows' – on this banked version in 1937. An idea of just how fast the AVUS track was can be gained by the fact that the average race speed of Mercedes driver Hermann Lang (260 km/hour) was not beaten for three decades!

However, by early 1938 the AVUS race track was deemed too dangerous for Grand Prix racing cars, especially after the legendary Auto Union driver Bernd Rosemeyer was killed in a land speed record attempt on a similar track. Additionally, it was now planned to connect the AVUS to the growing *Reichsautobahn* network by extending it to the south, as a result of which the south curve at Nikolassee was demolished in 1940 and replaced by a road junction (the line of the old curve can still be detected at the junction of Kronprinzessinnenweg and Havelchaussee).

In July 1945 President Harry Truman reviewed the 2nd Armored Division on the northbound track of the AVUS just prior to the Potsdam Conference. In October of the same year the AVUS was used by bus convoys bringing mothers and children out of Berlin to special camps set up to ensure they survived the harsh winter ahead. From 1961 onwards the Berlin Wall, with its Checkpoint Bravo at nearby Dreilinden Drewitz, ran a kilometre or so away from the old south curve (see no. 70). During this period a new south curve (*Südschleife*) was created in the middle of the track, just before the exit at Hüttenweg, reducing the track length to 8.3 kilometres. The first post-war race was held on this shortened track in July 1951 and in 1959 the AVUS hosted its only Formula One world championship, which was won by the British driver Tony Brooks. Unfortunately, this particular race weekend saw the death of driver Jean Behra, as his Porsche flew over the top of the unfenced north curve during a sports car race prior to the main event (German driver and journalist Richard von Frankenberg walked away unscathed from a similar crash).

The banked north curve was now also considered too dangerous by international racing standards and was dismantled in 1967 to be replaced by an expanded flat road junction, best viewed from the top of the nearby Radio Tower (Funkturm). Racing continued on the AVUS although it was now limited to German Touring Car Championships (Deutsche Tourenwagen Meisterschaft) and Formula Three events.

As racing on straights became unpopular so the length of the AVUS circuit was reduced by half yet again, in both the 1980s and 1990. Chicanes were also added in order to reduce entry speed into the north curve yet despite this accidents still occurred. The BMW of Dieter Quester, for example, rolled over when exiting the last corner and crossed the finish line on its roof! John Winter narrowly escaped when his car hit a barrier on the north curve and exploded into a fireball. British driver Kieth Odor was not so lucky when his car spun out of control and was rammed by another car causing his death.

The former control tower of the AVUS racetrack today

The last real race on the AVUS circuit took place in 1998 and in 1999 a farewell event for veterans was held. Since 2000 the AVUS has been replaced officially by the new EuroSpeedway Lausitz in Brandenburg, and the AVUS race track has become a part of the A115 Autobahn, the site of its once deadly north curve now used as a lorry park. The cylindrical race control tower (1936) that once overlooked the curve is now a Motel (Rasthof AVUS) and nearby can be seen one of the old trackside grandstands, known as a 'Bleacher' because it was open to the elements. The original spectator entrance that was located at the corner of Messedamm and Halenseestrasse also remains and is marked today by a stirring sculpture of two motorcyclists.

Other places of interest nearby: 39

34 The Villas of Charlottenburg

District IV (Charlottenburg-Wilmersdorf), a tour of historic villas from the New Pavilion (Neuer Pavillon) at Schloss Charlottenburg to the Villa Harteneck at Douglasstrasse 9
U2 Sophie-Charlotte-Platz

On the eastern side of Schloss Charlottenburg, the vast Baroque palace commissioned by King Frederick I (1701–1713) for his second wife Queen Sophia Charlotte, there stands a relatively tiny and unpretentious royal residence called the New Pavilion (Neuer Pavillon). It was erected in 1825 as a summer residence for King Frederick William III (1797–1840) and his second wife, Princess Auguste of Liegnitz. The building was designed by Carl Frederick Schinkel (1781–1841), the architect responsible for pioneering the neo-Classical style in Prussia, who based his design on the Villa Reale del Chiatamone in Naples, which had impressed the king greatly during a stay there in 1822. Like much of Schinkel's work it is a simple structure enhanced with a few clean and elegant flourishes, in this case pilasters, a cornice, and a cast-iron balcony.

The presence of Schloss Charlottenburg guaranteed that the surrounding area would in time become a wealthy and fashionable district, with clusters of grand garden villas erected during the mid to late 19th century in Schinkel's elegant regal style. Although once-rural Charlottenburg was absorbed into Greater Berlin in 1920, and inevitably transformed into a built-up city suburb, a few of the old villas remain and it makes for an interesting journey to locate them.

Our search begins on Schlossstrasse, the tree-lined approach road to Schloss Charlottenburg, which was once lined with villas. Most are long gone although a splendid example built in 1873 still remains at number 67, its restored neo-Classical façade and verdant front garden giving an impression of how the area must have looked during the 1870s; of interest too are the frontages at 15a-23.

The village that predated the construction of Schloss Charlottenburg was called Lietzow, of which nothing now remains. However, its old village square is the location of another neo-Classical villa, the Villa Kogge at Alt-Lietzow 28. Again in the style of Schinkel, it was built in 1866. Like the Schinkel Pavilion it has four façades, on this occasion adorned with columns, friezes and statuary.

It is difficult to imagine that villas with spacious gardens were built

along and around Kurfürstendamm, too, before huge tenement blocks smothered everything from 1890 onwards.
One remaining example can
be found at Fasanenstrasse
23, a red-brick building in the
style of a Renaissance *palazzo*
that today contains the Kohlhaas & Company/Café im
Literaturhaus, a charming
bookshop and café. Built in
1889 for Richard Hildebrandt,
a participant in several German North Pole expeditions,
the villa has since served as

Carl Frederick Schinkel's New Pavilion (Neuer Pavillon) in Charlottenburg

everything from a military hospital to a brothel! Next door at number
24 there is a country villa built in 1871, which is today home to a
museum dedicated to the sculptress Käthe Kollwitz (1867–1945). Her
poignant *Mother with her Dead Son* can be found in the Neue Wache
at Unter den Linden 4, a former Prussian royal guardhouse now the
Federal Republic of Germany's official Memorial to the Victims of War
and Tyranny.

We finish at the delightful Villa Harteneck at Douglasstrasse 9, on
the eastern edge of the Grunewald, marking the farthest reach of the ur-
banisation of Charlottenburg in this direction. The villa and its garden
were created in 1911–1912 in the style of an Italian country residence
for the successful businessman Carl Harteneck. The neo-Classical design was by the architect Adolf Wollenberg, who again harked back
to ideas pioneered by Schinkel. The beautiful garden was completely
restored during the 1980s, having been all but abandoned, and the villa
has now been taken over by an interior design company enabling visitors to walk through the splendid ground floor rooms.

> More garden villas are clustered south of the Tiergarten, including the elegant Villa
> von der Heydt, once a society salon, then a sweet factory, and now headquarters of the
> Foundation for Prussian Cultural Heritage (Stiftung Preussischer Kulturbesitz).

35 Truffles, Marzipan and Perfume

**District IV (Charlottenburg-Wilmersdorf),
a tour of some idiosyncratic shops beginning with Confiserie
Melanie at Grolmannstrasse 20
U2 Ernst-Reuter-Platz; Bus 101**

Berlin is a consumer's paradise boasting more than 30 000 shops that offer a vast and seductive array of products. The shops themselves vary enormously, from classic department stores and modern shopping arcades to traditional food halls and unique independent retailers (see no. 19).

Since the early 20th century the city's main centre for shopping and entertainment has been bustling Kurfürstendamm (known locally as Ku'damm) in the affluent district of Charlottenburg-Wilmersdorf. The area originally attracted those wealthy bourgeoisie who lacked the aristocratic credentials required to live in the city centre. Although not graced with much monumental architecture, Ku'damm's cafés, cinemas, shade-giving trees, and broad walkways have ensured its enormous popularity with shoppers to this day. Ku'damm's retail opportunities even spread onto the pavement itself, in the form of glass display cabinets first installed in 1936 as part of a Third Reich beautification plan!

Strong as the lure of Ku'damm is, it is always worthwhile strolling along the surrounding backstreets, where a more idiosyncratic selection of shops can be found. At Grolmanstrasse 20, for example, Confiserie Melanie has been in the handmade truffle business for well over half a century. More than sixty varieties are on offer including many with extraordinary ingredients: horseradish, garlic, fennel, chilli, and wasabi, to name but a few.

Around the corner at Knesebeckstrasse 88 there can be found another specialist, namely the lead soldier supplier Berliner Zinnfiguren, its window filled with miniaturised marching armies. Crossing onto Pestalozzistrasse a walk westwards passes a Russian grocer's shop (Russische Lebensmittel) at number 37 and a Polish equivalent (Polnische Lebensmittel) directly opposite at number 71. At the far end of the street at number 54a is the Königsberger Marzipan shop, where 'Wald' brand marzipan has been made to a traditional East Prussian recipe for the last fifty years. Next door at number 54 is Schneidersitz, a traditional haberdashery with a seamstress.

Running parallel to Pestalozzistrasse is Kantstrasse, the two connected by Windscheidstrasse, where at number 25 is Hase Weiss ('White Rabbit') offering dolls' houses, puppets and children's furniture, all handmade by a female architect and a sculptress. On Kantstrasse itself are two further specialist shops, including the florist and perfume maker Harry Lehmann at number 106. The business was founded in 1926 and has occupied the current premises since 1958, where perfumes are mixed to order from a selection of fifty scents; one of the house specialities is perfume number 65 called 'Eau de Berlin'! A little farther along is Heidi's Spielzeugladen at number 61, specialising in traditional wooden toys for children, and at nearby Savignyplatz 3 is C. Adolph, a hardware store and locksmith founded in 1898 offering a mind-boggling array of nuts and bolts. Farther south, at Güntzelstrasse 47 is Fleischerei Bachhuber, with its fine selection of German hams and sausages, and Horenstein at Fechner Strasse 3, which specialises in hard-to-find old vinyl records and has a café attached.

This tour of unusual shops in Charlottenburg-Wilmersdorf concludes where it began – with another confectioner. Chocolatier Erich Hamann founded his business in 1912 on Kurfürstendamm but since 1928 his shop has resided at Brandenburgische Strasse 17, where it retains both its old-fashioned furnishings and traditional Bauhaus-

Handmade truffles and other delights at Confiserie Melanie on Grolmannstrasse

style packaging: a blue ribbon signifying the high quality of its handmade bittersweet chocolate.

Those with a sweet tooth will want to extend their journey to Mitte and visit Fassbender & Rausch at Charlottenstrasse 60, boasting the longest praline counter in the world, and Konditorei Buchwald at Bartningallee 29, renowned for its rich and buttery *Baumkuchen*.

Other places of interest nearby: 36, 37

36 From *Kasseler* to Currywurst

District IV (Charlottenburg-Wilmersdorf), some historic Berlin restaurants including Restaurant Leibniz-Klause at Mommsenstrasse 57
S5, S7, S75 Savignyplatz; U1 Uhlandstrasse, U7 Adenauerplatz

It is often said that neither Berlin nor the surrounding rural area of Brandenburg have ever been culinary centres. This is because the Hohenzollern court was generally more focussed on its army than on cuisine. During the 19th century both the Prussian aristocracy and the working class preferred hearty food, using simple ingredients taken from the region's farms, rivers, forests and lakes. This reflected the fact that the city was still relatively poor and its winters notoriously harsh. However, that is not to say that during these times a distinctive Berlin kitchen did not emerge; it is just that not until after the fall of the Berlin Wall did renewed access to the countryside facilitate its rediscovery.

Traditional Brandenburg food is always available at Restaurant Leibniz-Klause

Pork is Berlin's most popular main dish and a traditional way of serving it is *Kasseler Nacken*. Created by a Berlin butcher called Cassel in the late 19th century, it consists of salted and dried pork served with *Sauerkraut*, mashed potatoes and spicy mustard. A variation known as *Brauhausknüller* consists of tender pork knuckle (*Eisbein*) served with mashed split peas (*Erbsenpuree*), *Sauerkraut*, potatoes – and plenty of beer! Other pork dishes include *Eisbeinsülze* (knuckle of pork in aspic), *Sauerfleisch* (pickled pork in aspic), and *Berliner Leber* (pork or veal liver on a bed of mashed potatoes with fried onions and sliced apple). In addition to pork there is *Brandenburger Landente* (roast apple-stuffed duck with red cabbage and dumplings), *Rinderrouladen* (rolled and stuffed roast beef), and *Havel-Zander* (pan-fried pike-perch).

Despite the justifiable temptations of Berlin's many new international restaurants, it would be a pity if visitors did not sample this traditional fare, available in a number of good city restaurants. A fine example is the Restaurant Leibniz-Klause at Leibnizstrasse 46 (Charlottenburg-Wilmersdorf), which has been serving high quality regional cuisine to the likes of actor Hardy Kruger and numerous visiting politicians for more than three decades. In the city centre there are other good traditional restaurants, too, including the Art Deco Dressler at Unter den Linden 39 and Zur Letzten Instanz at Waisenstrasse 14–16, Berlin's oldest tavern (1621), which contains a tiled stove on which Napoleon once warmed his hands. Farther south, on the tranquil banks of the Landwehrkanal, is the Altes Zollhaus in a former half-timbered customs house at Carl-Herz-Ufer 30 (Friedrichshain-Kreuzberg), and out in the western suburbs is the leafy Waldhaus at Onkel-Tom-Strasse 50 (Steglitz-Zehlendorf).

No less traditional are the numerous snacks available in Berlin's old pubs (*Altberliner Kneipe*), beer gardens, and former country inns, for example Zum Nussbaum at Am Nussbaum 3, an early 16th century tavern reconstructed as part of the St. Nicholas Quarter (Nikolaiviertel) (see no. 83). They include pork meatballs (*Buletten*), marinated herring (*Rollmöpse*), pickled eggs (*Soleier*), black pudding (*Blutwurst*), meatballs in white sauce with capers (*Königsberger Klopse*), meatloaf (*Falscher Hase*), and potato soup (*Kartoffelsuppe*). Guten Appetit!

Out on the streets, Berlin's most traditional snack is *Currywurst*, available in roadside kiosks across the city. Consisting of a pork sausage (*Bratwurst*) covered in spicy tomato sauce sprinkled with curry powder, it is served with a roll or French fries. Exactly when and where it was invented is a matter for debate although it is commonly attributed to one Herta Heuwer, a sausage seller in Charlottenburg. Out of boredom one rainy day in 1949 she experimented with various ingredients and the Currywurst was born (others claim that it was invented even earlier at Konnopke's Imbiss, a snack bar beneath a railway bridge at Schönhauser Allee 44a (Pankow)). Although today outnumbered 100:1 by the ubiquitous Turkish-style *Döner kebap*, *Currywurst* has its afficionados and there is even a dedicated website at www.currywurst-berlin.com. A recommended kiosk is Bier's at Kurfürstendamm 195 (Charlottenburg-Wilmersdorf).

Other places of interest nearby: 35, 37

37 Sheltering from the Cold War

District IV (Charlottenburg-Wilmersdorf), the civil protection shelter beneath the Ku'damm Karree shopping centre at Kurfürstendamm 207–208
S5, S7, S75 Charlottenburg; U1 Uhlandstrasse, U2 Adenauerplatz

The use of the term 'Cold War' to describe emerging post-war tensions between the United States and the Soviet Union was first coined by the American financier and presidential economic advisor Bernard Baruch (1870–1965), during a congressional debate in April 1947. The phrase is now widely used to describe the period of conflict, tension and competition between the two superpowers and their allies from the mid-1940s until the early 1990s.

The origins of the conflict and the reasons for the rapid unravelling of wartime alliances against Nazi Germany has long been a matter for intense discussion. Stalin has been accused of going back on the promises he made at Yalta and pursuing a policy of expansionism in Eastern Europe; in his defence it might be said that he was trying to protect the Soviet Union from encirclement by America and her allies. The United States, on the other hand, has been charged with deliberately attempting to isolate and provoke the Soviet Union since well before the end of the Second World War; in their defence it could be claimed that they were trying to keep foreign markets open for US goods and attempting to stem the spread of Communism around the world. The most likely cause was probably a plethora of conflicting political and commercial interests about how a post-war Europe should be shaped, compounded by misunderstandings on both sides.

Fortunately, despite serious crises such as the Korean War (1950–1953), the Cuban Missile Crisis (1962), and the Vietnam War (1964–1975), the Cold War never escalated into a global conflict in its own right. In reality it was played out by means of proxy wars, military coalitions, espionage, propaganda, and a nuclear arms race, the stockpiling of deliverable weapons on both sides ultimately proving enough to deter direct military engagement between the Soviet Union and the United States.

The tensions and paranoias of the times were felt nowhere greater than in Berlin, especially after the city was abruptly divided in 1961 (see no. 70). As well as the border guards, surveillance equipment and other paraphernalia that the Berlin Wall brought with it, the most tangible manifestations of the threat of another war was the construction of 30 radiation-proof shelters (*Atomschutzbunker*) on both sides of the city. That the shelters could in reality only hold 29 000 people in total (just 1% of the city's population), on a first come-first served basis, suggests that their provision was more for propaganda than practical reasons.

In some cases it was possible to modify and reuse existing air raid shelters constructed during the Second World War, for example one reaching four storeys below Alexanderplatz, which the East German leadership selected as their personal nuclear fallout shelter (see no. 65). The refurbishment of this particular shelter was abandoned in the 1970s for financial reasons and a reduction in the perceived threat of war. Similarly, a huge concrete Second World War shelter on Pallasstrasse (Tempelhof-Schöneberg) was earmarked as a nuclear fallout shelter for use by the West Berlin government. This shelter also doubled as a secure NATO foodstore in which large quantities of tinned food were stockpiled in case of another Soviet blockade of the city, like the one that led to the Berlin Airlift in 1948–1949. A similar store was established in a former Second World War civilian shelter constructed inside a disused gasometer on Fichtestrasse (Friedrichshain-Kreuzberg). Used until 1990 it contained 7000 tons of comestibles, such as tinned beans, sardines and apple purée. With the end of the Cold War and the fall of the Berlin Wall such stores were deemed unnecessary and removed.

Elsewhere, brand new radiation-proof civil protection shelters were constructed, a

Triple-decker bunks inside the Cold War civilian shelter under the Ku'damm Karree shopping centre

good example being the one built in 1974 as part of the Ku'damm Karree shopping centre at Kurfürstendamm 207–208 (Charlottenburg-Wilmersdorf). Still fully operational it can be visited on a tour that forms part of the highly atmospheric Story of Berlin multimedia exhibition. The shelter is entered through four airlocks operated from a separate control room, which also contains a telephone for contacting the outside world and a field-phone system for communications within the shelter itself. Capable of sustaining 3592 people for 14 days the shelter is equipped with row-upon-row of folding metal bunks, as well as two kitchens, two infirmaries, and separate washing facilities for men and women (which lack glass mirrors to prevent suicide bids). It is also provided with four tanks capable of holding 666 000 gallons of drinking water, which in the event of an interruption in the outside supply can be augmented by water pumped and purified from an underground well. Breathable air is drawn into the shelter by means of a shaft leading from the outside down through the roof via sand and coal decontamination filters. In the event of the external power supply faltering the shelter is provided with two 185 horsepower diesel engines capable of generating enough energy for all the lighting and ventilations systems. Should war ever break out in Berlin again, this is probably the safest place to be!

A similar shelter to the one on Kurfürstendamm can be found at the Pankstrasse U-Bahn station (Mitte) on the U8 and it too can be explored (together with another below nearby Blochplatz) as part of a guided tour hosted by the Berlin Underworlds Association (Berliner Unterwelten e.V.). This shelter was capable of supporting 3346 people, again for a mere 14 days, with no contingency plan for what happened afterwards.

Other places of interest nearby: 35, 36, 38

38 The Wilmersdorf Taj Mahal

District IV (Charlottenburg-Wilmersdorf), the Ahmadiyya
Mosque (Ahmadiyya-Moschee) at Brienner Strasse 7–8
U3, U7 Fehrbelliner Platz

Sometime during the mid-1870s, in the Punjab region that today strad-
dles the border between India and Pakistan, Mirza Ghulam Ahmad
(1835–1908) began claiming that he was in direct communication with
his God (*Allah*). He believed himself to be the 'Second Coming of the
Prophet Jesus', the Messiah predicted by the Holy *Quran*, the holy
book of Islam, to return to Earth in the final days to defeat the anti-
christ. The Messiah will be accompanied by another messianic figure,
the *Mahdi*, who will then transform the world into a perfect Islamic
society: Ahmad believed himself to be this figure, too. Ahmad additionally appointed himself *Mujaddid*, that is a *Caliph*, scholar or thinker (in
Ahmad's case the latter) sent by God in the first half of every century
of the Islamic calendar to reform Islam.

Based on his beliefs, and with the stated aim of reviving Islam
in its pristine form, Mirza Ghulam Ahmad
founded the Ahmadiyya movement in 1899.
The name was derived from 'Ahmad', an alternative name for the Prophet Mohammed.
However, whereas 'Mohammed' meant 'the
praised one', 'Ahmad' referred specifically to
the peace that Mohammed's teachings could
bring to the world. More specifically, Mirza
Ghulam Ahmad believed that his message
had special relevance for the West, which he
felt had slipped into materialism.

Not surprisingly Mirza Ghulam Ahmad's
strident claims were rejected by many Muslims, who branded him a false prophet and
heretic. Traditional Islam holds that Jesus is
the Messiah and that he himself will return
in the flesh. Mirza Ghulam Ahmad coun-
tered this by claiming that Jesus was dead,
having survived the crucifixion and dying
eventually in Kashmir. Additionally, most
Muslims believe the *Mahdi* to be a military

The Ahmadiyya Mosque in Wilmersdorf

leader, in line with the idea of militant *Jihad*, or struggle; again Mirza Ghulam Ahmad went against convention by stating that the *Mahdi* was a spiritual leader and that *Jihad* should only be used against extreme religious persecution.

After Mirza Ghulam Ahmad's death in 1908 controversy continued to surround his beliefs. This caused a split in the movement between those who believed he was a genuine prophet, although not a law-bearing one as Mohammed had been (the Ahmadiyya Muslim Community), and those who followed conventional Islamic wisdom that there could be no prophet after Mohammed and that Mirza Ghulam Ahmad was no more than a *Mujaddid* (the Lahore Ahmadiyya Movement).

It is a little-known fact that during the First World War a small community of Indian and African Muslim prisoners who had fought on the side of the British lived in the village of Wünsdorf near Zossen, 30 kilometres south of Berlin, where they were permitted to erect a wooden mosque for themselves in the hope that they would change sides. With its demolition after the war Muslim diplomats mooted the idea of constructing a new mosque in Berlin, in order to spread the word of Islam to Germany. The building was commissioned and financed by the governing body (*Anjuman*) of the Lahore Ahmadiyya Movement and completed in 1927. Designed by the Berlin architect K. A. Hermann in the style of a Mughal prince's tomb (similar in style to the Taj Mahal), the Ahmadiyya Mosque (Ahmadiyya-Moschee) is today the oldest mosque in Germany.

It stands amongst trees on a corner in the suburb of Wilmersdorf and is easily recognisable by its pair of 32-metre high, whitewashed *minarets*, whose name originates from the Arabic *alminar*, or 'place of light'. It is from here that the *muezzin* traditionally sings his five-times-daily call to prayer and dispels the darkness with the word of the *Quran*. Unfortunately, the minarets were reduced to rubble during the Second World War, when German soldiers used them to shoot at Russian troops entrenched in the nearby Wilmersdorf Cemetery; they were not restored until 2001.

The Ahmadiyya Mosque is now a peaceful place once more and although it only serves a relatively small Muslim congregation, due to the divisions of the past, it endeavours to reach into the community in an effort to placate and educate. It is unfortunate that most Berlin Muslims avoid the mosque and that many Muslim countries judge Ahmadis to be non-Muslims.

Other places of interest nearby: 36, 37, 53

39 Concrete Cadillacs and Other Modern Art

District IV (Charlottenburg-Wilmersdorf), the Concrete Cadillacs (Beton-Cadillacs) sculpture on Rathenauplatz
S41, S42, S46 Halensee

Travellers arriving into Berlin from the west along the busy E51 might choose to leave the Autobahn at junction 12, taking them to the western end of Kurfürstendamm, named after the Electors (*Kurfürsten*) of Brandenburg (see no. 6). Once a rough track used to gain access to the Grunewald forest, Ku'damm is today Berlin's premier shopping street and is invariably clogged with both pedestrians and vehicles. The motor age has transformed such thoroughfares beyond recognition and so perhaps that is why the German modern artist Wolf Vostell (1932–1998) chose this busy intersection for one of his famous sculptures incorporating large American cars: *Two Concrete Cadillacs in the Shape of the Naked Maja* (*Zwei Beton-Cadillacs in Form der nackten Maja*). Vostell undoubtedly realised that the sheer volume of passing traffic was sure to generate a healthy discourse on his work!

Vostell's unusual sculpture stands on Rathenauplatz and depicts two Cadillacs upended and partially entombed in concrete. It was created in 1987 to mark the 750th anniversary of the founding of Berlin and caused a storm of controversy from the moment it was unveiled. The title of the work, with its seemingly obscure reference to the famous painting by the Spanish artist Francisco Goya (1746–1828), suggests a measure of self-parody and mockery: undoubtedly for some the thought of a big American car is as enticing as a reclining female nude! The sculpture seems to pass comment not only on the stultifying and quite literally solidifying effects of gridlocked cars on the urban landscape but also on some modern character traits perhaps shared by both Europeans and Americans. Despite the best efforts of Vostell's vociferous critics to get the sculpture removed it is still standing today – and still making people think: surely the best response a modern artist can hope for. No stranger to extending the borders of art it is perhaps worth noting that in 1959 Vostell became the first artist ever to incorporate a television set into one of his works (*Deutscher Ausblick*).

At the eastern end of Ku'damm near Marburger Strasse can be found another, rather less provocative piece of modern sculpture, again

Wolf Vostell's controversial concrete cadillacs on Rathenauplatz

erected for the city's 750th anniversary of Berlin. The work of Brigitte and Martin Matschinsky-Denninghoff it is called simply *Berlin* and depicts two chain links, connected but with visible breaks: the allusion to Berlin as a divided city and Europe as a divided entity is all too clear.

A wholly different but no less arresting piece of modern sculpture is *The Deserted Room* (*Der Verlassene Raum*) on Koppenplatz (Mitte), in what was a thriving Jewish neighbourhood before the Second World War. This subtle piece of public art by the sculptor Karl Biedermann (1947) won a competition organised by the GDR regime to memorialise the 50th anniversary of the Nazis' notorious 'Night of Broken Glass' (*Reichskristallnacht*), a 1938 pogrom in which Jewish religious institutions and commercial premises were destroyed and their occupants arrested. Not actually unveiled until 1996, several years after German reunification, the bronze sculpture depicts an old-fashioned table and two chairs, one of which has been knocked over. The message of sudden abandonment is conveyed subtly, reinforced only by the lines written around the edge of the 'room' by the winner of the 1966 Nobel Prize for Literature, the Berlin-born poet Nelly Sachs (1891–1970): her mention of "die Wohnungen des Todes" ("the houses of death") and

"Israels Leib im Rauch durch die Luft!" ("the body of Israel going up in smoke!") speaks volumes about what happened here during the Nazi era.

Another understated piece by Biedermann can be found several streets north on Zionskirchplatz. In the grounds of the Zion Church (Zionskirche) is a bronze kneeling torso commemorating the theologian Dietrich Bonhoeffer (1906–1945), who was vicar here when the Nazis came to power and who was executed for sedition (he was arrested in his house at Marienburger Allee 43 (Charlottenburg-Wilmersdorf)). The church itself was a focus for the 1980s GDR dissident scene, cultivated by the fact that the Protestant Church was one of the few institutions permitted to organise its affairs free from state interference. Having attracted the unwelcome attentions of the Stasi, the GDR's ministry of state security, Biedermann's work once again had to wait until after reunification to be unveiled.

A mural on the Tommy-Weissbecker-Haus at Wilhelmstrasse 9

By far Berlin's most prolific genre of modern art is unofficial, ranging from casual graffiti to full-scale works gracing the blank fire walls of apartment houses, violently revealed during the Second World War. A magnificent example is the lively gable-end mural of the Tommy-Weissbecker-Haus at Wilhelmstrasse 9 (Mitte), home to a work collective named after a member of the disbanded 'Movement 2nd June' anarchist group (see nos. 21. & 41).

Other places of interest nearby: 33

40 Treasures from the Silk Road

District VI (Steglitz-Zehlendorf), the Museum of Asian Art
(Museum für Asiatische Kunst) in the Museen Dahlem at
Lansstrasse 8
U3 Dahlem-Dorf

For over two thousand years the fabled Silk Road has borne camel trains across the inhospitable deserts, mountains and steppe of Central Asia, from the old Chinese capital of Xi'an westwards more than 4500 miles to Tyre on the Mediterranean coast. However, it was only given its romantic name in 1877, by the German explorer and geographer Baron Ferdinand von Richthofen (1833–1905). In reality, Richthofen's Silk Road (*Seidenstrasse*), one of the world's earliest highways, is a

series of interconnecting tracks criss-crossing a vast area, used to transport not only silk but also jade, musk, diamonds, pearls and even rhubarb, the goods passing through many hands before arriving eventually in far-off Rome. The number of people to traverse the full length of the Silk Road was very small, but from the late 19th century onwards this number was bolstered by a handful of intrepid European explorers, geographers and archaeologists. For these men the term 'Silk Road' conjured up both a vast unmapped geographical area and a rich undocumented cultural history, the ruined civilisations of which were known to lie alongside the region's desert tracks and oases.

Statue of a seated Buddha in Dahlem's Museum of Asian Art

One such European was Albert von Le Coq (1860–

1930), the son of a successful German wine merchant, who having studied commerce in London decided at the age of 40 to study oriental languages in Berlin instead. As a mature student he worked as a volunteer at Berlin's Ethnological Museum (Museum für Volkerkunde), serving as assistant to the director of the museum's Indian Department, Professor Albert Grünwedel. Le Coq helped plan and organize the museum's first expedition into Central Asia in 1902, specifically along that part of the Silk Road skirting the northern flank of the mountain-girt Taklamakan Desert, in the area surrounding the oasis town of Turfan. When Grünwedel fell ill prior to the departure of the second expedition in 1904, Le Coq stepped in as its leader. His account of the so-called Second Royal Prussian Turfan Expedition was published in English in 1928 as *Buried Treasures of Chinese Turkestan* and it is a thrilling account of the prizes and pitfalls he encountered along the way. The expedition uncovered extensive networks of cave temples carved out by Buddhist monks from the 4th century AD onwards, notably at Bezeklik, in what is today northwest China. The many manuscripts recovered in the caves prompted von Le Coq to believe he had unearthed a major Manichaean (ancient Babylonian-Persian) library. More fancifully, some of the cave paintings he found depicting figures with blue eyes and red hair led him to speculate that he had uncovered evidence of an Aryan culture related to the Franks.

With the help of the expedition's handyman, Theodor Bartus, Le Coq cut away over 360 kilograms (305 cases) of painted wall plaster, stucco sculptures and rock carvings from the caves, which were shipped back to the Ethnological Museum in Berlin. Le Coq accounts for these "borrowings" as a matter of necessity, citing the turbulent nature of Turkestan at the time of his expeditions, as well as the local habit of using wall plaster from temples as field fertiliser! Whatever one thinks of the legality of removing such objects from their original location, their sheer artistry and workmanship cannot be disputed. Ironically, many of the artefacts were subsequently destroyed during Allied bombing raids on Berlin in the Second World War.

Today, Le Coq's Silk Road treasures, together with those found during the third (1905–07) and fourth (1913–14) Royal Prussian Turfan Expeditions, can be found in Dahlem's Museum of Asian Art (Museum für Asiatische Kunst), one of the world's most important Indo-Asian collections, with exhibits dating from the 4th millennium BC up to the present.

The formative influence on Indian art has always been religion and the Sub-Continent's three main religions – Hinduism, Buddhism, and

Ceiling fresco from the Buddhist Cave Temple of the Ring-Bearing Doves at Kizil

Jainism – are superbly represented in the museum in the form of stone sculptures and reliefs, bronzeworks and terracottas. Additionally, there are prehistoric grave goods, Islamic metalwork and ceramics, Mughal miniatures, and painted fabric wall hangings (*Thangkas*) from Tibet and Nepal. However, the heart of the museum remains the Turfan Collection, named after the expeditions that Albert von Le Coq participated in. The various murals, paintings on fabric and paper, and clay and wood sculptures, extracted predominantly from Buddhist temples dating from the 3rd to the 13th centuries AD, are stunning. At the centre of the collection is the restored Cave Temple of the Ring-Bearing Doves, brought back in its entirety from the Silk Road oasis of Kizil, three hundred miles west of Turfan, and dated to 431–533 AD.

The Museum of Asian Art will eventually be transferred to the new Humboldt Forum in the reconstructed Stadtschloss in Schlossplatz (Mitte), where together with the collections on Museum Island, a world-class museum landscape will come into being. The Museum of Ethnology (Ethnologisches Museum) and Museum of European Cultures (Museum Europäischer Kulturen) will follow later.

Other places of interest nearby: 41, 42, 52

41 "Scars As Nowhere Else"

District VI (Steglitz-Zehlendorf), the Ruin of Arts (Ruine der Künste) at Hittorfstrasse 5
U3 Thielplatz

"In good and in evil, Berlin is the trustee of German history, which has left its scars here as nowhere else." Thus wrote Berlin's former Mayor of West Berlin, Richard von Weizsäcker, in 1983. It was a time when German reunification seemed a long way off and the city's fabric still bore the open wounds of its violent liberation at the end of the Second World War. Today, those scars are gradually being erased, admittedly only slowly in the former East Berlin but more rapidly in what are now the city's affluent central and western suburbs, where any remaining signs of conflict have often been purposefully left, as a reminder of the city's darkest chapter.

Examples of this deliberate policy of preserving the scars of war include the New Museum (Neues Museum) at Bodestrasse 1–3 on Museum Island (Museum Insel), the Jüdische Galerie next to the New Synagogue (Neue Synagoge) at Oranienburger Strasse 31, the Art Library (Kunstbiblothek) at Sigismundstrasse 4, the Martin-Gropius-Bau at Stresemannstrasse 110, and an office building at Zimmerstrasse 14–15, the walls of all of them still peppered with shrapnel marks and machine gun fire. Other examples of the deliberate retention of war-damaged fabric include the restored Moltke Bridge (Moltkebrücke), with its broken sculptural fragments from the Red Army's assault on the Reichstag lying alongside it, and the renovated Reichstag itself, whose rooftop parapets still carry Russian *graffiti* praising Stalin and damning the Germans.

An extraordinary example of a battle-scarred building that has been left exactly as it looked at the end of the war is the so-called Ruin of Arts (Ruine der Künste) at Hittorfstrasse 5, a villa in the upmarket residential suburb of Dahlem. During the last weeks of the war the villa was hit repeatedly by gunfire. After the fighting was over the building was abandoned to the elements for the next 40 years, during which time most of the surrounding villas were gradually restored to their original appearance. By the early 1980s the crumbling walls and overgrown garden of the ruined villa stood in stark contrast to the pristine white façades and manicured flower beds of its neighbours.

It was at this time that the villa came to the attention of the self-

The Ruin of Arts, a war-damaged villa in Dahlem

styled 'intermedia artist' Wolf Kahlen (b. 1940), a professor in the Department of Architecture at Berlin's Technical University. Between 1981 and 1985 Kahlen installed an exhibition space and studio within the villa's ruined shell, which he called the Ruin of Arts (Ruine der Künste). In total sympathy with the villa's derelict state, so as not to detract from its impact as a war ruin, the workspace took on an inherent sense of both decay and creativity: the dynamic balance of such polar-opposed themes having long been a feature of Kahlen's other work. Since its inauguration Kahlen has invited numerous artists to work, exhibit and lecture in his ruin, each creating unique, site-specific installations, details of which are inscribed on an interior wall. One of Kahlen's own contributions to the project was his Ruin of Arts Radio, which for more than five years transmitted a round-the-clock, computer-generated, philosophical discussion.

Other places of interest nearby: 40, 42, 52

42 Where the Atom was Split

District VI (Steglitz-Zehlendorf), the former Kaiser Wilhelm Institute (Kaiser-Wilhelm-Gesellschaft) in Dahlem
U3 Thielplatz

In January 1945 Josef Stalin launched his great Russian winter offensive against Nazi Germany. Nearly seven million Red Army soldiers massed along a line between the Baltic and the Adriatic, supported by 7500 aircraft, 6000 tanks and 41 000 guns. Far mightier than the force used by Hitler to invade the Soviet Union in June 1941, it was the greatest concentration of military firepower ever assembled.

By the time Russian troops reached the gates of Berlin, the "lair of the Fascist beast", some eleven million German refugees had preceded them and a mere 85 000 Wehrmacht, Waffen-SS, Volksturm, and Hitler Youth fighters remained to man the city's defences. Armed with little more than hand-held *Panzerfausts* and the "Total War" propaganda of Joseph Goebbels (1897–1945) these war-weary soldiers, old men and children stood no chance against the 1.8 million Russian shells that would soon be fired into the city.

History relates how Stalin relentlessly urged his commanders, Marshalls Zhukov and Konev, on into Berlin, with the intention not only of planting a red hammer-and-sickle flag atop the Reichstag in time for the May Day parade in Moscow but also to assert the Soviet Union's right to a territorial buffer as protection against any possible future Western aggression. Stalin was also concerned that given the chance Germany would attempt to sue for peace with the Allies rather than surrendering unconditionally to a vengeful Red Army.

Another important reason for Stalin's headlong charge to Berlin was that anything seized along the way, both possessions and people, instantly became Russian property, as justifiable restitution for the destruction wrought during Germany's invasion three years earlier. Dismantling factories, raping women, sending prisoners back to the Soviet Union to work as forced labourers, and seizing large quantities of gold from Berlin's Reichsbank on Werdescher Markt were all cases in point.

A fascinating, and until recently little-written about, aspect of the Soviet Union's eagerness to asset-strip German territory concerns the Kaiser Wilhelm Institute (Kaiser-Wilhelm-Gesellschaft) in Dahlem. In 1938, in the institute's department of chemistry, German nuclear scientist Otto Hahn (1879–1968) had succeeded in splitting the nucleus of a uranium atom for the very first time. However, it was only after corresponding with his former Jewish colleague Lise Meitner (1878–1968), then in Swedish exile from the Nazis, that Hahn realised he had achieved what became known as nuclear fission. The resulting two nuclei emitted surplus neutrons, with the potential for a chain reaction from which atomic energy – and so plutonium for atomic bombs – could be produced. Although the wooden table on which Hahn made his momentous discovery is now in Munich, the institute in Dahlem is still standing, at Thielallee 63.

Fortunately, whilst the Nazis seem to have grasped the implications of Hahn's discovery, for reasons still unclear they were hesitant in funding further research. Institute director Werner Heisenberg (1901–1976) and his team were thus stymied in their quest to create the sustained fission reactions necessary to build a nuclear reactor. Stalin, meanwhile, was also aware of the potential of nuclear technology. In May 1942, furious after his spies informed him that America was well-advanced with the production of an atomic bomb, he gathered his country's leading nuclear physicists to ask them why Soviet nuclear science lagged so far behind. One reason was that the Soviet Union lacked its own source of uranium, which explains why Stalin was so desperate for his troops to reach the institute in Dahlem and its stores of uranium *before* the Western Allies, in whose sector the institute would eventually find itself. This might also explain why Stalin encouraged the Americans into thinking that Hitler would retreat to Bavaria for his last stand thereby reducing Berlin's strategic importance.

Unbeknown to Stalin, however, the Nazis had already moved Dahlem's seven tons of uranium oxide out of Berlin to the Black Forest. Similarly, Otto Hahn, Werner Heisenberg, and most of their fellow nuclear scientists had been smuggled to Bavaria, to prevent them from falling into Soviet hands; Hitler had in fact wanted them all executed (the scientists would later surrender to the Allies and be interned in England). However, due to a German administrative error a further three tons of uranium oxide were misdirected back to the institute at Dahlem, where it was seized by Red Army troops on 24th April. Together with dismantled laboratory equipment it eventually found its way back to the Soviet Union, kick-starting work on the eventual production of Russia's own atomic bomb.

The terrifying detonation of the world's first atomic bomb over Japan in August 1945, killing 150000 people in the process, greatly distressed Otto Hahn because he was vehemently opposed to the development of nuclear weapons. The event also demonstrated to Stalin and the rest of the world just how far advanced the Americans were in their own development and deployment of nuclear weapons – and how different the world might have been had Nazi Germany ever done the same.

In November 1945 Otto Hahn was belatedly awarded the 1944 Nobel Prize for Chemistry and in January 1946 he and the other scientists were released back to Germany as free men. In December 1946 Hahn officially received his prize in Stockholm and took the opportunity to speak out strongly against the misuse of nuclear energy. Meanwhile, back in Berlin the Kaiser Wilhelm Institute was absorbed into the Freie Universität, established in Dahlem in 1948 and renamed the Max Planck Institute after the father of quantum theory. Planck himself, whose son had been executed for his part in the failed Stauffenberg plot against Hitler, nominated Hahn as the institute's new president (see no. 12).

Dahlem's former Kaiser Wilhelm Institute, where scientists first split the atom

Under the Nazis, Ihnestrasse 22–24 was home to the Institute of Anthropology, Human Genetics and Eugenics (Institut für Anthropologie, menschliche Erblehre und Eugenik). A wall plaque records that director of the institute, Otmar von Verschuer, was a racial hygienist, who pursued his grisly profession at Auschwitz together with his assistant Josef Mengele, the notorious *Angel of Death*.

Other places of interest nearby: 40, 41, 52

43 The Changing Fortunes of Schwanenwerder

District VI (Steglitz-Zehlendorf), Schwanenwerder Island
(Schwanenwerder Insel)
RE1, RE7 Wannsee or S1, S7 Nikolassee, then walk along
Wannseebadweg and cross by bridge to Inselstrasse

Schwanenwerder Insel (Swan Isle) is a tiny residential island in the Wannsee, one of the lakes formed by the River Havel, and is linked to the mainland by a short bridge. Archaeologists have found evidence for Stone Age human habitation on the island dating to around 5000 B.C. The first mention of the island in written records dates back to the early 17th century, when it was known as Sandtwerder, or Sandy Isle, and belonged to the estates of the Brandenburg Electors. The French novelist Henri Stendhal described the island as a "pinnacle full of nobility and grace" after visiting it as a soldier during the Napoleonic Wars.

Throughout the 18th and 19th centuries esteemed visitors made a point of calling at the little island. However, it wasn't until 1870 and the advent of improved transportation in line with Berlin's industrial revolution that the real estate potential of Schwanenwerder was recognised. Friedrich Wilhelm Wessel, the owner of a successful petroleum lamp company, purchased the island in 1882, with the intention of enabling Berlin's ruling commercial class to work in the city by day and retire to the country in the evening. Wessel and his heirs invested huge amounts of their own money in creating an infrastructure for the island and then set about selling generous-sized residential plots along Inselstrasse, the island's only street. Most of the plots were bought by successful German-Jewish entrepreneurs and businessmen, who built a series of elegant villas, each with glorious views across the water. They included Dr. Walter Sobernheim (Director of the Schultheiss-Patzenhofer Brewery), Alfred Guggenheim (co-owner of a silk mill and textile department store), and Dr. Arthur Salomonsohn (Director of the Disconto Company).

As if to emphasise the exclusivity of Schwanenwerder as a residential address it was even given its own museum, wherein prehistoric artefacts and architectural curiosities from Germany's colonial empire were exhibited. Still remaining on Inselstrasse is a fragmentary column from the Tuileries Palace (Die Tuilerien-Säule), removed after the destruction of the palace during the Paris Commune of 1871. The inscription on the back reads: "This stone hails from Seine's strand, Planted here on German land, Traveller, it warns you from afar, Luck, how changeable you are!" Ironically, within the next few decades the fortunes of Schwanenwerder would change quite dramatically.

During the Golden Twenties (*Goldene Zwanziger*) the island became a popular meeting place for politicians, bankers, actors and aristocrats of the Weimar Republic. Legendary parties were hosted here and business deals were done over champagne and cigars. One of the luminaries was Dr. Oscar Schlitter, a member of the Board of Directors of Deutsche Bank, who bought a plot of land at Inselstrasse 8–10 and built himself a villa there. In 1936 the Schlitter family sold the villa to Hitler's Propaganda Minister Joseph Goebbels (1897–1945), who ensconced his wife Magda, her son, and their six children here soon after. A dark chapter for Schwanenwerder then ensued during which the villas of Berlin's commercial elite were confiscated for use by top ranking Nazis. They

The Tuileries Column on Schwanenwerder Island

included Hitler's personal doctor, Theodor Morell (1886–1948), who lived at Inselstrasse 16, and the architect Albert Speer (1905–1981), who bought a site at Inselstrasse 7 on which he planned to erect a villa, whilst he and his family resided at Inselstrasse 18. Adolf Hitler himself had a plot earmarked at Inselstrasse 20–22 for the construction of a villa and there was also a *Reichsbräuteschule* on the island, a Nazi boarding school in which young girls were trained to be wives and mothers for the Fatherland.

Reports of the decadent lifestyle led by Goebbels on Schwanenwerder abound, notably concerning his affair with the actress Lida Baarova, who lived nearby. The seemingly idyllic Goebbels' family photographs taken on the island at the time were part of a deliberate attempt to counteract adverse publicity. Goebbels continued to live here until 1943, when he moved his family to his country seat at Lanke on Bogensee. They returned to the island in 1945 in the face of the

A view across the Wannsee to Schwanenwerder Island

advancing Red Army and only abandoned it days before their deaths in Hitler's Führer Bunker (*Führerbunker*).

After the war, the Goebbels villa was occupied by American army personnel and then demolished to prevent it becoming a Nazi shrine, its timbers allegedly used to provide lamp posts for the island. In 1957 the plot was divided into two, the former outbuilding once used by SS guards at Inselstrasse 8 becoming a base for the Berlin river police (Wasserschutzpolizei). Inselstrasse 10 became the site of a new villa, which between 1974 and 2010 was home to the Berlin branch of the Aspen Institute of Humanitarian Studies, an organisation so dramatically different in its aims from those of the villa's earlier incumbents.

Another of Schwanenwerder's villas, at Inselstrasse 24–26, was built for the vociferously anti-Communist newspaper publisher, Axel Springer (1912–1985), who founded the Conservative tabloid *Bild* in 1952.

44 Suicide on Lake Wannsee

**District VI (Steglitz-Zehlendorf), the Kleist Grave
(Kleist-Grab) between Bismarckstrasse 2 and 4
RE1, RE7 Wannsee; S1, S7 Wannsee**

Most visitors to Berlin's leafy southwestern suburbs make for the area's pretty lakes and islands along the River Havel, drawn by the prospect of tree-fringed shores and pleasure boats. The sandy banks of the Grosser Wannsee, for example, known as the Strandbad Wannsee, can accommodate 50 000 people and is the biggest inland beach in Europe. It is strange to think that swimming was once forbidden here by law, and that watch towers were set up to spot illegal bathers! Eventually the authorities softened and in 1907 official bathing was sanctioned.

Just before crossing the bridge to Wannsee Island, a narrow street called Bismarckstrasse will be seen running south from the viaduct of the Wannsee S-Bahn station. A short distance along on the right-hand side, amongst a grove of sturdy oak trees, can be found the grave of Romantic poet and writer Heinrich von Kleist (1777–1811), who together with his close friend Henriette Vogel, committed suicide here on 21st November 1811.

Bernd Heinrich Wilhelm von Kleist was born in Frankfurt an der Oder to a family of stalwart Prussian soldiers, who shared little of his intellectual, creative and melancholic temperament. He entered the Prussian army himself in 1793 but gained leave in 1799 in order to immerse himself in literature, philosophy and teaching. In 1800 he became engaged to one of his students and took a modest finance post in Berlin to satisfy her parents. It was at this time, however, that his faith and personal world view were shattered by the works of the philosopher Immanual Kant (1724–1804), who contended that man was unable to know the true nature of things even with the power of reason. Reflecting on his life Kleist abandoned thoughts of a bureaucratic career and instead travelled to Paris and Dresden with his sister. He eventually settled in Switzerland and began developing his literary ambitions; the engagement by this time had been called off.

Dogged by a restless spirit and a tendency towards despair and frustration Kleist was soon on the move again, settling back in Berlin in 1804, where his first play *Die Familie Schroffenstein* was published to some acclaim. Despite being imprisoned by the occupying French forces, who thought he was a spy, further plays and short stories followed,

A sign leads to the secluded grave of Heinrich von Kleist

typified by his timeless depictions of individuals in crisis and doubt. Unfortunately, by 1811 Kleist's difficult temperament had lost him family and colleagues, and the collapse of his newspaper, the *Berliner Abendblätter*, had ruined him financially. Eventually, with no-one willing to produce his plays and not even the army interested in his desperate petition to rejoin he began to contemplate suicide as his only option. He found a willing partner in Henriette Vogel, a young married society woman suffering terminal ovarian cancer. The two decided to end it together on the shores of Lake Wannsee, spending their last day at an inn, which once stood on the banks of the Kleiner Wannsee, down a steep flight of stairs beyond where Kleist's grave now lies. After taking tea they disappeared into the woods and lay down in a hollow made by a fallen tree. Kleist shot Vogel in the chest and then turned the pistol on himself. Only in death, a century later, was Heinrich von Kleist eventually recognised as a major figure in German literature and a precursor to literary modernism.

Originally Kleist and Henriette were buried side by side, surrounded by a grove of poplar saplings, Vogel's last letter to her husband containing the request "…trenne Kleist ja nicht von mir im Tode" ("Do not separate Kleist and me in death"). Kleist's headstone was inscribed with the following lines: "Er lebte, sang und litt in trüber schwerer Zeit, er suchte hier den Tod und fand Unsterblichkeit" ("He lived, sang and suffered in gloomy and difficult times, he sought death here and found immortality"). However, by the time one of the Grimm Brothers visited the site several years later, the graves were overgrown and the trees withered; shortly afterwards, Vogel's grave disappeared altogether.

Kleist's grave has undergone several transformations since. When the novelist Theodor Fontane (1819–1898) visited in 1889 he reported that the opening of a tram line out to Wannsee had made the grave into a site of pilgrimage. As a result, the grave was renovated periodi-

Where a poet sought
death and found
immortality

cally, for example in 1936 in time for the influx of visitors to the Berlin Olympic Games. Most signiicantly, in 1941 the original inscription was replaced by a more upbeat verse from Kleist's own *Prince of Homburg*: "Nun, O Unsterblichkeit, Bist Du Ganz Mein" ("Now, Immortality, you belong to me"). During the 1950s and 60s Kleist's date of birth was corrected twice, the headstone was turned around, and its metal railings were opened out towards the path. However, not until 1980 was any memorial to Kleist's companion Henriette Vogel re-instated, several hundred metres away at the start of Bismarckstrasse. Although today Bismarckstrasse is sometimes bustling with traffic down to the nearby rowing clubs, the leafy corner where Kleist and Vogel chose to die still retains its solemn air of melancholy and seclusion.

Other places of interest nearby: 45

did not succumb to the rigours of forced labour in the east, namely the strongest and most wilful, had "to be treated accordingly" so as to eliminate any possibility of a new Jewish revival. In order to avoid legal and political difficulties Heydrich went on to stress the importance of defining Jewishness for the purpose of "evacuation". The result was a complicated set of rules based on the number of Jews within a person's family tree, which at best led to forced sterilisation and at worst to deportation. It was even discussed how the "final solution" would be concealed from the international community by sending Jews over 65 years of age, as well as some First World War veterans, to the 'model' concentration camp at Theresienstadt, which would be open to visits from the Red Cross.

With the concluding of the Wannsee Conference a new phase in the destruction of Europe's Jews began. To mass murder and starvation a third method of killing was now added: poison gas. Two months before the conference 1200 German political prisoners had been gassed at a euthanasia institute in Bernburg, south of Berlin, using a technique that would soon become a horrifying feature of the death camps of occupied Poland. It would be the world's first case of genocide using industrial means.

After the war the Villa Wannsee was occupied by the Soviet army, and then by the United States army as an officers' club, then it became the Centre for Political Education of the Berlin Social Democratic Party, with a children's summer camp in its grounds. Eventually, in 1992, on the 50th anniversary of the conference, Jewish lobbyists succeeded in having the building turned into a permanent memorial and education centre dedicated to the study of the Holocaust. Forever tainted by just one day in history, the villa's most chilling exhibit is a copy of Eichmann's list of the numbers of Jews to be exterminated in each European country (including many in countries not yet under German control), typed as if it were nothing more than a grocery list.

Near the Villa Wannsee is the Liebermann Villa (Liebermann-Villa am Wannsee) at Colomierstrasse 3. It was built in 1910 as a summer retreat for the German Expressionist painter Max Liebermann (1847-1935), who in 1920 became president of the Prussian Academy of Arts. He resigned in 1933, when the academy decided to no longer exhibit works by Jewish artists. After being forced to sell the villa in 1940 his wife comitted suicide in 1943 and was buried alongside her husband in the Jewish Cemetery (Jüdischer Friedhof) at Schönhauser Allee 23–25 (see no. 84).

Other places of interest nearby: 44

46   The Follies of Peacock Island

District VI (Steglitz-Zehlendorf), Peacock Island (Pfaueninsel)
RE1, RE7 Wannsee or S1, S7 Wannsee, then Bus 218 to Pfauen-
insel ferry terminal

Peacock Island (Pfaueninsel) on the River Havel near Wannsee is an explorer's paradise. A former royal seat, whose owners indulged their architectural whims without bounds, it retains a special atmosphere to this day since cars, shops, and even smoking are prohibited. The origin of the island's name will become apparent when disembarking the ferry from Wannsee, since the island is home to a small colony of peacocks, the last vestige of a royal menagerie that in 1844 formed the core of Berlin's famous zoo (Zoologischer Garten) in the southwest corner of the Tiergarten (Mitte).

After leaving the ferry a path immediately to the left runs past the Castellan's House, with its peacock-topped flagpole, and then uphill to the Swiss House, erected in 1830 for the gardener. The path continues onwards to a clearing with a flower garden and the island's most extraordinary building, namely Schloss Pfaueninsel. This sham castle was built between 1794 and 1797 (to a design by court joiner Johann Gottlieb Brendel) for King Frederick William II (1786–1797) and his

mistress Wilhelmine Encke (the future Countess Lichtenau), whose sketches are said to have inspired the building. Sited so as to be visible from the King's main residence, namely the Marble Palace (Marmorpalais) in distant Potsdam, the castle's most unusual feature is its deliberately ruined upper storey, set between two towers connected by an arched bridge.

After the king's death in 1797, by which time Prussia had been seriously weakened as a result of its ill-advised involvement in the affairs of Poland and France, the castle became the preferred summer residence of the king's son and heir, Frederick William III (1797–1840). In the 1820s he commissioned the royal

An artificial Gothic ruin ('the dairy') on Peacock Island

gardener Peter Joseph Lenné (1789–1866) to landscape the island in the informal English style, at which time many of the pavilions and follies seen today were constructed. The first of these is James's Well, a tiny, deliberately ruined, pedimented 'eyecatcher' set in a meadow towards the centre of the island, reached by bearing right at the green bench. Continuing onwards a left turn leads through an avenue of trees (past a disused circular fountain on the left) to the neo-Gothic Kavaliershaus, used to provide the royal household with accommodation. It was rebuilt in the 1820s by the architect Carl Frederick Schinkel (1781–1841), who added the late Gothic façade of a 16th century house brought all the way from Danzig (modern Gdańsk) in Poland.

Continuing onwards again a crossroads is eventually reached from where the Parschenkessel bay can be viewed on the left, its numerous dead trees used by nesting cormorants. The sandy path straight ahead runs alongside the bay towards the northern tip of the island. Here stands a *faux* Gothic ruin called the dairy, built in 1795 to resemble a partially-ruined medieval abbey; nearby is the red-roofed Dutch House, a cow shed dating to 1802.

Following the path southwards, down the eastern shore of the island, a right-hand turn is reached leading to the edge of the forest and a Greek style neo-Classical pavilion called the Luisentempel. It is faced with a Doric sandstone portico created in 1812 that was brought here in 1828 from the Schlosspark Charlottenburg, when the royal mausoleum of Queen Louisa, wife of Frederick William III (1797–1840), was given a new granite façade by Schinkel (see no. 66).

Continuing along the main path an inscribed boulder is passed commemorating Johannes Kunckel (1630–1703), glassmaker and alchemist to Frederick William, the Great Elector (1640–1688). Kunckel built a laboratory on the island in 1685 and is remembered for discovering how to prepare phosphorous and for the creation of ruby glass. Beyond, the path leads upwards across another path to an aviary (Vogelhaus) in which pheasants, peacocks and other birds are kept. Finally, the path returns to the ferry landing where our journey began.

Peacock Island has witnessed not just architectural follies but historical ones, too. In 1936 the island was commandeered by Hitler's Propaganda Minister, Joseph Goebbels (1897–1945), for a huge party to celebrate Nazi Germany's staging of the Olympics in Berlin. Using his film industry connections Goebbels decked out the island like a giant film set, with music provided by the Berlin Philharmonic Orchestra!

47 Princely Towers and Far Pavilions

District VI (Steglitz-Zehlendorf), Klein-Glienicke Schlosspark and Park Babelsberg off Königstrasse on Wannsee Island
RE1, RE7 Wannsee or S1, S7 Wannsee, then Bus 118 Schloss Glienicke

For a fascinating three hour walk that illustrates not only the constructional whims and fantasies of the Prussian royal family but also the penchant for architectural Historicism during the 19th century, a visit should be made to the palace-park estates of Klein Glienicke and Babelsberg.

The Klein-Glienicke Schlosspark lies at the western end of Königstrasse on Wannsee Island and was created by Prince Carl of Prussia, younger son of King Frederick William III (1797–1840), after he acquired the estate in 1824. Prior to this it had been owned by Chancellor Carl von Hardenberg, who had hired the prominent gardener Peter Joseph Lenné (1789–1866) to landscape the property as an English-style pleasure garden. The park is entered through the Griffin Gate (Greifentor), its gateposts suitably crowned with mythological eagle-headed lions. The first garden structure to be encountered is the so-called Stibadium, a semi-circular pavilion with seating erected in neo-Classical style in 1840 to a design by Ludwig Persius (1803–1845), a follower of the renowned architect Carl Frederick Schinkel (1781–1841), Prussia's foremost exponent of neo-Classicism.

Schloss Glienicke itself stands just beyond, on the left-hand side, but far from being a castle it is actually an Italianate villa above which rises a *Campanile* tower. This time the work of Schinkel himself it was constructed between 1825 and 1828 and features a courtyard with a collection of sculptural fragments built into its walls. The Schlosspark is entered to the rear of the courtyard where on the left-hand side Schinkel's gilded Lion Fountain (Löwenfontäne) can be seen, added in 1838 on the same axis as the castle.

Following the path on the right-hand side out of the courtyard Persius once again leaves his mark in a long, glazed Orangery (1839), immediately beyond which can be found a mock monastery known as the Klosterhof. This garden fantasy was created in 1850 by Ferdinand von Arnim in order to house Prince Carl's collection of Byzantine and Romanesque sculptural fragments, which are cleverly incorporated into

A detail of the Griffin Gate leading into the Klein-Glienicke Schlosspark

its walls. A gateway from here leads north, along the riverbank, to a former gardener's house, and then on to the extensive rear section of the park – called Volkspark Klein-Glienicke – that stretches as far as Schinkel's Hunters' Hall (Jägerhof, 1828) and Persius's Moorlake House (1841) (see no. 81).

Staying inside the park a further three Schinkel structures follow in quick succession, commencing with the Italianate *Casino* built as a guesthouse above the banks of the Havel in 1824–1825. Following the main path to the left along the boundary of the park reveals Schinkel's so-called 'Large Curiosity' (Grosse Neugierde), a circular pavilion with Doric columns erected in 1835 as a place from which to view the Glienicke Bridge (see no. 48); it is based on the Athenian monument to Lysicrates from the 4th century B.C. Thereafter follows Schinkel's 'Small Curiosity' (Kleine Neugierde), a rectangular temple-like pavilion built originally in 1796 as a teahouse and reworked in 1827 as a repository for Roman sculptural fragments and mosaics.

Leaving the Schlosspark by the Griffin Gate a short walk southwards down Mövenstrasse brings into view the Jagdschloss Glienicke, a hunting lodge erected in 1889, this time in the neo-Baroque style for Prince Frederick Leopold. It replaced an earlier lodge built in 1682 for Crown Prince Frederick, whose estate house once stood where Schloss Glienicke now stands.

Mövenstrasse now leads onto Waldmüllerstrasse and the Park Bridge (Parkbrücke), which crosses over the narrow Glienicker Lanke into Park Babelsberg (a series of display panels remind passers-by that during the Cold War Klein-Glienicke was an East German enclave only accessible by this bridge). Following the path to the right passes another series of royal garden structures, this time created in the neo-Gothic style as part of a summer residence for Crown Prince William, later King and Emperor William I (1861–1888). The first looks like a lakeside medieval castle but is in fact an engine house (Maschinenhaus) with a tall chimney, once used to supply water to the park's fountains. The park itself was landscaped in the 1830s (again by Lenné) and further shaped by Prince Hermann von Pückler-Muskau a decade later.

Most remarkable of the estate's architectural features is Schloss Babelsberg a little farther up the hill. It was begun in the 1830s to a design once again by Carl Frederick Schinkel, in a Tudor-Gothic style based on ideas he had gained whilst in England. The building was completed in the 1840s by Persius and Johann Heinrich Strack (1805–1880), the latter another of Schinkel's former students. These two architects designed most of the other neo-Gothic structures on the estate, including the Kleines Schloss, a guesthouse for ladies at court far-

The so-called Gerichtslaube on a hill in Park Babelsberg

ther along the lakeside, and a crumbling stable block directly behind it. Farther up the hill on the right-hand side is something quite unexpected. The Gerichtslaube is a *bona fide* Gothic structure, as opposed to an idealised recreation, being a 13th century arcaded courthouse from Berlin's old town hall, brought here when its successor was erected in 1868 (see no. 1).

The path continues now to the Flatowturm, again a neo-Gothic structure, put up between 1853 and 1856. Based on a medieval tower in Frankfurt am Main it has a viewing platform at the top from where the emperor's boat house can be seen on the shore far below. This walk concludes at an easy-to-miss, scaled-down version of Berlin's famous Victory Column (Siegessäule), from where the path leads downhill to the S-Bahn station at Babelsberg.

On the southern shore of the Grunewaldsee, far to the northeast, stands another royal building, the Grunewald Hunting Lodge (Jagdschloss Grunewald). Built for Elector Joachim II (1535–1571) in 1542 to a design by Caspar Theyss it is one of Berlin's oldest civic buildings and retains the city's only surviving Renaissance hall.

Other places of interest nearby: 48

48 Bridge of Unity, Bridge of Spies

District VI (Steglitz-Zehlendorf), the Glienicke Bridge
(Glienicker Brücke)
RE1, RE7 Wannsee or S1, S7 Wannsee, then Bus 118
Glienicker Brücke

The Glienicke Bridge (Glienicker Brücke), which crosses the Havel on the border between Berlin and Potsdam, seems a quiet and almost inconsequential place today. Appearances, however, can be deceptive since the bridge is one of Germany's most storied.

By the mid-17th century the growth of Berlin-Cölln, the capital of the March of Brandenburg, had been checked by a series of plagues and famines, as well as the ravages of the Thirty Years War (1618–1648). The population had fallen to just 6000 and Potsdam was viewed as little more than a remote island a day's coach journey away, and then accessible only across a wooden bridge. Things started to change with the accession of Frederick William, the Great Elector (1640–1688), whose linking of the Spree and Oder rivers turned Berlin into the hub of Brandenburg trade. In 1660 Frederick William selected Potsdam as his secondary residence (after Berlin) with a daily coach link between the two royal capitals inaugurated in 1754.

The introduction in 1838 of a rail link between Berlin and Potsdam prompted the construction of a new, sturdier bridge, which was undertaken in 1831–1834 to a design by the architect Carl Frederick Schinkel (1781–1841). The stone bridge had a wooden section that could be raised to allow steamers to pass along what had now become a busy waterway. However, as the volume of traffic using the bridge increased so in 1904 a competition was held to design a new steel suspension bridge, which opened on 16th November 1907 (a graceful colonnade from the original stone bridge still stands on the Potsdam side of the river).

After being damaged in late April 1945 the bridge was reopened in December 1949, shortly after the foundation of the German Democratic Republic and the Federal Republic of Germany, whose borders ran across it: as such it was named the Brücke der Einheit ('Bridge of Unity'). From now on the bridge was primarily used by the Allies as a link between their Berlin zones of occupation and the military liaison missions in Potsdam (residents of Berlin and Potsdam preferred to use the S-Bahn).

On 27th May 1952 the Glienicke Bridge was closed to citizens of West Berlin and the Federal Republic. Later, after the Berlin Wall was erected on 13th August 1961, citizens of the GDR were also prevented from using it: ironically, the 'Bridge of Unity' had now become a symbol of division (see no. 70).

The bridge was one of the very few places in the world where the United States and the Soviet Union stood facing each other directly. It was thus deemed the ideal location for the exchange of prisoners during the the Cold War (1949–1989), especially since other nations would not get any say in the matter. The media dubbed it the 'Bridge of Spies' and it gained lasting celluloid fame in the 1966 Harry Palmer film, *Funeral in Berlin*, starring Michael Caine.

The first and most famous prisoner exchange happened on 10th February 1962, when the American pilot Francis Gary Powers was swapped for the KGB spy Colonel Vlyam Fisher (aka Rudolf Ivanovich Abel). Powers set out from the eastern end of the bridge and Abel from the west, the two simply nodding at each other as they passed. Powers had been captured on 1st May 1960 after his U-2 aircraft was shot down by a surface-to-air missile over Sverdlovsk in Soviet airspace. Since the U-2 was designed for covert photographic surveillance, the Soviet government imprisoned him for espionage. Although later cleared by

Looking across the Glienicke Bridge from Berlin to Potsdam

American pilot Francis Gary Powers

a Senate Armed Services Select Committee Powers was cold-shouldered by the CIA for neither having operated his aircraft's self-destruct mechanism nor having used his suicide pin (sealed inside a hollow silver dollar). Powers went on to work for Lockheed as a test pilot and died in 1977, at the age of just 47, when a television helicopter he was piloting crashed in Los Angeles. In 2000, on the 40th anniversary of his being shot down, Powers' family was presented with his posthumously awarded Prisoner of War Medal, Distinguished Flying Cross, and National Defense Service Medal.

A second exchange of prisoners occurred on 12th June 1985, in a hastily arranged operation during which four East European "scouts" arrested in the West were swapped for 23 American secret agents held in Eastern Europe; it was the largest prisoner exchange since the end of the Second World War. On the first of December in the same year the GDR agreed to the bridge reverting back to its original name, in return for assistance in its upkeep. So it was that the Glienicke Bridge became the scene for the third and final exchange of prisoners on 11th February 1986. Nine people were involved, namely five agents from the East, including the Soviet spy Karl Koecher, and four from the West, including human rights campaigner and political prisoner Anatoly Sharansky.

In the face of mass demonstrations against the East German regime, and an increasing number of attempted border crossings (including one in 1988 by three Potsdam citizens who forced their way across the Glienicke Bridge in a lorry), the Berlin Wall was opened on 9th November 1989. At 6pm the following day, the bridge was opened, too. Its border defences were dismantled after unification was declared on 3rd October 1990.

Other places of interest nearby: 47

49 Exploring Garrison Town

Potsdam, a tour of the former garrison town commencing on Lange Brücke
RE1 Potsdam Hauptbahnhof; S1, S7 Potsdamer Hauptbahnhof

Most of today's visitors to Potsdam come to see the royal palaces of Sanssouci Park and nearby New Garden (Neuer Garten), erected by a succession of Hohenzollern kings from the time of King Frederick II, 'the Great' (1740–1786) up until the abolition of the German monarchy in 1918. However, it should not be forgotten that whilst Potsdam served as a second home to the Hohenzollerns, it was also their second most important garrison town. Although seriously damaged during the last months of the Second World War, a walk around the Old Town (Alt-Stadt) still provides a glimpse of this other face of Potsdam, namely as a city of soldiers and barracks.

It was Frederick William, 'the Great Elector' (1640–1688), who had pulled Berlin and Potsdam out of obscurity but it was his grandson Frederick William I, 'the Soldier King' (1713–1740), who created the army that backed up Prussia's dream of becoming the most powerful kingdom in Europe. Little wonder that Prussia was described as an army with a state rather than the other way round! In reality, however, the 'Soldier King' never fought a war, his real contribution being the reorganisation of Prussia's near-bankrupt finances.

From Potsdam main station (Potsdamer Hauptbahnhof) the southern edge of what was 18th century Potsdam is reached by following Babelsbergstrasse onto the Long Bridge (Lange Brücke), which spans a narrow point on the River Havel. At the end of the bridge on the right-hand side is the old town square (Alter Markt), where once stood a fortress built in the 12th century to guard what was an important fording place: it prompted the eventual founding of Potsdam. In 1662 a town palace was erected here after the Great Elector had chosen Potsdam as his secondary residence in 1660. Reworked under Frederick the Great, and damaged during the Second World War, the palace was demolished by the GDR regime in 1960. All that remains of it today is its northern entrance, rebuilt as part of an as yet unrealised plan to reconstruct the entire building. Known as the Fortuna Portal it is crowned with a gilded statue of Fortuna celebrating the acquisition by the Great Elector's son, Elector Frederick III (1688–1701), of the Prussian royal crown in 1701, making him King Frederick I (1701–1713).

Opposite the square, on the other side of the busy main road and best reached via a nearby underpass, are the tantalising remains of a water feature called *Neptune's Triumph*, which adorned what was once the royal pleasure gardens (Lustgarten). Alongside it is a graceful 18th century colonnade (re-erected here in 1970) that originally connected the palace with the royal stables (Marstall), which extend westwards from here along Breitestrasse. Built originally as an Orangery in 1685, the stables are now home to Potsdam's Filmmuseum (see no. 51). Hidden away behind the stables is New Market (Am Neuen Markt), with its royal carriage house (Kutschstall) and fine 18th century houses still miraculously intact. Frederick William II (1786–1797) lived at Am Neuen Markt 1–2 on the south side of the square whilst crown prince.

Siefertstrasse leads out of the square to Yorckstrasse, with its canal commissioned in 1720 by King Frederick William I, to replace the town's old drainage ditches. The Soldier King was also responsible for the first Baroque town extension northwards from here in 1721, in order to provide housing for his growing garrison, which included a regiment of especially tall soldiers (*Lange Kerls*) gathered at great expense from across Europe (the houses at numbers 5–7 date from this period). A left turn along Yorckstrasse, and another left down Dortustrasse to its junction with Breitestrasse, reveals more of the Soldier King's additions to Potsdam, namely a Prussian military orphanage in which the children of dead soldiers were cared for (and eventually themselves recruited). Opposite the orphanage once stood Potsdam's Garrison Church (Garnisonkirche), marked today by a red-brick arch, in which the coffins of both the Soldier King and Frederick the Great were kept (see no. 50).

By continuing along Breitestrasse, away from the Long Bridge, the next street is Lindenstrasse, which leads up to Charlottenstrasse and the start of the second Baroque town extension begun in 1732 (at the junction is the ornate Old Guardhouse (Alte Wache) erected in the 1790s and finished off with suitably martial statuary). This part of garrison town retains some of its original architecture, notably its modest stuccoed wooden houses built to a royally prescribed model, two storeys high, five windows wide, with a central gable. Each homeowner was obliged to allocate an upstairs room for use by two to six soldiers, each bed to be shared by a pair of soldiers in order to discourage desertion. The rooms also had to face the street so that calls to arms sounded by drummers outside could not be ignored. In return for providing rooms, the king granted homeowners with subsidies and construction materials (the latter being pine since the Great Elector had already felled Brandenburg's oak forests in order to settle outstanding debts with England and Holland).

Lindenstrasse next crosses Brandenburgerstrasse, at the western end of which is Potsdam's own Brandenburg Gate, rebuilt in 1770 in the style of a Roman triumphal arch to commemorate victory in the Seven Years' War; it also provides a suitably grand

Equestrian sculptures adorn the royal carriage house in Potsdam

link between the once-walled town and Sanssouci Park. Back on Lindenstrasse at number 54 stands the former home of the commander of Potsdam's garrison, built in the 1730s. Between 1935 and 1941 the building served as a Nazi courthouse after which it became a prison, a function it retained under the Stasi until 1989.

Lindenstrasse terminates at the Hunter's Gate (Jägertor), the second of Potsdam's three remaining gateways (and the only one to retain its original appearance from 1733). The other gateway, the Nauen Gate (Nauener Tor), can be seen by backtracking to Gutenbergstrasse and following it eastwards to its junction with Friedrich Ebert Strasse. Rebuilt in 1755 during the reign of Frederick the Great it is considered to be Central Europe's first neo-Gothic structure.

The second Baroque town extension ends here with the so-called Dutch Quarter (Holländisches Viertel), a surprising group of 134 red-brick buildings reaching back along Mittelstrasse to the corner of Kurfürstenstrasse and Hebbelstrasse. They were built and occupied by Dutch artisans invited to Potsdam by the Soldier King in the 1730s because of their mercantile acumen. Another important immigrant community from the same period were the French Huguenots, whose oval French Church (Französische Kirche) of 1753 stands in the far left-hand corner of Bassinplatz at the end of Benkertstrasse (their story is told in a museum inside the church). This tour of the garrison town of Potsdam concludes around the corner at Posthofstrasse 17, where the existence of the crumbling Actors' Barracks, built in 1796 together with a now lost garrison theatre, reminds the visitor that nearly everything in Potsdam once had military connotations.

Other places of interest nearby: 50

50 A Well-Travelled Coffin

Potsdam, the grave of Frederick the Great at Sanssouci
Palace (Schloss Sanssouci)
RE1 Park Sanssouci; S1, S7 Potsdamer Hauptbahnhof,
then Bus 695 into Park Sanssouci

No other palace is more closely connected with the reclusive personality of King Frederick II, 'the Great' (1740–1786), than Sanssouci Palace (Schloss Sanssouci) in Potsdam. It is telling of the modesty of the man, who was responsible for transforming a small provincial kingdom into Europe's leading power, that the intimate palace remained his favourite summer retreat, even after the completion in 1769 of the nearby New Palace (Neues Palais), with its 200 richly decorated rooms and 428 Baroque sculptures on the façade.

Sanssouci Palace was erected in 1745–1747 to designs by Frederick himself, the charming Rococo structure being placed at the top of a series of vineyard terraces. Such was the calming effect of this Prussian Arcadia upon the king – the name Sanssouci meaning 'without a care' – that he made it known he wished eventually to be buried here, alongside his eleven beloved Italian Greyhounds. However, although Frederick's grave can indeed be found at Sanssouci, this is not where his coffin was originally placed. After his death in the palace on 17th August 1786 it was taken instead to the crypt of Potsdam's Garrison Church (Garnisonkirche) at the junction of Breitestrasse and Dortustrasse, where his father Frederick William I, the 'Soldier King' (1713–1740), had been buried; here it remained for the next one hundred and fifty nine years (see no. 49).

The Garrison Church reappears in the history books on 21st March 1933, when the newly appointed German Chancellor Adolf Hitler and the ailing Reich President Paul von Hindenburg (1925–1934) came here to bow before the coffin of Fredrick the Great. Known as Potsdam Day it was seen by many as a sign of Prussia's blessing of its Nazi successors. The church would be damaged during the ensuing Second World War and eventually demolished in 1968 by the Communist regime, striking a symbolic blow against both German militarism and Christianity.

Frederick the Great's coffin remained in the Garrison Church until 1945, when the rapid approach of the Red Army prompted Hitler to issue instructions that Germany's heritage must be protected against bombing and possible seizure. Consequently, the coffins of both Fredericks, together with those of President Hindenburg and his wife (recently disinterred from their graves at the Tannenberg Memorial in East Prussia), were carted westwards to Bernterode, 40 kilometres east of Kassel in Thuringia. Here, amidst great secrecy, the coffins were concealed in a 2000 foot-deep potassium mine.

When the mine was eventually commandeered by the US First Army, it was found to contain some 40000 tons of explosives and ammunition stored in its 23 kilometres of tunnels. More intriguing to the seven soldiers sent down to investigate the tunnels, however, was a freshly plastered wall built into the side of the main corridor, about 400 metres from the bottom of the lift shaft. After removing the plaster and tunnelling through five feet of masonry they discovered a padlocked door. Breaking through they found themselves standing in a chamber filled with paintings, tapestries, royal regalia, and hundreds of Prussian

A potato adorns the the grave of Frederick the Great at Sanssouci Palace

The "Berliner Strasse" backlot at the Babelsberg Film Studios

Berlin's own Marlene Dietrich (1901–1992). By the early 1930s, however, UFA had been taken over by right-wing press magnate Alfred Hugenberg, whose early support of Hitler saw the company increasingly being controlled by Propaganda Minister Joseph Goebbels (1897–1945) for the production of Nazi propaganda films. By 1937 the Nazi Party had acquired 72% of UFA's shares and in 1942 it was nationalised by the Third Reich as the country's only film production company. Despite the departure for America of many of German cinema's leading practitioners, hundreds of feature films were still produced at Babelsberg between 1933 and 1945, including several notoriously anti-Semitic films such as *Jud Süss* (1940).

In September 1944 pre-production began in Berlin on an all but forgotten Nazi propaganda film called *Life Goes On* (*Das Leben geht weiter*). The director Wolfgang Liebeneiner was coerced into making the film by Goebbels, who not only controlled production but possibly even wrote the script. The fact that 350 000 Reichsmark was spent on developing the script, the largest amount ever for a Third Reich-era film, emphasises the importance Goebbels placed on the film's subject matter, namely the promise that rocket-powered wonder weapons (*Wunder Waffen*) could still turn the war around in Germany's favour. Filming began in mid-December although Allied bombing raids meant that outdoor filming was soon abandoned in favour of the studios at Babelsberg, where the city's bombed streets were reconstructed in safer surroundings. In March 1945, with the Red Army advancing rapidly toward Berlin, the entire production moved to the Lüneburger Heide in Lower Saxony, where ironically Nazi Germany's surrender would be taken two months later (see no. 79). Needless to say, the Third Reich's last film was never finished, never mind released, and the negatives are thought to have been hidden and then burned: only two production stills remain.

After the war, however, life did go on for the Babelsberg Film Studios, although not quite in the way Goebbels had hoped. Falling into the Soviet zone of occupation UFA became DEFA (Deutsche Film-Aktiengesellschaft), the GDR's film studio, which produced 700 feature films and 600 television shows. DEFA itself ceased to exist after German reunification in 1990 since when the Babelsberg studios have reinvented themselves once more, this time by attracting Hollywood-style big budget co-productions, such as *The Pianist* (2002), directed by Roman Polanski, *The Bourne Supremacy* (2004), *Mission Impossible III* (2006), *The Bourne Ultimatum* (2007), and *Valkyrie* (2008), starring Tom Cruise as the failed Hitler assassin Claus von Stauffenberg (see no. 12).

On one side of the studios today, and entered from Grossbeeren-strasse, is the Filmpark Babelsberg, although it is more of a theme park for children than a serious studio tour. However, it does allow a glimpse of the famous Studio West (Atelier West) (today Stage 7 Sound West), towards the rear of the park on the right-hand side, where Josef von Sternberg (1894–1969) directed Marlene Dietrich (1901–1992) in *The Blue Angel*. The red-brick building is today marked with a modest stone wall plaque. Of greater interest is a stroll around the grounds of the modern studios themselves, especially Marlene-Dietrich-Allee, at the end of which can be found a backlot with several reconstructed street scenes. One of them, dubbed 'Berliner Strasse', has been used for several major films. Look out, too, for a statue of the famous golden robot, Maria, played by actress Brigitte Helm in the film *Metropolis* (see front cover).

For an in-depth look at the work of the Babelsberg Film Studios visit the Filmmuseum Potsdam.

Many notable films have used Berlin as a backdrop and it is fascinating to see how they reflect the politics of the day. For Berlin before the destruction of the Second World War see Berlin, *Symphony of a Great City (Berlin, die Symphonie der Grossstadt)* (1927). For the city during the 1930s watch *Mephisto* (1981) and *Cabaret* (1972). *Germany, Year Zero (Germania Anno Zero)* (1948) and *The Ballad of Berlin (Berliner Ballade)* (1948) depict post-war Berlin, whilst *Wings of Desire (Der Himmel über Berlin)* (1987), *Goodbye Lenin!* (2003), and *The Lives of Others (Das Leben der Anderen)* (2006) cover the Cold War period.

52 The Secrets of Lichterfelde

District VI (Steglitz-Zehlendorf), the former Lichterfelde Barracks (Lichterfelde Kaserne) on Finckensteinallee S1 Lichterfelde West, then walk along Kadettenweg

The leafy southwestern suburb of Lichterfelde, straddling the banks of the Teltowkanal, is rarely visited by tourists. It was created in the 1870s by the developer J. W. von Carstenn as Berlin's first railway suburb. Although little remains from this time, a few of Carstenn's suburban villas can still be identified, clustered around the Lichterfelde West railway station (1872), which itself is built in the style of an Italianate villa.

Running south from the station are Kadettenweg and Kommandantenstrasse, their names hinting at a longstanding military presence in the area. Hoping to elevate the prestige of his new suburb, Carstenn granted a large pocket of land on Finckensteinallee (at the southern end of Kadettenweg) to the army for the construction in 1873 of an academy for the Royal Prussian Cadet Corps. Still standing today, the Lichterfelde Barracks (Lichterfelde Kaserne) were used to train 12-year-old boys, typically the sons of the rural gentry, to be future officers in the Prussian army. The original barracks building forms a long, three-winged range, easily identified by its arched windows. In front of the range was the parade ground (now grassed over), at the eastern end of which once stood the Isted Lion. This Danish monument commemorating victory over the Prussians at the Battle of

Third Reich statuary adorns a building at the former Lichterfelde Barracks

Isted in Schleswig-Holstein in 1850 was brought back in triumph by the Prussians after their defeat of the Danes in 1864 (the statue is today in Copenhagen). It was on this parade ground on 9th March 1920 that the Royal Prussian Cadet Corps was eventually disbanded, marking the end of a chapter in German history.

Another, darker chapter in the history of Lichterfelde opened in 1933, when Hitler's Nazis commandeered the barracks. On 30th June 1934, during the so-called 'Night of the Long Knives', Hitler ordered the SS (*Schutzstaffel*), the Nazi party's blackshirted protection squads formed to police political meetings, to arrest the insufficiently loyal leadership of the brownshirted SA (*Sturmabteilumg*). Despite having helped Hitler to power, the SA remained disgruntled at not having precipitated a Socialist as well as a nationalist revolution. Not able to tolerate such internal conflict Hitler had 200 senior members of the SA, executed over a three day period, not only at the barracks but also at Gestapo Headquarters on Prinz-Albrecht-Strasse, as well as the Columbiahaus detention centre at Columbiadamm 1–3, near Tempelhof Airport.

Once a mere subsidiary of the SA, the SS was now the most powerful organisation in Nazi Germany, its members used exclusively for Gestapo security forces, concentration camp guards, and Waffen-SS combat troops. Another function of the SS was to supply handpicked men for Hitler's special chancellery guard, the 'Stabswache Berlin', which had been created in March 1933 by SS Lieutenant General Josef 'Sepp' Dietrich. Within six months it became Hitler's personal bodyguard unit – the Leibstandarte-SS 'Adolf Hitler' – with its base at the Lichterfelde Barracks.

To provide the regiment with imposing new headquarters the barracks were enlarged between 1935 and 1938 in typical Third Reich style, the new extension easily identified by its large rectangular windows and pared-down neo-Classical pilasters. A plinth at the top of the pilasters once bore the regiment's name, above which was a huge martial eagle clutching a swastika. In front of the wing there was a parade ground, entered by a wide gateway from Finckensteinallee. The two gateposts are especially interesting since they were originally fronted by a pair of stone sentinels wearing SS longcoats and helmets and clutching rifles. The statues were dubbed *Reichsrottenführer* after an SA-SS paramilitary rank created in 1932.

On 24th April 1945 after the barracks were captured by the Red Army, the Nazi eagle was quickly removed. The Soviets then handed the barracks over to the Americans, in whose sector it lay, in July 1945 and they erased the regimental name. The stone guards, however,

SS motifs on the back of a gatepost leading into the former Lichterfelde Barracks

were left *in situ* and simply covered over with concrete, where they remain to this day, sealed inside the thickness of the gateposts. The only clue as to the original symbolic significance of the gateway is the oakleaf-entwined sword carved on the back of each post.

After 1945 the Americans renamed the complex Andrews Barracks in memory of Lieutenant General Frank Maxwell Andrews, the wartime deputy commander of the US European Theater of Operations, who was killed in a plane crash in May 1943. It was just another step in neutralising the potent history of a place where in 1942 many Jews had been executed as part of a widespread revenge for the assassination in Prague of SS Lieutenant General Reinhard Heydrich (1904–1942), Chief of the Reich Main Security Office (Reichssicherheitshauptamt). When the Americans themselves departed in 1994 several of the former barracks buildings were taken over by the federal government to store their archives (Bundesarchiv). It seems that peace has finally descended once and for all on the former Lichterfelde Barracks.

One of Nazi Berlin's numerous, anonymous-looking administration buildings in which murder was planned on a huge scale can be found north of the Lichterfelde Barracks at Unter den Eichen 128-135. The SS Economic and Administrative Central Office was the central office for the management of the death camps, as well as for SS business enterprises. Its director General Oswald Pohl was responsible for transferring the plundered assets of those murdered into the Third Reich's bank account.

Other places of interest nearby: 40, 41, 42

53 "I Still Keep a Suitcase in Berlin"

District VII (Tempelhof-Schöneberg), the grave of
Marlene Dietrich in Städtischer Friedhof III at
Stubenrauchstrasse 43–45
S41, S42, S45, S47 Bundesplatz; U9 Bundesplatz,
U3 Rüdesheimer Platz

In the far northwestern corner of the suburb of Friedenau, well away from Berlin's busy tourist routes, lies a quiet cemetery called Städtischer Friedhof III. Here can be found the grave (Plot 34/363) of actress and singer Marlene Dietrich (1901–1992), an entertainment icon of the 20th century named as one of the American Film Institute's 'Greatest Female Stars of All Time'. Her simple headstone is inscribed "Hier steh ich an den Marken meiner Tage" ("Here I stand on the border of life"), words written by the young German poet and soldier Theodor Körner (1791–1813) after being wounded in battle.

Marie Magdalene Dietrich was born on 27th December 1901 at Leberstrasse 65 in the Schöneberg district of Berlin (the house is long gone, as is the original street name – Sedanstrasse – recalling the defeat of the French army by Prussia in 1870). Nicknamed 'Lena' by her family, whilst still a teenager she contracted her first two names to form 'Marlene'. For a while she was a promising student of the violin, until a hand injury forced her to give up playing. In 1924 her destiny was re-defined, when she married Rudolf Sieber, a film director who introduced her to the world of acting. Soon a mother and living in an elegant apartment at Bundesallee 54 she worked as a chorus girl and actress for theatre director Max Reinhardt (1873–1943), although it was Austria's great Svengali director, Josef von Sternberg (1894–1969), who would be the most powerful influence on her career. Whilst still relatively unknown he cast her as Lola Lola in *The Blue Angel* (1930), Germany's first major talking film, in which she sang what would become her signature tune, *Falling in Love Again* (see no. 51). Dietrich's character symbolised the harsh and unfeeling decadence of the 1920s, which threatened to both captivate and destroy German innocence. Her performance as a dangerously sexy *femme fatale*, with a husky voice and a cool exterior, would define her stage persona for the rest of her career.

Against a background of rising National Socialism, von Sternberg

The grave of Marlene Dietrich in Friedenau

whisked Dietrich off to Hollywood, where she signed a seven-year contract with Paramount Pictures and starred in such films as *Blonde Venus* (1932), *Shanghai Express* (1932), and *The Scarlet Empress* (1934). Their intense collaboration introduced the soft focus close-up, which all female stars would eventually aspire to during Hollywood's golden age. Dietrich also scandalised American society, as much by wearing trousers in public as by her many love affairs – with both men and women – including Frank Sinatra, John F. Kennedy, Douglas Fairbanks, Yul Brynner, the playwright Mercedes de Acosta, and *Gone with the Wind* actress, Ona Munson; the great love of her life was said to have been the French actor Jean Gabin.

In 1937 Dietrich became an American citizen having refused several lucrative offers from Hitler's Propaganda Minister Joseph Goebbels (1897–1945) to return to Nazi Germany (it is telling that by this time half the actors on *The Blue Angel* and a third of the production crew had fled Germany).

During the Second World War Dietrich denounced the German government and its anti-semitic policies and made many personal appearances in support of American troops near the front lines. It was at this time that she made her own recording of *Lili Marleen*, a German song that was popular on both sides of the conflict. After the war she continued her film career – although never with quite the same success as in the early 1930s – alongside a blossoming cabaret act that proved popular around the world. Many of her songs were about her home town, for example *In the Ruins of Berlin*, which she sang in Billy Wilder's 1948 film *A Foreign Affair*. Another, *Ich hab noch einen Koffer in Berlin* (*I Still Keep a Suitcase in Berlin*), describes the singer's bittersweet longing for her native city, using a suitcase as a suitable metaphor. She finally toured Germany again in 1960 and also undertook a tour of Israel, during which she performed some songs in German, breaking an unofficial taboo in the process.

In 1975 an on-stage fall resulted in a broken leg and the now ageing Dietrich retired from public performance. She moved to Paris and lived out her remaining days in semi-seclusion, visited by her daughter and surrounded by mementos of her career and romantic exploits. It is said that she kept in telephone contact with world leaders such as Ronald Reagan and Mikhail Gorbachev during this period. Following her death at the age of 90 she was buried, at her own request, near her mother's grave in Berlin.

Although criticised by neo-Nazi groups for her seemingly anti-German stance during the war, the majority of Berliners welcomed back their greatest diva. Marlene-Dietrich-Platz was named in her honour in 1997 and is today the focal point of the Quartier Daimler, the largest of the Potsdamer Platz building projects (aptly it contains Berlin's largest musical stage). The Deutsche Kinemathek at Potsdamer Strasse 2 holds Dietrich's personal effects, including her gowns, handbags, private correspondence, and her complete luggage set. Perhaps most telling is the cigarette case given to her by the director von Sternberg, which bears the following inscription: "Marlene Dietrich, Weib, Mutter und Schauspielerin wie noch nie" ("Marlene Dietrich, woman, mother and actress like no other").

Before leaving the Städtischer Friedhof III one should visit the grave of another Berlin original, Helmut Newton (1920–2004), who lies to the left of Marlene Dietrich. As the son of a Jewish button factory owner he fled Nazi persecution and went on to become a world class fashion photographer noted for his female nudes. Although he never lived in Berlin again, as a sign of reconciliation he donated a large number of his works to the city in 2004, which are today displayed in the Museum for Photography (Museum für Fotografie) and the Helmut Newton Foundation at Jebensstrasse 2 (Charlottenburg-Wilmersdorf), the last building he saw from the departing train in 1938.

Also remembered for singing *Ich Hab Noch Einen Koffer in Berlin* is the German songstress and actress Hildegard Knef (1925-2002), who is buried in the Waldfriedhof Potsdamer Chaussee (Steglitz-Zehlendorf). Liberated and self-confident like Dietrich, she is remembered as Marina in *The Sinner (Die Sünderin)* (1951), in which she performed the first nude scene in German cinema.

54 Lost Jewish Worlds

District VII (Tempelhof-Schöneberg), the former
Jewish Quarter around Bayerischer Platz
U4, U7 Bayerischer Platz

Berlin's first Jewish community lived on the east bank of the Spree, just south of what is today Alexanderplatz. It was expelled in a series of pogroms after the Black Death (1348–1350), as happened in many European cities. By the early 1900s the area had become a notorious slum, known as the Krögel. It was eventually levelled during the 1930s and today the only reminder of the Jews is a street called Jüdenstrasse.

Meanwhile, in 1671 fifty wealthy Jewish families expelled from Vienna were invited back to Berlin by Frederick William, the 'Great Elector' (1640–1688). Despite considerable discrimination the descendants of these families established a small but successful community over the following two centuries, which then expanded rapidly across several neighbourhoods during the industrial boom of the 19th century. Numbering 160 000 it was all but wiped out during the Nazi regime, these lost Jewish worlds having since been memorialised in a variety of ways.

An especially effective example can be found around Bayerischer Platz, west of Martin-Luther-Strasse (Tempelhof-Schöneberg). Bounded by Badensche Strasse to the south, Hohenstaufenstrasse to the north, and Kufsteiner and Bamberger Strasse to the west, the area is known as the Bavarian Quarter (Bayerisches Viertel) because its streets were named after southern German towns. Until 1933 it was also known as Jewish Switzerland, since many of the well-to-do apartments attracted wealthy Jewish renters. In 1963 the former site of the local synagogue at Münchener Strasse 34 was marked by an abstract stone sculpture, the first postwar memorial to Berlin's destroyed Jewish community. In 1993 another memorial project was launched only this time it was decided not to erect a conventional monument. Instead signs were mounted on the neighbourhood's lamp posts to remind passers-by of how the Nazis made life impossible for the Jews. Each block has one or two signs, with each sign having a figurative image on one side and a related Nazi decree on the other. Thus, the image of a cat is explained by a 1942 decree stating that Jews could not own pets; a telephone dial explains that Jews could not use public phones; a bench illustrates that Jews could only use park benches painted yellow; a thermometer recalls how Jews were forbidden from practising medicine, likewise a rubber stamp represents the ban on Jews being state officials. Another sign at Haberland Strasse 8 recalls that Albert Einstein lived here from 1918 to 1932, and how the street was renamed Nördlinger Strasse by the Nazis because the property developer Georg Haberland was Jewish.

Somewhat similar in concept, in that they deter passive observance, are the so-called *Stolpersteine* ('stumbling stones') embedded into many of Berlin's pavements. The brainchild of Cologne artist Gunter Demnig these inscribed, brass-covered cobblestones are some of the 12 000 he is installing across Germany in front of the former homes of Jews and others murdered during the Holocaust. In Kreuzberg, for example, they can be found to the north of the remaining wing of a demolished synagogue at Fraenkelufer 10–16, as well as around Oranienstrasse, and along nearby Dresdener Strasse.

Berlin's main post-medieval Jewish community was the *Scheunenviertel* ('Barn Quarter'), which occupied the eastern part of the Spandauer Vorstadt, so-called because its main street, Oranienburger Strasse, led to Spandau. The name dates back to 1671, when the Great Elector moved his hay barns outside the town wall due to them being a fire hazard. From this time onwards the area became a refuge for Jews fleeing Russia and Eastern Europe, and by the 19th century it had become a well-established Jewish neighbourhood. Since the fall of the Berlin Wall the district has enjoyed a revival and today Germany's largest Jewish community lives here; numbering 11 000 they are predominantly immigrants from the former Soviet Union.

The community's cultural life is focussed around the New Synagogue (Neue Synagoge) (now Berlin's oldest!) at Oranienburger Strasse 30. Opened in 1866 in the presence of Chancellor Otto von Bismarck (1815–1898) it was damaged in 1938 during *Reichskristallnacht*, a Nazi pogrom carried out on 9th November 1938, and again in 1943 during a bombing raid. Partially restored in 1995 it now serves as the Centrum Judaicum, a Jewish cultural centre. Next door at number 31 is the Jüdische Galerie, where Berlin's first Jewish Museum was opened on 24th January 1933, just six days before Hitler as-

Stolpersteine ('stumbling stones') mark the former homes of Jews murdered by the Nazis

sumed power (Berlin's new Jewish Museum (Jüdisches Museum Berlin) designed by Daniel Libeskind opened in 2001 at Lindenstrasse 9–14 (Friedrichshain-Kreuzberg), its zig-zag plan recalling an exploded Star of David). Nearby at Oranienburger Strasse 28 is the Kadima kosher restaurant above which are the offices of the Jewish community, where they were located prior to 1933.

Not surprisingly, the streets around Oranienburger Strasse hold many memorials – both conventional and unconventional – to the area's pre-war Jewish community. A traditional wall plaque at Krausnickstrasse 6, for instance, marks the former home of the world's first female rabbi, Regina Jonas, who died in Auschwitz. An old inscribed door lintel at Grosse Hamburger Strasse 27 identifies a former Jewish boys' school, founded by the enlightened philosopher and social activist Moses Mendelssohn in 1778 and rebuilt in 1906. Opposite the school, at Grosse Hamburger Strasse 15–16, there is an empty lot, where a building was destroyed by a bomb in 1945. Since 1990 it has been an 'installation' by Christian Boltanski known as *The Missing House*, its blank firewalls mounted with plaques giving details of the building's all-but-forgotten residents (at the northern end of the street at Koppenplatz 6 there is another firewall carrying the names of vanished Jews, close to an unusual sculpture called *The Deserted Room* (see no. 39)).

Next to Mendelssohn's school there is another empty lot, once occupied by Berlin's first Jewish old people's home, which was used by the Gestapo in 1942–1944 to detain thousands of Jewish prisoners before deporting them to the concentration camps at Theresienstadt and Auschwitz. There is a plaque marking the spot (Gedenkstätte Grosse Hamburger Strasse) as well as a haunting group of bronze figures. They were created originally for the anti-Fascist memorial at Ravensbrück concentration camp for women and moved here in 1957. Immediately behind is the former site of the oldest of central Berlin's three main Jewish cemeteries (see no. 84).

Most of Berlin's 14 pre-war synagogues were damaged or destroyed in 1938 during *Reichskristallnacht*, their former presence marked today by various memorials. Of those that survived, most escaped destruction only because they were a part of apartment blocks that would have caught fire had the synagogues been torched.

Other places of interest nearby: 37, 55

55 Through Quiet Colonnades

District VII (Tempelhof-Schöneberg), the King's
Colonnades (Königskolonnaden) in Heinrich von Kleist Park
on Potsdamer Strasse
U7 Kleistpark

Modern Berlin is a city lit-
tered with architectural fragments from its past. A monumental apect of this built
heritage is its handful of
decorative colonnades, several of which once adorned
entrances across the long-
vanished moat that formerly
encircled the city (see no. 2).
Their chequered histories are
indicative of the fluctuating
fortunes of the city itself.

The best preserved are
the Baroque sandstone King's
Colonnades (Königskolon-
naden) that form the centrepiece of Heinrich von Kleist
Park on Potsdamer Strasse
(Tempelhof-Schöneberg).
They were designed by Carl
von Gontard (1731–1791),
architect to Frederick II, 'the
Great' (1740–1786), and were
erected originally in 1780 on
the King's Bridge (Königs-
brücke), near what is now

The King's Colonnades in Heinrich von
Kleist Park

Alexanderplatz. They remained in place until 1910, when they were
dismantled and moved in order to widen the street. In their new location the colonnades act as an approach to the park's other main structure, namely the Prussian Court of Appeal (Kammergericht), erected
between 1909 and 1913. Still used as a court the building has a sinister
past: it was here that many of the co-conspirators of the failed 20th July

57 The Ghosts of Germania

District II (Friedrichshain-Kreuzberg), the heavy load
testing body at the corner of Loewenhardtdamm and
General-Pape-Strasse
U6 Platz der Luftbrücke

"Give me ten years and you will not recognise Germany," Adolf Hitler promised in 1933, reflecting not only his dissatisfaction that Germany's industrialised cities lacked dominating public monuments but also his interest in architecture as an expression of power. Hitler's promise would indeed be fulfilled – but only in so much as his cities were reduced to rubble by Allied bombing raids, the inevitable response to the Nazis' aggressive policy of territorial conquest.

Had events turned out in Hitler's favour, cities such as Nuremberg, Munich, Hamburg, Linz, and the Reich capital Berlin would have been transformed by the construction of overblown, neo-Classical monuments and public buildings that harked back to ancient Rome and Greece, which according to the Nazis' own spurious racial ancestry was the origin of the superior Aryan race from which they were descended. Such structures, which would represent the cultural and spiritual rebirth of the new German order, would be built in granite, limestone and marble, so that when they themselves eventually became ruins a thousand years hence, they would appear as impressive as the wreckage of imperial Rome.

As early as September 1933 Hitler had told the mayor of Berlin that his city was "unsystematic" but it was not until January 1937 that he officially enlisted the services of architect Albert Speer (1905–1981) to rebuild Berlin as *Germania*, the new world-class capital of Nazi Europe. As Inspector General for Construction in the Reich Capital Berlin, Speer based his design for the city on Roman planning principles, envisaging a monumental new boulevard – the North-South Axis (Nord-Süd-Achse) – stretching from outside the Reichstag all the way down to Tempelhof Airport five kilometres away. With a width of 120 metres it would be lined with the main administrative offices of the Third Reich, together with important cultural institutions.

The North-South Axis would be crossed at right angles (precisely where the main Soviet War Memorial was constructed in November 1945) by an East-West Axis (Ost-West-Achse), running 13 kilometres along existing thoroughfares between Alexanderplatz and the Olympic Stadium (Olympiastadion): Unter den Linden, Charlotten-burg Chaussee, Berliner Strasse (today Strasse des 17. Juni), Bismarck Strasse, Kaiserdamm, and Heerstrasse (see no. 32). Between the Brandenburg Gate (Brandenburger Tor) and Ernst Reuter Platz, Speer increased the width of the East-West Axis to 60 metres and unveiled it officially for Hitler's 50th birthday on 20th April 1939. Immediately west of the S-Bahn bridge it is still lined with Speer's distinctive candela-bra street lamps, beyond which is Ernst Reuter Haus, one of the very few Third Reich structures to actually be completed on the axis. Farther west, beyond the Landwehrkanal, a grandstand was constructed in front of the Technical University (Technische Universität) from where military parades could be reviewed.

Albert Speer's model of Germania, Hitler's new Berlin

In what was Königsplatz, north of where the axes intersected, a vast forum 350 000 square metres in size was to be created, capable of holding a million people and to be called Adolf Hitler Platz. Around it would be erected Berlin's most politically potent edifices: a vast domed *Volkshalle* ('People's Hall') on the Spree bend (*Spreebogen*) to the north, with room for 180 000 spectators; Hitler's own palace on the site of the Kroll Opera (Krolloper) to the west; the old Reichstag building and a new parliamentary building to the east; whilst to the south, the entrance to the forum would be framed on one side by a brand new Reich Chancellery (to replace Speer's earlier effort on Vossstrasse) and by the High Command of the Wehrmacht on the other. In preparation the Prussian Victory Column (Siegessäule) and its attendant avenue of statues (Siegesallee), which the North-South Axis would obliterate, was dismantled and moved onto the East-West Axis in the Tiergarten in 1938 (see no. 63). The column is today reached by tunnels under the road accessed via four ceremonial guardhouses: designed by Speer

Albert Speer's heavy load testing body near Tempelhof Airport

they are notable for being the only remaining examples of his work still standing in Berlin.

The 320 metre-high *Volkshalle* would be 16 times larger than St. Peter's Basilica in Rome, on which it was modelled, and would even boast its own microclimate! As the largest building in the world it would be the focal point of the ceremonial centre of *Germania*. Speer later admitted in his memoirs that his architecture quite deliberately "represented an intimidating display of power", the colossal dimensions of Third Reich buildings, like Roman ones before them, serving to emphasise the authority of the power that erected them, the importance of the community that would use them – and the insignificance of the individual that would gaze upon them. Nowhere would this display of power be more apparent than to visitors arriving from the south, either from a new central railway station, which would be built to replace the Anhalt and Potsdam stations, or Tempelhof Airport (which itself would eventually be replaced by four airports on the outskirts of the city). For now Tempelhof Airport would be integrated into Speer's grand plan by widening Dudenstrasse into a suitably impressive connecting boulevard. At the western end of the boulevard there would be a colossal triumphal arch (*Triumphbogen*), based on Hitler's own sketches, giving access to the North-South Axis and a clear view to the *Volkshalle* in the distance. The arch would be 117 metres high, 170 metres wide, and nine times larger than its main antecedent, Napoleon's Arc de Triomphe in Paris. It would also be inscribed with the names of the 1.8 million Germans (excluding Jews) who died during the First World War.

Like most of Speer's plans, Hitler's arch never left the drawing board, although the site of its planned northeast corner can still be found today at the junction of Loewenhardtdamm and General-Pape-Strasse. Here there is a huge cylinder of solid concrete that is not an air raid shelter, as many believe, but rather the world's largest 'heavy load testing body' (*Grossbelastungskörper*), poured in 1941 to ensure that the sandy ground could bear the immense weight of the finished arch. Weighing 40 000 tons and with a diameter of 21 metres it rises 14 metres above ground and reaches 21 metres beneath it. By 1944 the cylinder had sunk 18cm against a maximum allowable settlement of 6cm, demonstrating clearly that the sandy soil of Berlin could not support the weight of Hitler's *Germania* unaided.

Of the *Volkshalle* only a foundation trench was ever dug. There is also an unfinished U-bahn tunnel, which would have transported visitors to the *Volkshalle*, as well as several partially constructed road tunnels, to convey traffic north under the Spree. Only re-discovered in 1967 the tunnels are today sealed off and hidden from view.

Unfinished, too, was Speer's model housing project for the 8000 workers needed to build the *Volkshalle*, its remains now incorporated into the Waldkrankenhaus psychiatric hospital on Stadtrandstrasse (Spandau).

From 1937 Albert Speer used the Academy of Arts (Akademie der Künste) on Pariser Platz as his office, a wing of which built in 1907 is still standing. It was here that a 30 metre-long, 1:1000 scale model of *Germania* was constructed, which Hitler could visit unnoticed by crossing the ministerial gardens behind his Chancellery on Vossstrasse. This he continued to do long after any real work on the new city had been abandoned because of the war. He remained encouraged by a statement from Speer's office stating that Allied bombing raids were actually assisting in the destruction of the 80 000 buildings that needed clearing for *Germania* to be realised.

Other places of interest nearby: 55, 56, 59, 60, 61

58 Schöneberg's Urban Jungle

District VII (Tempelhof-Schöneberg), the South Schöneberg Nature Reserve (Natur-Park Schöneberger Südgelände) on Priesterweg
S2, S25 Priesterweg

An abandoned railway shunting yard in the Berlin district of Schöneberg, sandwiched between a noisy S-bahn line and several apartment blocks, may seem an unlikely setting for a wildlife park. However, the so-called South Schöneberg Nature Reserve (Natur-Park Schöneberger Südgelände) on Priesterweg has defied the odds and become just that: Berlin's first visitor-friendly urban jungle.

Over the last 20 years, conservationists, city planners and eco-artists have pooled their talents and transformed what had become an unsightly wasteland of rusting rails and derelict buildings into a haven for plants, animals and birds. Visiting this highly unusual park and witnessing nature's slow re-colonisation of what had been a wholly man-made landscape makes for a fascinating experience. The roots of Birch (*Betula*) and Black Locust (*Robinia pseudoacacia*) saplings have now taken hold, under foot there is a carpet of rare wild flowers with exotic names such as Spotted Lady's Thumb (*Persicaria maculosa*) and Queen Devil Hawkweed (*Hieracium glomeratum*), in the air are bumblebees, endangered butterflies and silken spiders' webs, and overhead fly Goshawks, Kestrels and Nightingales. Close scrutiny of the vegetation will also reveal evidence of Europe's most northerly breeding colony of Praying Mantis.

The creators of the South Schöneberg Nature Reserve offer little in the way of traditional signposting beyond the information board at the entrance. Instead they rely on the innate ability of their visitors to tune in quickly to their natural surroundings despite the urban context. In this respect, man's contribution to the park in the form of rotting metal and masonry, together with contemporary sculptures made from the same materials, sits surprisingly well alongside nature's burgeoning greenery, the two seeming to be a part of the same endless process of decay and renewal.

One of the aims of such urban nature parks is to correct the view that cities are biologically barren. On the contrary, urban ecologists are discovering that cities can be hot spots of animal and plant life. Indeed, it has been recently demonstrated that animal numbers and bio-

Railway tracks leading nowhere in the South Schöneberg Nature Reserve

diversity are often greater today in urban areas than in the countryside. Cities have become cleaner, greener places and wildlife has quickly adapted to it; by contrast, the countryside has been increasingly turned over to single-strain, chemically-maintained crops, destroying habitats and driving out species. A case in point concerns Germany's 280 bird species, two thirds of which are now found in Berlin: they include Peregrine Falcons and Ospreys, which have all but disappeared from the German countryside. Another startling statistic is that agriculture and forestry are responsible for 80% of species loss worldwide, whereas just 15 percent is caused by human settlement and urban sprawl. Flora and fauna are seeking refuge in the varied habitats provided by modern cities, from back gardens to abandoned factories, as well as industrial areas like the old shunting yard in Schöneberg.

59 Hitler's Eagles

District VII (Tempelhof-Schöneberg), a collection of
Third Reich eagles including several at Berlin-Tempelhof
Airport (Flughafen Berlin-Tempelhof)
U6 Platz der Luftbrücke

Following German reunification on 3rd October 1990 the country's
parliament, the *Bundestag*, chose Berlin over Bonn as the future seat
of government. As a result, the Reichstag building, which had stood
empty since being torched in 1933, was earmarked for full reconstruction. Not surprisingly, the project courted some controversy, for example over whether anti-German graffiti, added by Red Army soldiers
during the storming of the building in 1945, should remain visible
(see no. 41). Concerns were also raised over a huge aluminium eagle
planned by the architect Sir Norman Foster to adorn the Plenary Chamber (*Plenarsaal*), directly below his new glass dome. A similar eagle
designed for the *Bundestag* in Bonn, where the federal government had
been based since 1949, had been jokingly dubbed the *Fette Henne* ('Fat
Hen'). To avoid a similar scenario it was suggested that the Reichstag
eagle be made slimmer, although this solution raised the possibility of
comparisons with Prussian imperial eagles, or even worse, the lean,
stylised eagles of Hitler's Third Reich: an acceptable compromise was
eventually found somewhere between the two.

The controversy over the Reichstag eagle was an entirely understand-
able one for a newly unified country committed both to building itself
a bright future as well as coming to terms with its dreadful past. It was
an especially sensitive issue on this occasion since the Reichstag was
one of the few institutions permitted to retain the word *Reich* (meaning
land or domain) in its name, the word having been strongly associated
with the Nazis. The use of potent historical symbols such as eagles in
contemporary German architecture also needed extra-careful handling.

The eagle as the national emblem of Germany dates back to the
time of Charlemagne, the King of the Franks (768–814AD), who was
crowned Emperor of the Romans in 800, claiming direct succession
from the emperors of ancient Rome for whom the eagle was a symbol of strength and invincibility. In 1433 the Holy Roman Emperor
Sigismund (1410–1437) adopted the double-headed eagle, which was
used in varous forms until 1867, when the Kingdom of Prussia adopted
a single spread eagle once again. This was retained during the Ger-

man Empire (1871–1918) and the Weimar Republic (1918–1933) until Hitler over-stylised it and placed an oak wreath containing a swastika (*Hakenkreuz*) in its talons. In 1950 the Federal Republic of Germany incorporated the Weimar-era eagle into its coat of arms and it is this version, known as the Federal Eagle, which continues to serve as the state symbol of reunified Germany today.

The head of Ernst Sagebiel's eagle at Tempelhof Airport

The swastika is an even older symbol than the eagle, having first appeared as a decorative motif on Neolithic pottery and then as a Sanskrit sacred symbol (meaning 'something good') across the Hindu world. It was only subverted when the Nazis used it to support their spurious theory of the Aryan racial ancestry of the German people from the ancient Greeks and Proto Indo Europeans before them.

Known as the national emblem (*Hoheits(ab)zeichen*), the powerful combination of martial eagle and swastika was used initially as the emblem of the National Socialist German Workers' Party (Nationalsozialistische Deutsche Arbeiterpartei, or NSDAP) and only later as a symbol of the Third Reich (1933–1945), symbolising German renewal and the strength of the Nazi state. It found countless official applications, from rubber stamps and headed notepaper to military uniforms and buildings.

After the war the Allies ordered that all Nazi emblems in Germany be removed and that the swastika be banned: it was erased wherever possible, with or without the less contentious eagle. Buildings in Berlin shorn of such Nazi iconography included Joseph Goebbel's Ministry of Public Enlightenment and Propaganda at Mauerstrasse 45–53/Wilhelmstrasse 49, Reichsmarschall Hermann Göring's Reich Air Ministry (Reichsluftfahrtministerium) at Wilhelmstrasse 97, Robert Ley's German Labour Front headquarters at Potsdamer Strasse 182 (Tempelhof-Schöneberg), the Reich Railways' Central Office at Schöneberger Ufer 1–3 (Friedrchshain-Kreuzberg), and the Lichterfelde Barracks on Finckensteinallee (Steglitz-Zehlendorf), once home to Hitler's personal guard unit (see no. 52). The stone eagle atop Fritz Todt's towering Armaments Ministry building at Friedrichstrasse 34–37 was presumably left intact because of its inaccessibility. An eagle on a pylon outside the House of German Sports (Haus des Deutschen Sports) at the Olympic Stadium (Olympiastadion) has survived because its swastika was chiselled off, as was the case over the doorway of a Charlottenburg tax office built in 1939 at Bismarckstrasse 48 (Charlottenburg-Wilmersdorf), and a postal sorting office at nearby Knesebeckstrasse 95. So long as the swastikas were gone the eagles lived on.

Needless to say, there were numerous 'national emblems' incorporated into Hitler's New Reich Chancellery (Neue Reichskanzlei) on Vossstrasse (see no. 9). Modelled by sculptor Kurt Schmid-Ehmen in gilded wood, bronze and stone, those that could be moved were taken away as trophies by the liberators of Berlin and can still be found in museums today, including the Central Museum of the Soviet Armed Forces in Moscow, London's Imperial War Museum, and the US Airforce Museum in Daytona, USA.

An especially interesting example of the post-war de-Nazification of Third Reich buildings concerns the Berlin-Tempelhof Airport (Flughafen Berlin-Tempelhof). First designated an airport in 1923, Tempelhof became not only Germany's largest international airport but also the world's largest building when its old terminal was replaced between 1937 and 1941. With an overall length of 1230 metres it was designed by the architect Ernst Sagebiel (1872–1970), a former assistant of German-Jewish Modernist architect Erich Mendelsohn (1887–1953), who had fled Germany in 1933. Together with the Reich Air Ministry (Reichsluftfahrtministerium) (also by Sagebiel) and the Olympic Stadium (Olympiastadion), Tempelhof typefies the pared-down classical forms that identify Third Reich public architecture.

The airport's reconstruction was taken advantage of by the architect Albert Speer (1905–1981), who planned to integrate it temporarily into his designs for the transformation of Berlin into *Germania*: he eventually planned for Tempelhof to be replaced by four new airports on the outskirts of the city (see no. 57). In reality, the Red Army seized Tempelhof Airport in April 1945 during the Battle for Berlin, handing it over to US troops shortly thereafter. In 1962 the Americans removed Sagebiel's 4.5 metre-high aluminium eagle, modelled by the sculptor Walter Lemke, from the roof of the terminal building and shipped it to the museum of the United States Military Academy at West Point in New York State (several stone eagles built into the building's façade were left untouched and remain in place today).

An intact Nazi eagle on the roof at Friedrichstrasse 34–37

During the Berlin Blockade, which lasted from 26th June 1948 to 12th May 1949, Tempelhof Airport was used by American, British and German pilots, who landed their so-called 'raisin bombers' here every 90 seconds in order to sustain Berlin's two million starving citizens. The success of the Berlin Airlift, and the lives lost during the 277,728 flights involved, were commemorated not only by Edward Ludwig's sculpture on the Platz der Luftbrücke, representing the three westward-pointing air corridors, but also by the return in 1985 of the head of Sagebiel's eagle, no longer a symbol of Nazism but rather a monument to German-American friendship.

Other places of interest nearby: 56, 57, 59, 60, 61, 62

60 A Pair of Little Theatres

District II (Friedrichshain-Kreuzberg), the English Theatre Berlin at Fidicinstrasse 40
U6 Platz der Luftbrücke

Thanks to director Max Reinhardt (1873–1943) and dramatist Bertolt Brecht (1898–1956), Berlin became an important focus for the burgeoning European theatre scene of the 1920s. Its success is still evident today, despite many of those working in the business having been killed persecuted under the Hitler regime. After the Second World War a revival occurred, with theatre numbers even doubling following the construction of the divisive Berlin Wall. Despite some closures after reunification Berlin still boasts more than 50 theatres and a few of them are rather unusual.

The English Theatre Berlin at Fidicinstrasse 40 (Friedrichshain-Kreuzberg) is a case in point. Founded in 1990 and known formerly as the Friends of Italian Opera, after the alias taken by the Mafia in Billy Wilder's *Some Like It Hot*, it is Berlin's only exclusively English-speaking theatre. It is located at the back of an industrial courtyard of the type so typical of Kreuzberg. The intimate auditorium contains 120 seats and stages productions that change every three to four weeks, ranging from one-person shows to full-blooded dramas or comedies performed by local or visiting groups. The theatre also shares the venue with Theater Thikwa, which works with disabled actors.

A second little theatre, this time in the former East Berlin, is the Orph Theatre (Orphtheater) at Ackerstrasse 169/170 (Mitte). Also founded in 1990 it is named after Orpheus, the mythical Greek musician. The theatre is one of Berlin's oldest 'alternative' theatres, its original purpose being to mirror the intellectual reawakening of the former GDR. Like the English Theatre its premises are modest and industrial in origin, being the ground floor of a disused chocolate factory in an old tenement courtyard. There are seats for around 60 people and the theatre's 100 or so annual performances – described as *Bewegungstheater* ('Expressive Theatre') – are never less than thrilling, with works by Brecht, Beckett and Chekov.

Berlin's better-known theatres hold a few surprises too. The Komische Opera at Behrenstrasse 55–57 (Mitte), for example, was built in 1892 but lost its original facade during post-war reconstruction: its gilded neo-Baroque interior therefore comes as quite a shock. The Theater des Westens built in 1896 at Kantstrasse 9–12 (Charlotten-burg-Wilmersdorf) is interesting not only for its extravagant architecture but also for its original artists' apartments and studios at nearby Fasanenstrasse 13. The Wintergarten Theater at Potsdamer Strasse 96 (Mitte) continues the 1920s tradition of variety shows over dinner, whilst a similar atmosphere is maintained in the Admiralspalast

The English Theatre Berlin

at Friedrichstrasse 101–102, built originally as a swimming pool over a thermal spring in 1911 and converted into a theatre in 1922. The colossal 2000-seater Friedrichstadtpalast at Friedrichstrasse 107 (Mitte) replaced an even larger theatre on the same site demolished in 1985, which held 5000 people and was adorned with a sumptuous Expressionist interior dripping with artificial stalactites. A couple of streets to the west is the Deutsches Theater at Schumannstrasse 13A, which is where Max Reinhardt began as an actor before taking over as director in 1905. Also of interest is the Volksbühne on Rosa Luxemburg Platz, Berlin's first Modernist theatre opened in 1914 at the instigation of the Free People's Theatre Society (Freie Volksbühne) to bring serious drama to the working classes. It was managed in the 1920s by radical director and theatre reformer Erwin Piscator (1893–1966) and restored after the war by the GDR regime as part of their Socialist theatre tradition. Piscator also worked at the former theatre at Nollendorfplatz 5 (Tempelhof-Schöneberg), which was used in 1930 to host the Berlin premiere of *All Quiet on the Western Front*. The film so upset the Nazis that they secretly released mice into the auditorium causing a riot thereby getting the film banned for causing a public disturbance!

Bertolt Brecht founded the Berliner Ensemble in 1949. His *Threepenny Opera* premiered in the Theater am Schiffbauerdamm at Bertolt-Brecht-Platz 1. He lived at Chausseestrasse 125 (Mitte) – now the Brecht-Weigel Memorial (Brech-Weigel-Gedenkstätte) – and is buried in the nearby Dorotheenstadt Cemetery (Dorotheenstädtischer Friedhof).

Other places of interest nearby: 56, 57, 59, 61, 62

61 Riehmer's Hidden Hofgarten

District II (Friedrichshain-Kreuzberg), Riehmer's Hofgarten
at Yorckstrasse 83–86
U6, U7 Mehringdamm

During the latter half of the 19th century, with industrialisation in full swing, Berlin witnessed a massive influx of new workers – and a corresponding increase in demand for housing. A plan was drafted for the controlled enlargement of the city by constructing capacious tenement blocks, laid out along a grid of right-angled streets (see no. 21). Since the state had to pay for all new roads, costs were minimised by encouraging deep as well as long tenement blocks. By the end of the 19th century, Berlin had been dubbed the "largest tenement complex in the world".

In the absence of any regulations regarding the internal layout of these new tenement blocks, except that a small courtyard for firefighting equipment was required, most property developers maximised their profits by building high. The resulting accommodation was usually fairly well-constructed but also dark and inward-looking, especially in the larger blocks (see no. 21). Occasionally, however, an alternative was found to the traditional gloomy blocks, an unusual example of which is known as Riehmer's Hofgarten.

Wilhelm Ferdinand August Riehmer was a master bricklayer and property developer, who acquired a plot of land in Kreuzberg bounded by three streets: Yorckstrasse, Grossbeerenstrasse and Hagelberger Strasse. He planned originally to build a very deep, traditional tenement block, stretching back from Yorckstrasse. However, the authorities expressed concern about traffic on Yorckstrasse, which was a main thoroughfare into Berlin, and insisted on a change in design. As a result, Riehmer deconstructed the usual rear courtyard layout and incorporated a private, T-shaped road, running right through the development and connecting all three surrounding streets.

The façades of the 18 five-storey apartment blocks that Riehmer constructed were fairly conventional, if somewhat grand, with plastered ornamentation in the prevailing Historicist tradition. Inside the complex, however, where smaller and cheaper apartments would traditionally have looked out onto a gloomy courtyard, Riehmer planted an attractive courtyard garden (*Hofgarten*) either side of his private road. The façades here were equally grand and all the apartments – each containing three or more rooms – offered higher-than-usual residential standards, which proved popular with well-heeled middle-class tenants from the civil service, military and bourgeois classes.

Although Riehmer's Hofgarten was built over two decades, between 1881 and 1899, its overall appearance is similar throughout. Despite falling into disrepair after the Second World War, during which a part of the Yorckstrasse façade was destroyed, the complex was listed as an historical monument and restored during the 1980s. Although some of the ground floor apartments have subsequently been converted to office, retail and hotel use, Riehmer's Hofgarten looks much as it did when first built. It also continues to offer the same leafy tranquillity, away from the bustling streets outside, that Mr. Riehmer's tenants found so appealing more than a century ago.

From Yorckstrasse looking into Riehmer's Hofgarten

Immediately adjacent to Riehmer's Hofgarten is the red-brick Church of St. Boniface, designed in neo-Gothic style by the architect Max Hasak (1856–1934). Unlike most Protestant churches of the time, which were freestanding and built on public land, it is an integral part of another housing complex, built by the church in a matching style. A couple of streets south of Riehmers Hofgarten, at Methfesselstrasse 7, is the former workshop of engineer Konrad Zuse (1910–1995). Frustrated at having to perform endless calculations by hand Zuse built the world's first programme-controlled computing machine here (known as the Z3) in 1941.

Other places of interest nearby: 56, 57, 59, 60, 62, 63, 64

62 From the Hebrides to the Halle Gate

District II (Friedrichshain-Kreuzberg), the Halle Gate Cemeteries (Friedhöfe am Halleschen Tor) at Mehringdamm 22
U6, U7 Mehringdamm

After the construction of Berlin's so-called Customs Wall in 1735 all new burials in the city had to be made outside it (see no. 2). The location chosen for this new extramural cemetery was just beyond the Halle Gate (Hallesches Tor), across the ancient drainage ditch known as the Landwehrkanal. Bounded today by Mehringdamm, Blücherstrasse, Baruther Strasse and Zossener Strasse, the secluded burial ground actually comprises six individual cemeteries, known collectively as the Halle Gate Cemeteries (Friedhöfe am Halleschen Tor).

It is best to enter the cemetery from Zossener Strasse, following the wall on the left-hand side as far as a second entrance, beyond which lies the Holy Trinity Cemetery I (Friedhof der Dreifaltigkeits I). Here on the right-hand side can be found the last resting place of the German composer and conductor Felix Mendelssohn Bartholdy (1809–1847), grandson of the Jewish philosopher Moses Mendelssohn (see no. 84). Felix's father had him baptised a Lutheran in an attempt to break with the past, and encouraged the use of the surname 'Bartholdy' on the grounds that "there could no more be a Christian Mendelssohn than there could be a Jewish Confucius"; despite this Felix retained the name Mendelssohn. A child prodigy in the mould of Mozart, he came to typify the music of the early Romantic period. One of his most famous works is undoubtedly the concert overture *Fingal's Cave* (known also as the *Hebrides Overture*) (1830), inspired by visits he made to Scotland in the late 1820s as part of the Grand Tour. He took a boat to the famous cave on the Hebridean island of Staffa and was so impressed that he wrote the opening theme on the spot. Similarly his *Symphony No 4 in A major*, known as the *Italian*, was inspired by a visit to Italy and was premiered by the composer himself in 1833. Popular too is the *Wedding March* from his incidental music to Shakespeare's *A Midsummer Night's Dream*, composed in 1843. His chamber music is also to be admired, notably his string quartets and the *Octet* written when he was just sixteen.

Mendelssohn was a skilled conductor, too, and performed a major service to music by reviving the works of Johann Sebastian Bach, in particular the *St. Matthew Passion*. Although he became something of a European celebrity, and a favourite of Queen Victoria, he died young from nervous problems and overwork, griefstricken over the death of his beloved sister, the pianist and amateur composer Fanny Hensel (1805–1847): together with other members of the family she is buried alongside him.

In the opposite corner of the same cemetery is the grave of Rahel Varnhagen von Ense (1771–1833), a German writer of Jewish descent, who was great friends with the daughters of Moses Mendelssohn. Whilst Napoleon's troops occupied Berlin and the Prussian King was in exile, she toured Paris, Hamburg, Prague and Dresden hosting literary salons, before returning to Berlin after Napoleon's defeat at Waterloo. Now married and having converted to Christianity she became the centre of a circle of eminent writers, scholars and artists but never forgot her ancestry: her husband, who is buried with her, made a sizable donation to the city's Jewish poor on her death.

An exit next to a plain cemetery chapel leads into another of the Halle Gate Cemeteries, namely the Jerusalem and New Church Cemetery III (Friedhof der Jerusalems- und Neuen Kirche III). By following the path straight ahead a clump of trees is reached and the grave of botanist and writer Adelbert von Chamisso (1781–1838). Escaping the French Revolution he arrived in Berlin with his parents and entered the Prussian army. In 1803 he sought distraction by founding a literary journal with German biographer Karl August Varnhagen von Ense (1785–1858), the future husband of Rahel Varnhagen. Chamisso then spent the next decade writing prose and studying botany. In 1815 he was appointed botanist to the Russian scientific ship *Rurik* on its journey around the globe. His diary records trips to the Pacific Ocean and the Bering Sea and tells of new species found along the way. He also became the first writer to use the Inuit word *Parka*, being a hooded wind-

The grave of botanist and writer Adelbert von Chamisso

proof jacket. On his return he was made custodian of Berlin's Botanical Gardens returning to his love of literature in later life.

Turning right at this point and passing two sets of intersecting paths the headstone of influential Romantic writer, composer and caricaturist Ernst Theodor Wilhelm Hoffmann (1776–1822) can be found. He is better known by his pen name of E. T. A. Hoffmann, the 'A' being in homage to Amadeus Mozart. Hoffmann is remembered as much for his own work as for the works of those he influenced, most notably Tchaikovsky's ballet *The Nutcracker* (1892), based on Hoffmanns *Nutcracker and Mouse King* (1816), which inspired not only Delibes's ballet *Coppélia* (1870) but also Jacques Offenbach's *Tales of Hoffmann* (1881). Underlying many of his works are philosphical musings on the dark side of the human condition lurking behind the hypocritical harmony of bourgeois life.

A couple of streets south of the Halle Gate Cemeteries there is a similar group of walled burial grounds, known as the Friedhöfe an der Bergmannstrasse. Accessible from the Südstern U-Bahn station, the first is the Old Luisenstadt Cemetery (Alte Luisenstädtische Friedhof) containing the imposing grave of Gustav Stresemann (1878–1929), chancellor and foreign secretary during the Weimar Republic; it lies along the main path to the left of a bell-tower. Continuing onwards and turning sharp right towards the top of the cemetery is the family grave of Franz Späth (1839–1913), head of the Späth horticultural dynasty (see no. 74). Doubling back to the bell-tower and turning left the path leads through a wall into the Jerusalem and New Church Cemetery IV (Friedhof Jerusalems- und Neuen Kirche IV), the last resting place of Wilhelm Riehmer (1830–1901), remembered for his Hofgarten, an ensemble of late 19th century houses overlooking a garden courtyard on Yorckstrasse (see no. 61).

Continuing onwards, a path parallel to Bergmannstrasse passes through the neighbouring Friedrichswerder Cemetery (Friedrichswerderscher Friedhof) and into a final burial ground, the Holy Trinity Cemetery II (Friedhof der Dreifaltigkeits II). A sharp left after entering the cemetery passes the grave of Martin Gropius, architect of the neo-Renaissance Martin-Gropius-Bau at Stresemannstrasse 110 (Mitte). It was constructed in 1881 to house an arts and crafts museum, as reflected in the reliefs still visible on the building's facade. From 1922 the building accommodated the city's Museum of Ethnology but it was abandoned after the Second World War until its reconstruction in the 1980s as an exhibition centre. Gropius's great nephew, Walter, was the first chairman of the Bauhaus movement, dedicated to creating a new and better society through architectural form and function. In the same row beyond is the tomb of artist Adolph von Menzel (1815–1905), considered one of Germany's foremost realist painters. Born in Breslau he illustrated the great events of contemporary history, for example the 1848 Revolution in Berlin and the Franco-Prussian War, as well as the more mundane events of daily life; he is closely associated with Berlin having lived and painted here for 75 years.

Finally, turning right along the cemetery's main path to the far end is the grave of another long-term Berlin resident, the historian Theodor Mommsen (1817–1903), who was awarded the Nobel Prize for Literature in 1902. His great passion was Roman history, as reflected in the highly regarded *Römische Geschichte* and the 17-volume *Corpus Inscriptionum Latinarum*. His involvement in the 1848 Revolution led to his expulsion from the city but in 1858 he returned and was made Professor of Ancient History at the University of Berlin.

Felix Mendelssohn's grave in one of the Halle Gate Cemeteries

Other places of interest nearby: 59, 60, 61, 64, 65

63 Berlin's Moving Statues

District II (Friedrichshain-Kreuzberg), the former
sewage pumping station at Hallesches Ufer 78
U2 Mendelssohn-Bartholdy-Park

Between 1961 and 1989 Berlin was effectively two distinct cities, separated by the Berlin Wall (see no. 70). One of the tangible ways in which this east-west divide manifested itself was in the duplication of many of the city's cultural institutions, which goes some way to explaining why reunified Berlin has quite so many museums, galleries, and libraries. Indeed, a separate book could be written about the countless journeys made during this period by the city's cultural artefacts, paintings and books, as they were ferried from one building to another. However, it should not be forgotten that Berlin had been in a state of cultural flux long before the erection of the Wall, as its different rulers sought to impose a cohesive and imposing urban plan on what had originally been a handful of separate settlements, spread out along the River Spree.

The deliberate relocation of the city's iconic monuments in order to satisfy the whim of an incumbent ruler is perhaps nowhere better illustrated than in the unlikely setting of a former sewage pumping station at Hallesches Ufer 78, close to the Schöneberger Brücke on the bank of the Landwehrkanal (see no. 78). It was constructed in 1873–1876 as part of a radial, city-wide wastewater treatment system designed by city planner James Hobrecht (1825–1902), which explains why Hobrecht's name can be seen on a plaque outside the building today (see nos. 21 & 78). Known as Station III because it was located on the third radial, its superstructure was designed by the municipal architect Hermann Blanckenstein, who was responsible for many of Berlin's market halls, which share a similar use of ornate brickwork. The station is further embellished with an Orientalised minaret-like chimney. Such attention to detail ensured that the structure was listed as a historic building after its decommission in 1972.

In 1978 the former pumping station was pressed into service as a lapidarium, wherein an unusual collection of statuary was displayed alongside the abandoned pumping engines. These marble statues once lined the so-called Avenue of Victory (Siegesallee), a wide boulevard that ran south from the Victory Column (Siegessäule), which stood originally in front of the Reichstag (see no. 13). The avenue was commissioned by the last Emperor, King William II (1888–1918), and its 32

statues, depicting Brandenburg-Prussia's rulers dating
back to Margrave Albert I
(1157–1170), were added between 1889 and 1901. Each
statue was originally set on
a high pedestal and flanked
by smaller figures of distinguished personages from
each era. The project was
never popular, modern artists
perceiving it as a declaration
of imperial opposition to their
work, the public viewing it
as an overblown propaganda
exercise, which they cynically
dubbed *Puppenallee* (Puppet
Avenue).

Only broken statues remain from the Avenue of Victory

In 1938 Hitler ordered that
the entire ensemble of column
and statues be removed to the
Tiergarten, so that his architect, Albert Speer (1905–1981), could commence construction of his North-South Axis, as part of the new city
of *Germania* (see no. 57). The plan scarcely left the drawing board although the column and statues were indeed moved, the column to the
so-called Great Star (Grosser Stern) and the statues to the Neue Siegesallee, which ran off to the southeast (now re-named the Grosse Sternallee). The column has stood there ever since but the statues, which were
deemed too militaristic after the war, were removed by the British Army
to Schloss Bellevue, a little to the north, where they were unceremoniously buried.

In 1979 the statues were exhumed and put on display in the lapidarium, where they remained for almost last three decades. Their journey, however, was still not over. In 2006 the lapidarium closed and the
statues removed to a new exhibition space in the Zitadelle Spandua at
Am Juliusturm 64 (Spandau). Perhaps this time they will remain there.

Other places of interest nearby: 9, 10, 12, 56, 60, 61, 62, 64

64 The Remains of a Great Railway Station

District II (Friedrichshain-Kreuzberg), the former
Anhalt Railway Station (Anhalter Bahnhof) at the corner
of Stresemannstrasse and Schöneberger Strasse
S1, S2, S25 Anhalter Bahnhof

During the 20th century Berlin's architects were thwarted by war, economic crisis, and division in their efforts to give the city a central railway station. The situation was only rectified in 2006, with the opening of the Berlin Hauptbahnhof on the site of the former Lehrte Station (Lehrter Bahnhof), built in 1870 to service northwest Germany. A new north-south rail link has subsequently been built from the station, southwards beneath the River Spree, Tiergarten and Potsdamer Platz, to re-emerge at Yorckstrasse.

By contrast, Berlin during the 19th century had numerous railway stations spread across the city, each servicing different parts of Germany and beyond. The city's first ever train was hauled in 1838 by a British-built locomotive called the *Adler* ('*Eagle*'), from Potsdam Station (Potsdamer Bahnhof) on Königgrätzer Strasse (now Stresemannstrasse) out to Potsdam. In 1902 the station was linked by a pedestrian tunnel to Berlin's first U-Bahn, which ran from the now defunct Stralauer Tor station on the Oberbaum Bridge (Oberbaum Brücke) to a station on Potsdamer Platz. In 1939 the Potsdam Station was also connected to a new, north-south stretch of the S-Bahn, running entirely underground between Unter den Linden and Yorckstrasse. As a result, Potsdam Station became the busiest railway station in Berlin, catering for 80 000 travellers a day. Despite this the above-ground station buildings were demolished in the late 1950s after suffering serious bomb damage in 1944, and the site is now occupied by the Tilla Durieux Park.

The only first generation railway station still extant in Berlin is the neo-Classical Hamburg Railway Station (Hamburger Bahnhof), built in 1846 at Invalidenstrasse 50–51. After losing most of its traffic to the Lehrte station it was closed in 1884 and in 1906 became a transport museum. Abandoned for 40 years it reopened in 1996 as the Museum for the Present (Museum für Gegenwart), which contains a collection of modern art.

Another first generation railway station was the Anhalt Station (Anhalter Bahnhof) – so-called because its trains passed through the

Duchy of Anhalt (later Saxony-Anhalt) – which began life as the terminus for a line opened in 1841 going as far as Jüterbog, southwest of Berlin. The line quickly developed into a network handling services to and from Leipzig, Frankfurt am Main and Munich, and in 1880 a vast new station building was unveiled to a design by Franz Heinrich Schwechten (1841–1924); at the time it was the largest railway station in Europe.

In 1882, with the closure of the inconveniently-sited Dresden station (Dresdener Bahnhof), south of the Landwehrkanal, the Anhalt station inherited services to Dresden, Prague and Vienna, and later Rome, Naples and Athens. By 1930 trains were departing Berlin's "Gateway to the South" every three to

The shattered façade of the Anhalt Railway Station

five minutes. Though always less busy than Potsdam Station, Anhalt Station excelled in its opulence, its façade embellished with zinc sculptures called *Day and Night* by Ludwig Brunow (1843–1913), and its huge 34 metre-high iron-and-glass train shed stretching back 171 metres, under which 40 000 people could stand on six platforms. The station by this time was also connected to Europe's largest hotel, the 600-room Excelsior opposite, by means of the world's first pedestrian tunnel containing shops.

As with the neighbouring Potsdam Station, in 1939 a stop on the new north-south S-Bahn was opened at Anhalt station, and in 1943 a huge civilian air raid shelter (*Reichsbahnbunker*) was built alongside it (see no. 65). By 1943, however, Allied bombing raids had terminated all long-distance journeys and in February 1945 the station was closed altogether after its roof was destroyed. The S-Bahn continued to be used until early May 1945, when it was used to evacuate the shelter.

Immediately thereafter the tunnels were deliberately flooded to prevent the Red Army following (see no. 65). Even had the station not been bombed it would have eventually ceased to be used as such since the projected North-South Axis of Hitler's dream city *Germania* would have severed its lines (see no. 57); Albert Speer's plans proposed the station be converted into a swimming pool!

Incredibly, the north-south S-Bahn link was back in service by 1947 and limited services even began running from Anhalt Station after the remains of its roof were cleared – but it was not to last. The station was now serviced by trains arriving from Soviet-controlled East Germany but the station itself lay in West Berlin. In May 1952 the Soviets switched all trains to the Ostbahnhof and Anhalt Station closed forever. Despite a public outcry, the station was demolished in 1960–1961, its main portal being left as a symbol of Berlin's broken connection to its past; it is crowned by replicas of Brunow's sculptures sitting either side of a circular hole that once contained a large clock.

Opposite the ruins the 18-storey Excelsiorhaus now occupies the former site of its namesake hotel, the connecting tunnel destroyed during roadworks in the 1980s. Behind the façade a synthetic sports field covers the site of the train shed and platforms, beyond which is a multi-spired concert venue called the Tempodrom, opened in 2001. More interesting is the area of woodland extending southwards from here down to the Landwehrkanal, where there is still evidence for the platforms that once stretched out beyond the train shed. A pedestrian bridge now stands where a bridge once carried the railway lines over the canal and into the station.

On the south bank of the canal stood the Anhalter Güterbahnhof, a goods station built at the same time and by the same architect as the main station. Of its twin administration blocks, once linked by a portal through which goods vehicles could enter, only one survives which is now home to the Spectrum Berlin Science Centre, a part of the German Technical Museum (Deutsches Technikmuseum Berlin). Nearby stand two old circular locomotive sheds, which are now used by the Technical Museum to house not only its collection of historic locomotives but also a superb model of the entire Anhalt station complex: the perfect place to end this tour of a once great railway station.

Other places of interest nearby: 8, 9, 10, 60, 61, 62, 63

65 Bunker Capital of the World

District II (Friedrichshain-Kreuzberg), a tour of Second World War air raid shelters including the Gasometerbunker on Fichtestrasse 4–12
U7 Südstern

Inside the Second World War civilian shelter at the Gesundbrunnen U-Bahn station

In August 1939 Reichsmarschall Hermann Göring (1893–1946) made the arrogant claim that no Allied bomber would ever reach the River Ruhr, never mind Berlin. When the first Allied aircraft successfully bombed the German capital in June 1940 Hitler responded by initiating a crash programme of air raid shelter building across Germany to protect himself, his staff, his armaments factories, and his people: using 200 million cubic metres of concrete it was the largest building project in history. This is not to say that shelters had not been constructed in Germany prior to 1940, indeed the first had been built beneath Göring's own Reich Air Ministry (Reichsluftfahrtministerium) at Wilhelmstrasse 97 in 1936. However, the majority date from the war years and it is estimated that by 1944 a thousand bombproof shelters had been constructed in the easily-excavated, sandy soils of the Greater Berlin area, giving rise to the urban legend that for every metre built above ground during the Nazi period three metres were excavated below: Berlin had become the bunker capital of the world.

Whilst Hitler and his immediate staff occupied relatively commodious air raid shelters located in and around the New Reich Chancellery on Vossstrasse, the German people had to make do with an assortment of cramped and uncomfortable shelters across the city (see no. 10). The simplest of these were individual house cellars, rudimentarily strengthened with wooden benches along the walls (an example can be seen in the basement of the Antiwar Museum (Antikriegsmuseum) at Brüsseler Strasse 21 (Mitte)). Those walls shared with adjoining buildings were whitewashed so that in the event of the building above collapsing they could be easily located and knocked through, giving the occupants a chance to escape.

Wherever possible, suitable existing structures were pressed into service as public shelters, for example 19th century brewing cellars and the stations of Berlin's extensive underground railway: an original sign from the period reading "Zu den Schutzräumen" ("To the Shelter") is visible in the stairwell of the Hermannstrasse station on the U8 railway line. In some cases a complete civilian shelter was excavated inside a station, a well-preserved example of which lies behind a green-painted steel door inside the southern entrance of the Gesundbrunnen U-Bahn station at Brunnenstrasse 108a (again on the U8). Still preserved are its original triple-decker bunk beds, as well as guidelines in luminous paint for use in the event of a power cut. Designed to hold 1500 people the shelter was often used by as many as 4000, highlighting the shortfall in the provision of civilian shelters. It can be visited on a fascinating guided tour with the Berlin Underworlds Association (Berliner Unterwelten e.V.).

Another unusual example of reusing existing structures as shelters is concealed behind a steel door in the Alexanderplatz U-Bahn station, where a labyrinthine four-level shelter was built in the foundations of an unfinished skyscraper, begun in 1928 to a design by the architect Peter Behrens. Divided up into 55 rooms (in order to give greater stability and minimise casualties should a bomb break through) the shelter could hold 3000 people: little wonder the GDR leadership later earmarked it for their personal use during the Cold War (see no. 37). Other examples of existing structures being adapted as civilian shelters include a 454-metre-long former tram tunnel under the River Spree, excavated in 1895–1899 between Treptower Park and the Stralau peninsula, and a 295-metre-long tunnel excavated in 1895 by the General Electric Company (Allgemeine Elektricitäts-Gesellschaft) beneath their factory on Hussitenstrasse (see no. 24). The latter was used between 1897 and 1914 to test electric underground railways and was the first of its type in Continental Europe; it can be visited as part of a guided tour offered every few months by the Under Berlin Association (unterberlin e.V.).

Most interesting is a shelter built inside a disused gasometer on Fichtestrasse in the district of Kreuzberg, tours of which are given by the Berlin Underworlds Association (Berliner Unterwelten e.V.). Built originally in 1876 for the Kreuzberg Gas Company, to supply gas to the city's street lamps, it is 56 metres wide and 21 metres high, topped with a low-domed cupola. With the widespread introduction of electric power during the early years of the Weimar Republic (1919–1933) it was decommissioned and remained empty until late 1940, when it was converted, together with two other former gasometers on Müllerstrasse (Wedding), into an air raid shelter for up to 6000 people. This use of a pre-existing structure was deemed a labour- and time-saving exercise, since the outer walls acted as a ready-made mould into which the bomb-proof concrete could be poured (to a thickness of 1.8 metres around the walls and 3 metres on the roof); four strengthened concrete entrances were also added to the original structure. The work was undertaken in less than a year by prisoners of war and slave labourers housed in on-site barracks.

The Gasometerbunker on Fichtestrasse

The gasometer's cavernous innards were thus transformed from a single open space into a six-storey, windowless shelter with 120 rooms on each floor, connected by 5 staircases and 3 lifts. Additionally there were 24 kitchens, a diesel driven power supply, and an independent air supply. It is said that 30000 people cowered here during the ferocious American bombing raids of 2nd–3rd February 1945. The Gasometerbunker was considered so secure that prisoners were even brought here from nearby police stations to prevent them escaping from bomb-damaged cells! After the war it served as a hostel for the homeless until 1963, when it then served as a secure NATO food depot until 1990.

With a civilian population of three million to protect, the Nazi administration also commissioned a series of purpose-built air raid shelters, which fall into four main types. The largest were those in the lower storeys of the city's six colossal anti-aircraft (*Flak*) towers, all of which are now either demolished or else covered with rubble (see no. 22). Next came the two so-called *Reichsbahnbunker* ('Railway Bunkers'), built for both railway personnel and civilians near the Friedrichstrasse S-Bahn station at Reinhardtstrasse 20 (Mitte), and at the Anhalt railway station (Anhalter Bahnhof) at Schöneberger Strasse 23a (Friedrichshain-Kreuzberg). The former was erected in 1942 and could hold 3000 people, its 1.8 metre-thick walls given an unusually decorative finish in an attempt to shore up public confidence in the wake of Allied bombing raids. By contrast, the Anhalt shelter built in 1943, which had a capacity of 12 000, was made of plain ferro-concrete 4.5 metres thick, with three storeys above ground and two below. Wooden seats and tables were provided together with tinned sardines. This shelter's great advantage in the last weeks of the war was its direct link to the nearby S-Bahn tunnel, enabling people to walk the five kilometres to the Nordbahnhof without being exposed (see no. 64). By 27th April 1945, with the Red Army almost at the door, most people had fled along this route. On 2nd May, in a desperate bid to prevent Red Army troops from following, SS engineers blew a hole in the tunnel below the Landwehr Canal (Landwehrkanal) at nearby Trebbiner Strasse, flooding 26 kilometres of tunnels as a result and drowning up to 200 civilians and wounded soldiers. Used after the war to store potatoes the shelter today contains a 'Chamber of Horrors' (*Berliner Gruselkabinett*), although its lower level has an informative exhibition about the history of the shelter itself.

More common were smaller above-ground shelters called *Hochbunker*, examples of which can still be seen at Friedrich Karl Strasse (Tempelhof-Schöneberg), Zwieseler Strasse (Lichtenberg), Wittenauer Strasse (Reinickendorf), and Eiswaldtstrasse (Steglitz-Zehlendorf). Another example on Pallasstrasse (Tempelhof-Schöneberg), built also to protect the main telephone exchange on nearby Winterfeldtstrasse, proved so difficult to remove after the war that an apartment block was built directly on top of it; during the Cold War it was designated a nuclear fallout shelter (see no. 37). A fourth, smaller type of shelter was predominantly subterranean, with only its reinforced roof and chimney-like air vents protruding. Examples of this type can be found on Wolffring, Arnulfstrasse, and in Bosepark, all of which lie in the Tempelhof district.

In 1946 the Allied Control Authority decreed that all structures with a potential military usage be demolished, as a result of which many of Berlin's air raid shelters were destroyed, especially in East Berlin where the Soviets were keen to obliterate all trace of Germany's military might. By contrast, the Allies in West Berlin bowed to pressure from homeless people still occupying the shelters to let them remain. Additionally they avoided dynamiting shelters in close proximity to public housing. This explains why most shelters remaining today are to be found in the city's western suburbs.

Other places of interest nearby: 62, 66, 71

66 All in the Name of Louisa

**District II (Friedrichshain-Kreuzberg), the Luisenstadt
Canal Gardens between Oranienplatz and Schillingbrücke
U8 Moritzplatz**

By the early 19th century the only large undeveloped area within Berlin's town wall (the so-called Customs Wall) was the southeast corner, which is today the eastern part of Kreuzberg. At that time it was known as Luisenstadt after Queen Louisa (1776–1810), wife of King Frederick William III (1797–1840), and one of the most beloved figures in Prussian history.

The former heart of old Luisenstadt can best be reached by taking the U8 railway to Moritzplatz, from where it is a short walk eastwards to Oranienplatz. Here is as good a place as any to reflect not only on how this area has changed over the last two cen-

An ornate fountain today adorns the Luisenstadt Canal Gardens

turies but also on the life of the woman after whom it was once named.

Louisa Augusta Wilhelmina Amelia was born in Hanover in 1776 to Grand Duke Charles II of Mecklenburg-Strelitz and Princess Friederike Caroline Louisa of Hesse-Darmstadt. In Frankfurt in 1793 Louisa met the crown prince of Prussia, later King Frederick William III, who it is said was so fascinated by her beauty, modesty and friendliness that he asked for her hand in marriage almost immediately: they were wed on 24th December of the same year.

As Queen of Prussia, Louisa soon gained the respect and affection of her people, especially during the Franco-Prussian Wars, when she displayed great dignity and courage in the face of adversity. After the crushing defeat of the Prussian army by Napoleon at the Battle of Jena in 1806 she accompanied her husband to Königsberg in East Prussia, where they fell on the mercy of Tsar Alexander I (1801–1825). In 1807, after the Russian army itself had been defeated at the Battle of Friedland, Queen Louisa made a personal appeal for clemency to Napoleon at his headquarters in Tilsit: the French emperor responded by confiscating all Prussia's Polish territories and extracting a large levy to pay for the billeting of French troops across what was left. He also attempted to destroy the now pregnant queen's reputation in the process but this only served to make her more deeply loved by her own people. Although the king seemed resigned to Prussia's fate, Queen Louisa encouraged the gradual reconstruction of the Prussian army under the guidance of Generals Scharnhorst (1755–1813) and Gneisenau (1760–1831); a rebuilt Prussian military would assist in significant victories against the French army in 1813 and 1814.

Not until 23rd December 1809 was Queen Louisa eventually able to return to Berlin, only to die aged just 34 on July 19th 1810, while visiting her father in Strelitz. Ten births in her 16 years of marriage had undoubtedly taken its toll. She was greatly mourned by her subjects and was buried in the garden of Schloss Charlottenburg, at the end of an avenue of pines in an elegant neo-Classical mausoleum designed by Heinrich Gentz. Although her remains are hidden from the public gaze in a subterranean crypt, it is possible to enter the Hall of Remembrance, with its accomplished recumbent statue of the queen by Christian Daniel Rauch (1777–1857). In 1828 the façade was reworked by Carl Frederick Schinkel (1781–1841), the original finding its way to Peacock Island (Pfaueninsel) on the River Havel, where it was used to front the so-called Luisentempel (see no. 46). In 1840 the body of the Queen's husband King Frederick William III (1797–1840) was buried by her side. Later, the emperor's second wife, Princess Augusta of Liegnitz, as well as King and Emperor William I (1861–1888), joined them. Despite these added attractions it is the statue of Louisa that draws the most attention, especially on 10th March when admirers gather to honour her memory.

Elsewhere at Schloss Charlottenburg the queen is recalled in her silk-lined bedchamber (Schlafzimmer Königin Luise), designed by Schinkel in 1810 and featuring his typically clean, neo-Classical lines, and also by a square called Luisenplatz in front of the palace. There is also the Louisa Church (Luisenkirche) on Gierkeplatz, several streets to the southeast, which was remodelled in the 1820s.

Queen Louisa is memorialised at several other locations in Berlin, including a statue outside the Roman Baths (Römische Bäder) at Schloss Sanssouci and another on Tiergartenstrasse (Mitte), as well as the octagonal Queen Louisa Memorial Church on Gustav-Müller-Platz (Tempelhof-Schöneberg). However, the most ambitious monument to carry the name of the much-loved queen was undoubtedly the Luisenstadt Canal (Luisenstädtischer Kanal), opened in 1852 to enable barges to pass between the Upper Spree and the Landwehrkanal. It was the creation of the royal landscape gardener Peter Joseph Lenné (1789–1866), to whom the urban planning of Berlin had been assigned in 1840 by King Frederick William IV (1840–1861). Oranienplatz, which is today surrounded by buildings dating mostly from the construction boom of the 1860s, was once bisected by the canal. North from here the canal ran between

The mausoleum of Queen Louisa at Schloss Charlottenburg

Leuschnerdamm and Legiendamm, although where once there was water, since 1926 there have been the Luisenstadt Canal Gardens, designed by the landscape gardener Erwin Barth (1880–1933) after the canal was filled in (see no. 29).

At Leuschnerdamm 25 is the venerable Henne Alt-Berliner Wirtshaus, one of the last of the city's traditional workers' taverns. Opened in 1907 it serves locally-brewed Schultheiss beer and *Milchmasthänchen*, white-fleshed roast chicken cooked to a secret recipe. The wood-panelled rooms are a history lesson in themselves, including a partition wall that once allowed banned Socialist groups to gather in private.

Other places of interest nearby: 4, 65, 71

67　Berlin's First Socialist Street

District II (Friedrichshain-Kreuzberg), Karl-Marx-Allee
U5 Strausberger Platz or Weberweise

By the end of the Second World War the centre of Berlin had been reduced to rubble. The subsequent partitioning of the city made it practically impossible to carry out any co-ordinated reconstruction and instead Berlin's two opposing regimes set about re-defining their territory architecturally in line with their political beliefs. Nowhere was this more apparent than in the construction of what is today Karl-Marx-Allee, in the former East Berlin.

The city planners of the newly-founded German Democratic Republic initially ignored Berlin's historical centre in favour of the devastated proletarian district of Friedrichshain to the east. The district was dissected by Frankfurter Allee, which stretched from Frankfurter Tor westwards as far as Alexanderplatz; in the other direction it led to Frankfurt an der Oder (hence its name) – and eventually Moscow. In 1949 Frankfurter Allee was renamed Stalinallee, in honour of Stalin's 70th birthday, and plans were drawn up to transform it into a showpiece boulevard to rival the Champs-Élysées. It would be the first step in the Socialist reconstruction of Berlin and in the provision of new housing for East Berlin's 'freed' Germans.

Between Frankfurter Tor and Strausberger Platz existing buildings were quickly torn down and the street widened to 90 metres (making it ideal for military and May Day parades). Over the next 12 months new buildings were constructed in the unadorned Modernist style of the 1920s, which had been suppressed under the Third Reich. Designed by Ludmilla Herzenstein and rising five storeys they can be found at numbers 102-104 and 126–128. However, by 1950 this style, too, was being decried, by the GDR leader Walter Ulbricht (1950-1971) for being capitalist: trees were soon planted to obscure them. From 1952 onwards the building of Stalinallee would instead be continued in the overblown neo-Classical style prevalent in the Soviet Union since the 1930s. Uniquely, Stalinallee would also reflect the local traditions of Prussian neo-Classicism, as pioneered by Carl Frederick Schinkel (1781–1841). Thus, the new seven-to-ten-storey buildings display Schinkel-esque entrances, bays and windows, and the upper storeys are clad in Meissenlike ceramic tiles: ordinary workers could thus enjoy the comforts of the old bourgeoisie.

The most prominent architect on the Stalinallee project was Hermann Henselmann (1905–1995), who was responsible for the dramatic pair of 13-storey tower blocks at Strausberger Platz. Running eastwards from them for more than a kilometre and a half were erected near-unbroken rows of buildings on either side of the street. Despite their monumentality, however, the buildings are actually very shallow, as decreed by the East German Politburo, since the primary goal of Berlin's first Socialist street was only to impress. Carved reliefs and mosaics adorning some of the façades depict heroic, happy people at work in the prevailing Socialist Realism style (see no. 8).

One of a pair of towers at Frankfurter Tor on the former Stalinallee

Although shops, restaurants and cinemas were built at ground level (for example the intact GDR-era Café Sybille at number 72) the blocks were essentially residential units (see no. 18). The roomy and comfortable apartments were allocated to those deemed to have provided valuable services to the state, and included both cultural figures and construction workers. However, building costs soon became unsustainable for the broader project of rebuilding East Berlin and in June 1953 the pressure to reduce costs and increase daily construction quotas proved too much for the site's 45,000 workers: unimpressed by the propaganda disseminated by the National Reconstruction Programme they downed their tools. By 17th June workers across East Germany had joined the strike to demand not only better working conditions but also free elections and German reunification. Over a hundred workers died as the GDR regime used Soviet tanks to restore order (the day of infamy is recalled by the Strasse des 17. Juni in the Tiergarten).

By the mid-1950s, following Stalin's death, the new Soviet leader Nikita Kruschev called for further industrialisation of the construction industry to meet the huge demand for new housing. East Germany followed suit and although the original part of Stalinallee was completed as planned (terminated by another pair of Henselmann towers at Frankfurter Tor), its extension westwards beyond Strausberger Platz to Alexanderplatz would be quite different. The continuous decorative façades were replaced by individual apartment blocks made from pre-fabricated concrete panels, requiring far less labour and skill to erect. Modernism was back and by comparison the original part of Stalinallee now appeared decadent. As if to emphasise the regime change it was re-named Karl-Marx-Allee in 1961 and a huge statue of Stalin removed overnight (see no. 8).

In West Berlin, Stalinallee was denounced as the embodiment of Communist ideology, parallels being made with Third Reich architecture to emphasise the similarity of the totalitarian regimes of Hitler and Stalin. West Berlin's architectural riposte was the Hansa Quarter (Hansaviertel) (Mitte), built in the northwest corner of the Tiergarten on the site of a neighbourhood flattened during the war. As the centrepiece of the 1957 International Building Exhibition (Internationale Bauausstellung) prominent architects from around the world conjured up a varied residential development set in a green landscape. Most noticeably it comprises individual housing blocks oriented to the landscape and the sun rather than each other, thereby avoiding regimentation and emphasising the virtues of Western freedom.

Ironically, around the time of German reunification in 1990 Western postmodernists began praising Stalinallee for its grandeur when compared with more recent modern architecture, making its 3,000 apartments fashionable once again. As one of its last pieces of legislation the East Berlin government declared Stalinallee a protected monument, as a result of which its crumbling façades have now been renovated.

It is not surprising that the GDR's Ministry for State Security (Staatssicherheit) – *Stasi* for short – was located not far from Stalinallee at Ruschestrasse 103 (Lichtenberg). Haus 1 in the sprawling former headquarters is maintained today as the Stasi-Museum Berlin; it includes the former office of Stasi chief Erich Mielke, from where he managed 50,000 operatives, and a museum displaying sealed flasks containing personal items stolen from dissidents, for later use by sniffer dogs. There is now public access to the millions of once secret files. The main Stasi Prison at Genslerstrasse 66 is also now a museum (Gedenkstätte Berlin-Hohenschönhausen), its rubber-lined, windowless cells still intact.

Other places of interest nearby: 2, 3, 4, 18, 83

68 The Factory Hostel and Other Unusual Accommodations

District II (Friedrichshain-Kreuzberg), some unusual places to stay including the Die Fabrik hostel at Schlesische Strasse 18 U1 Schlesisches Tor

Berlin's four million annual tourists are spoilt for choice when it comes to finding a room: the city currently offers around 600 hotels and guesthouses! Not surprisingly for a city with a reputation for reinvention, and a penchant for modern design, several of these accommodations are a little out of the ordinary.

The relaxed backpackers' hostel Die Fabrik ('The Factory') at Schlesische Strasse 18, in the heart of alternative Friedrichshain-Kreuzberg, is a case in point. It occupies the former five-storey Paul Michaelsen telephone factory built around 1900, which in 1994 was converted into a 45-room hostel, the architects ensuring that the original façade was retained. The existing coal-fired heating system was taken out and replaced by a solar-powered one, which has proved very popular with travellers looking for environmentally-friendly accommodation. Schlesische Strasse was once a busy high street but with the erection of the Berlin Wall it became a *cul de sac*: now the Wall has gone the street has regained some of its buzz, with cafés, fashion stores and galleries.

Other successful examples of Berlin hoteliers inventively reusing former industrial-era structures include the Arcona Hotel Am Havelufer at Zeppelinstrasse 136 inside an old granary, the Albion Spree-Bogen Waterside Hotel at Alt-Moabit 99 (Mitte) occupying an old dairy, and a converted cargo barge called the Eastern Comfort Hostel moored permanently on the River Spree at Mühlenstrasse 77 (Friedrichshain-Kreuzberg), downstream from the Oberbaum Bridge (Oberbaum Brücke). Rather more intimate is the 4-cabined *Anny*, a houseboat moored at Parkstrasse 13 (Spandau), which also offers leisurely river cruises through the Brandenburg countryside.

A far grander example of adaptive reuse is the conversion of a palace built in 1912 for Walter von Pannwitz, the Prussian Emperor's personal lawyer, into the Schlosshotel im Grunewald at Brahmsstrasse 10 (Charlottenburg-Wilmersdorf), with contemporary interiors by Karl Lagerfeld. Opened in 1951 its famous guests have included Robert Kennedy, Errol Flynn, Josephine Baker, and Romy Schneider. The Relexa

Schlosshotel Cecilienhof in Potsdam's Neuer Garten is also a hotel with a history, having been the last palace of the Hohenzollerns and the venue for the Potsdam Conference from 17th July–2nd August 1945. It was here that Prime Minister Winston Churchill (and later Clement Attlee), President Harry S. Truman and Communist Party General Secretary Joseph Stalin abolished the Nazi Party, reverted all German annexations, de-militarised Germany, agreed to punish war criminals, and established the political balance of power in Europe that would last for the next 45 years. (The rooms in which the conference took place are open to the public.)

A colourful welcome at the hostel Die Fabrik on Schlesische Strasse

Hotels known for their audacious design include the Radisson Blu Hotel Berlin at Karl-Liebknecht-Strasse 3 (Mitte), with its stunning 16 metre-high cylindrical aquarium containing 900 000 litres of seawater and 2600 tropical fish. Called the AquaDom it is serviced by two full-time commercial divers and contains a guest elevator running right through it, providing a thoroughly modern ripost to Berlin's venerable aquarium at Budapester Strasse 32 (Mitte), founded in 1911 and boasting a spectacular collection of jellyfish.

Almost as memorable is the Propellor Island City Lodge at Albrecht-Achilles-Strasse 58 (Charlottenburg-Wilmersdorf), which although located in a traditional 19th century apartment block, offers its guests 27 outrageously decorated guest rooms and the opportunity to sleep in floating beds, cages, and even coffins! Another singular place to stay is the Arte Luise Kunsthotel at Luisenstrasse 19 (Mitte), an early 19th century house that promotes itself as "a gallery where you can spend the night", each room uniquely decorated by a different German artist.

For a really traditional night in Berlin a room should be taken at one of the city's last remaining *Hotel-Pensionen*, which offer cosy high-ceilinged rooms in a 19th century setting, replete with heavy curtains, patterned carpets, chandeliers, and period furniture. Highly recommended is the 14-room Hotel-Pension Funk at Fasanenstrasse 69 (Charlottenburg-Wilmersdorf), which during the 1930s was the home of Danish silent film star Asta Nielsen (1881–1972): Greta Garbo once

The old-fashioned breakfast room of the Pension Funk on Fasanenstrasse

remarked of her that "in dramatic interpretation, in expressiveness and versatility I am nothing". Reached by an elegant hundred-year-old elevator the Pension was established by the Funk sisters in 1956 and later extended into the apartment next door, once the home of Ernst Udet (1896–1941), the second highest-scoring flying ace of the First World War. Together with the Hotel-Pension Dittberner at Wielandstrasse 26 and the Nürnberger Eck at Nürnberger Strasse 24a, the Funk hints at the pleasures once purveyed by Berlin's *grand dame* hotels such as the Fürstenhof, Esplanade, Kaiserhof, and the Adlon, all of which were damaged or destroyed during the Second World War. One of the very few to survive the conflict was the Hotel Askanischer Hof at Kurfürstendamm 53, which opened as the Pension Continental in 1930 and still retains the original décor once enjoyed by a host of German film stars, whose autographed pictures adorn the walls; more recent celebrity guests here have included author Arthur Miller, rock star David Bowie, and Helmut Newton, who took some of his best-known photographs here.

Other places of interest nearby: 69, 70, 71

69 History on the Banks of the Spree

District IX (Treptow-Köpenick), exploring the banks of the River Spree including Lohmühleninsel at the junction of Schlesische Strasse and Puschkinallee
S8, S9, S41, S42 Treptower Park; U1 Schlesisches Tor

The lakes and waterways of the River Havel in south-west Berlin are justifiably popular with Berliners and visitors alike, thanks to their tree-fringed shores, regular boat trips, and historical sights. However, to escape the crowds and gain a rather different riverine experience, a visit should be made to the less written-about banks of the Spree, east of the city centre. Here is a watery world of tributaries and former lagoons, which until the fall of the Wall had been all but forgotten; only today is this historic natural resource starting to be utilised once again.

Our journey begins far out in Old Köpenick on the banks of the Frauentog, a tiny tributary of the Spree that was once home to a thriving fishing community (see no. 76). Here can be found an unusual hotel called the Hostel am Flussbad at Gartenstrasse 50 (Treptow-Köpenick), which as its name suggests occupies the boathouse and changing rooms of an abandoned, 100-year-old riverside bathing pool. Such pools were only located in the clean waters *upstream* of the city centre, and it was here that commercial laundering was also carried out for the same reason. The Köpenick Local History Museum (Heimatmuseum) at Alter Markt 1 contains an exhibition illustrating the laundry trade from 1835, when one Henriette Lustig opened the first "laundry for payment". At the industry's peak in 1913 there were 399 laundries in the area!

Moving downstream into Friedrichshain-Kreuzberg, a modern take on the old riverside bathing pool can be found in the form of the *Badeschiff* ('bathing boat'), a 32-metre-long barge partially submerged at Eichenstrasse 4 and filled with fresh water. Nearby, on the left bank, there is a flood channel (*Flutgraben*) that connects the Spree to the upper end of the Landwehrkanal farther southwest. Originally a natural lagoon in which fish were bred, it was straightened out in the 18th century creating Lohmühleninsel, an island named after the tanning mills once located here. Today, busy Schlesische Strasse and Puschkinallee converge on the island but fortunately its riverbanks still retain a relaxed, rustic feel. The waterside pathways, simple wooden buildings, and landing stages have attracted some unusual new enterprises. They

The tranquil waters of the Flutgraben conceal a hive of activity

include the Club der Visionäre, a lively waterside bar at Am Flutgraben 2, and the Flutgraben e.V. at Am Flutgraben 3, a non-profit making artists' initiative inside an old car repair workshop. On the opposite shore at Vor dem Schlesischen Tor 2 is the Café Anhalt inside Berlin's oldest petrol station, and next door is the evocatively-named Freischwimmer Restaurant, where customers dine at the water's edge.

Back on the Spree, on the right bank, can be found the former site of the East Docks (Osthafen), which ran along Stralauer Allee between the Elsen and the Oberbaum Bridges; one of the buildings being re-developed here is a 1928 refrigerated warehouse once used to store 75 million eggs! The Oberbaum Bridge (Oberbaumbrücke) is named after a tree trunk placed across the river in medieval times to regulate boat traffic (the 'Lower Tree Bridge' was near where the Reichstag now stands). (Berlin, incidentally, has a hundred more bridges than Venice: counting the smaller ones there are 500!)

Downstream from the Oberbaum Bridge is a floating hotel called the Eastern Comfort moored at Mühlenstrasse 77, the street name reflecting the former presence of grain mills. Farther downstream again, where the Spree splits so as order to navigate Museum Island (Museumsinsel), there is a collection of old river craft moored at Märkisches Ufer. Called the Historic Port of Berlin (Historischer Hafen Berlin). It includes boats, barges and tugs that operated on the Spree during the late 19th century. One of the craft, a barge called the *Renate Angelika*, contains an exhibition illustrating the history of inland waterway transport, whilst another, moored outside the former Ermeler-Haus at Märkisches Ufer 10, is used as a summer café.

Other places of interest nearby: 68, 70, 71, 72

70 What's Left of the Berlin Wall?

District IX (Treptow-Köpenick), a tour of the former Berlin
Wall from the watch tower in Im Schlesischen Busch at
the junction of Schlesische Strasse and Puschkinallee to
Bernauer Strasse
S8, S9, S41, S42 Treptower Park; U1 Schlesisches Tor

In 1945, as part of the post-war peace settlement agreed at the Yalta
Conference, both Germany and Berlin were divided into four zones of
occupation (American, British, French and Russian). Trouble flared in
June 1948 when the Soviets, in whose zone occupied Berlin lay, block-
aded West Berlin in an attempt to gain control of the area. This resulted
in a year-long standoff, which saw the Berlin Airlift successfully staged
and the formation of both the Federal Republic of Germany (comprising West Germany and West Berlin) and the German Democratic Republic (East Germany and East Berlin), the latter governed by the German Socialist Unity Party (Sozialistische Einheitspartei Deutschlands).
With Germany and its old capital now officially divided it was the
start of the Cold War. The story of American, British and French forces
in Germany during these unusual times is told in the Allied Museum
(Alliierten-Museum) opened on the 50th anniversary of the Berlin Airlift at Clayallee 135 (Steglitz-Zehlendorf).

Although the GDR gained sovereignty in 1954, Russian troops remained there in order to counterbalance the ongoing American presence
in West Germany. By 1958, however, continuing economic problems and
an authoritarian government had prompted some three million people
to defect to non-Communist countries via West Berlin. In order to halt
this drain of labour, as well as the reduction in economic output arising
from the daily migration of workers from east to west, GDR leader Walter Ulbricht (1950–1971) decided to contain his population, and in doing
so to ensure the continuation of his own brand of tyranny. Thus, on 13th
August 1961 (known as 'Barbed Wire Sunday') West Berliners woke up
to find their city had become an enclave cordoned off by a 150-kilometre
-long boundary made from 18 200 concrete posts and 150 tons of barbed
wire: 68 out of 81 crossing points were barricaded, 193 streets straddling
the border were closed, and 12 railway stations were blocked. Known
as the Berlin Wall (Berliner Mauer) this boundary was the most prominent part of the GDR's border control system, which they dubbed their
"anti-Fascist protection barrier", claiming its function was to stave off a

capitalist invasion. President John F. Kennedy, relieved that the erection of a physical border meant the Soviet Union had no intention of seizing West Berlin, said famously: "A wall is a hell of a lot better than a war."

By 1975 the barbed wire fence had been replaced by a 3.6 metre-high, panel-built wall of reinforced concrete. Between it and a less formidable inner wall (the so-called 'Hinterland Wall') lay the 'Death Strip' (*Todesstreifen*), a swathe of land cleared by bulldozers and monitored permanently from watch towers. The entire ensemble was now known simply as 'The Wall' (*die Mauer*) and became an icon not only of the Cold War but also of cruelty and division around the world. It would remain in place for 28 years during which time 5075 people would successfully cross it and 192 would die trying. Not until 9th November 1989, in the face of mass demonstrations against the East German regime and rising numbers of refugees escaping to the West via Czechoslovakia, were the crossings between East and West Germany officially re-opened. The Wall's subsequent demolition generated a million tons of rubble and was seen as the first step towards German reunification, which was concluded on 3rd October 1990.

Today, the desolation left by the construction of the Wall has mostly disappeared, especially in the city centre, where little remains except memories. However, farther out there are three significant sections still extant, together with several other fragments, and here it is easier to trace the Wall's former course.

Our journey begins in a neglected park called Im Schlesischen Busch at the junction of Schlesische Strasse and Puschkinallee (Treptow-Köpenick). Here can be found one of the Wall's last remaining watch towers. Its upper floor has been preserved as it was during the Cold War, when it was used by border guards to monitor the Wall. The tower is administered today by the Flutgraben e.V., a non-profit making artists' initiative based nearby that uses the building as an innovative exhibition space (see no. 69).

From the tower the Wall trailed away southeastwards along what is today the border between Neukölln and Treptow-Köpenick. To the northwest the Wall crossed over

A watch tower from the Berlin Wall in Im Schlesischen Busch park

to the east side of the River Spree by means of the Oberbaum Bridge (Oberbaumbrücke), where a checkpoint was located. Here the first (and longest) remaining stretch of the Wall can be found, running for 1.3 kilometres along Mühlenstrasse (Friedrichshain-Kreuzberg), downstream as far as the Schillingbrücke. It has been called the East Side Gallery since 1990, when 118 artists from 21 countries daubed politically-themed paintings on its previously unapproachable east face; the most famous is Dimitri Vrubel's cynical *Brotherly Kiss* depicting Leonid Brezhnev and East German leader Eric Honecker enjoying an intimate embrace in a Trabant!

Crossing over the Schllingbrücke back onto the west bank the Wall now followed the former line of the Luisenstadt Canal (Luisenstädtischer Kanal), along Bethaniendamm and Leuschnerdamm (see no. 66). After another checkpoint on Heinrich-Heine-Strasse the Wall assumed a zig-zag course along Sebastianstrasse, Alexandrinenstrasse, Stallschreiberstrasse, and Alte Jakob Strasse. At the corner of Axel-Springer-Strasse and Kommandantenstrasse, the former named after the vociferously anti-Communist newspaper publisher whose offices were nearby, the line of the Wall is marked on the pavement.

From here it is only a short distance along Zimmerstrasse to the most famous feature of the Wall, namely Checkpoint Charlie, memorialised today by the Checkpoint Charlie Museum (Museum Haus am Checkpoint Charlie) at Friedrichstrasse 43–45. After the erection of the Wall, U.S. forces were ordered by President John F. Kennedy (1917–1963) to create three Allied checkpoints in order to exercise the right of free access to Berlin, as stipulated under the post-war quadripartite agreement. Named using the NATO phonetic alphabet, Checkpoint Alpha was located in Helmstedt, Lower Saxony and was the crossing point between the Federal Republic of Germany and the GDR. Checkpoint Bravo was at Dreilinden Drewitz, southeast of Wannsee, and was the crossing point from the GDR into West Berlin. The third was Checkpoint Charlie, the crossing point for foreigners between the American and Soviet sectors of Berlin (West Berliners and West Germans crossed elsewhere). It was here that American and Soviet tanks faced each other in October 1961 in a standoff that almost triggered another war. (A rusted steel pillar around the corner at Zimmerstrasse 26 marks where 18-year old Peter Fechter bled to death on 17th August 1962, the first victim of East Germany's shoot-to-kill policy for those attempting to flee to the West).

From Checkpoint Charlie the former line of the Wall westwards is marked in the road by a double row of cobblestones as far as Niederkirchnerstrasse, where the second significant remaining stretch of Wall can be found, running parallel to the Topography of Terror (Topographie des Terrors) Documentation Centre (see no. 9). Beyond, at its junction with Stresemannstrasse, the Wall then turned northwest towards Potsdamerplatz, again marked by a line of cobblestones that run as far as Köthener Strasse (in Potsdamerplatz itself can be found several concrete Wall panels placed on permanent display).

From here, northwards along Ebertstrasse as far as the Spree, nothing of the Wall remains although the Room of Silence (Raum der Stille), in the northern side pavilion of the Brandenburg Gate (Brandenburger Tor), offers the chance to reflect on the period when the iconic gateway stood inside East Berlin. On the southern

An iconic image on the East Side Gallery is the Brotherly Kiss

bank of the river, at the corner of Scheidemannstrasse and Ebertstrasse, a row of white crosses attached to a fence commemorate those drowned whilst attempting to swim to freedom.

The Wall traversed the Spree at Schiffbauerdamm, where a fragment of Wall remains together with an installation of trees and sculptures known as the *Parliament of Trees* (*Parlament der Bäume*). From here the Wall continued northwestwards along Alexanderufer and then along the edge of the Berlin-Spandau Ship Canal (Berliner-Spandauer-Schifffahrtkanal), to another checkpoint on Invalidenstrasse. Beyond lies the Invaliden Cemetery (Invalidenfriedhof) on Scharnhorststrasse, containing several further fragments of the Wall amongst its battered gravestones.

Continuing along the canal path another watch tower is now revealed, on Kieler Strasse, with its memorial to Günter Litfin, the second East German to die trying to cross the Wall on 24th August 1961. An East German border guard, Peter Göring, was later a victim of friendly fire here although his memorial, like several others to dead border guards, has since been removed.

At the end of Scharnhorststrasse the Wall turned right along Boyenstrasse, at the end of which a line of cobblestones at the junction of Liesenstrasse and Chaussestrasse again marks its former course; another border checkpoint once stood here. At the end of Liesenstrasse the Wall turned sharply onto Gartenstrasse and then sharply again onto Bernauer Strasse, where the third significant section of Wall remains. Standing between Ackerstrasse and Bergstrasse it is the most informative since it retains a complete section of main wall, 'Death Strip' and inner wall; it is now preserved as the Berlin Wall Memorial (Gedenkstätte Berliner Mauer) and includes the highly informative Berlin Wall Documentation Centre (Dokumentationszentrum Berliner Mauer). A poignant feature in the remaining 'Death Strip' a little to the east is the Church of Reconciliation (Versöhnungskirche), built to replace an earlier church that was demolished in 1985 in order to clear East German sight lines (the original church bells can be seen alongside the new church). In 1962 a tunnel was dug between nearby Wolgaster Strasse and Schönholzer Strasse7 through which 29 East Berliners escaped. This was followed in 1964 by a 120-metre-long tunnel between Strelitzer Strasse 55 and Bernauer Strasse 97, enabling a further 57 to flee. A guided tour of the area is offered by the Berlin Underworlds Association (Berliner Unterwelten e.V.).

Our journey terminates at the eastern end of Bernauer Strasse, where the Wall turned sharply northwards, along the boundary separating the districts of Pankow and Wedding. A further fragment of the Wall is still preserved here in Mauerpark ('Wall Park') along Schwedter Strasse.

The Invaliden Cemetery was once earmarked as a burial ground for Third Reich elite and that it was here that the assassinated Chief of the Reich Security Main Office (Reichssicherheitshauptamt) SS Lieutenant General Reinhard Heydrich (1904–1942), and the Minister for Armaments and Munitions Fritz Todt (1891–1942) were both buried, their grave markers removed by the Soviets after the war. Also buried here was Gerhard von Scharnhorst (1755–1813), the renowned Prussian general during the Napoleonic Wars, and First World War flying ace Manfred von Richthofen (1892–1918), better known as the 'Red Baron', whose remains were later moved to Wiesbaden by his family (one of his trademark Fokker Triplanes can be seen in Hangar 3 at the Air Force Museum (Luftwaffenmuseum) at Kladower Damm 182–188 (Spandau), on the former Gatow airstrip (Flugplatz Gatow).

Other places of interest nearby: 68, 69, 71, 72

71 Berlin's Turkish Quarter

District VIII (Neukölln), a tour of Turkish Berlin starting
at the Turkish Market on Maybachufer (Türken Markt am
Maybachufer)
U8 Schönleinstrasse

During the mid-1960s, West Germany's previously small Muslim community was increased dramatically in size as Turkish guest workers (*Gastarbeiter*) were recruited to help with the country's economic revival. They made up for a manpower shortage that resulted not only from the Second World War but also the erection of the Berlin Wall, which blocked the flow of German migrant workers from the east. By the mid-1990s many Turks had decided to make Germany their permanent home (despite the acquisition of citizenship being discouraged) and today there are 1.8 million Turks in Germany (out of a total of 3.4 million Muslims). Berlin's Muslim population stands currently at 220 000, of which 190 000 are Turkish, with notable communities in the old West Berlin working class neighbourhoods of Neukölln, Moabit, Wedding, and Kreuzberg, the latter the largest Turkish population outside Turkey itself.

Kreuzberg's Turkish Quarter is focussed either side of Oranienstrasse, having relocated here from Bergmannstrasse after the fall of the Berlin Wall. The area is sometimes cited as an example of peaceful coexistence and multiculturalism, in part because different social classes have lived and worked in close proximity in the area since the early 19th century. After the Second World War, Kreuzberg's old industrial lofts and deep courtyards continued to attract a diverse population, this time including students, dropouts, artists and, increasingly, immigrants. The resulting population has been dubbed the "Kreuzberg Mixture".

Despite multiculturalism having been being branded a failure in some parts of Europe, it has fared somewhat better in Germany. This is partly because it is a much larger place and also because few of its urban areas are dominated by a single ethnic group, avoiding the risk of ghettoization. The naturalisation programme for immigrants in Berlin has been especially ambitious and most Turks consider themselves true Berliners. Having said that, many German Berliners have little contact with the Turkish community and there are still radical Islamists in Germany, determined to prevent the integration of Turks into German society.

Kreuzberg's many authentic Turkish sights and sounds have turned the area into a fascinating and unconventional tourist attraction in itself, one which offers the sensitive visitor an opportunity to participate in, and perhaps even contribute to, Europe's elusive goal of ethnic interaction. A good example is Berlin's largest outdoor Turkish Market held every Tuesday and Friday on Maybachufer, just outside Kreuzberg in Neukölln on the south bank of the Landwehrkanal. Whilst the majority of stallholders and customers are Turkish the colourful array of fresh fruit and vegetables, fabrics and Turkish specialities always guarantees a significant non-Turkish presence.

Equally enticing are the area's array of bazaars, restaurants and takeaways, opened in order to escape the menial work offered to the original guest workers. Turkish takeaways can be found throughout Berlin today, each offering the ubiquitous *Döner kebap* (meaning 'rotating roast meat'), served with salad, yogurt and spices inside flat, unleavened bread (a traditional flat bread (Fladenbrot) bakery can be seen at Kottbusser Damm 6). Said to have been invented specifically for the German market in Kreuzberg in 1971 there are currently 15 000 *Döner kebap* shops in Germany selling 400 million *kebaps* each year: with an annual turnover of 1.8 billion Euros the German *kebap* business is worth more than McDonalds and Burger King combined! Some of the best are to be found in Kreuzberg, along Oranienstrasse and around Kottbusser Tor.

For a broader selection of Turkish cuisine, including delicious soups, pilafs, stuffed vegetables and sticky Middle Eastern pastries, try some of Kreuzberg's traditional Turkish restaurants, for example Hasir at Adalbertstrasse 10 and Defne at Planufer 92c. Unusual too is the Turkish-run Burg am See, a canalside beer garden at Ratiborstrasse

Ramadan cookies for sale at the Turkish Market on Maybachufer

Exotic fruit for sale at the Turkish Market on Maybachufer

14c, which includes a separate tea garden and an area for water-pipe smoking. A singular restaurant in the area is Die Weltküche at Graef-estrasse 18, established by immigrants from around the world as a means of creating sustainable jobs for themselves and furthering their integration into German society. The roster of chefs cook traditional dishes from their counties of origin.

Another Turkish institution is the steam bath, or *Hamam*, popular since Ottoman times as a place for cleansing and socialising. Since bathing in still water is forbidden in Islam, the Turkish baths offer steam and running water ablutions only. In Kreuzberg there is the women-only Hamam das Turkische Frauenbad, at Mariannenstrasse 6, whereas both men and women are welcome at the Sultan Hamam at Bülowstrasse 57 (Tempelhof-Schöneberg). Men also might like a tradi-tional Turkish shave, which is available at the Barbier- und Friseur-salon Kücük Istanbul at Oranienstrasse 176.

The most important area of Turkish life, and one traditionally for-bidden to non-Muslims, is of course the mosque. Being a temporary population Germany's Muslims worshipped at first wherever they could, creating modest prayer houses in disused apartments, old fac-tory buildings and community centres, quite invisible from the street. There are an estimated 2200 such prayer centres across Germany, for example the Muradiye Mosque in an old industrial courtyard in Neu-kölln.

Surprisingly there are still barely a hundred traditional mosque buildings in Germany, although this looks set to change following the recent consensus that the country's Turkish population is now a permanent one, with a legitimate need for convenient and identifiable places of worship. A manifestation of this has been the construction between 1999 and 2005 one of Germany's largest mosques, the Şehitlik Mosque (Şehitlik-Moschee) at Columbiadamm 128 (Neukölln). Constructed in the grand Ottoman style it can hold 1500 worshippers. The mosque is located next to Berlin's oldest Islamic cemetery (Islamischer Friedhof), wherein all the graves typically point towards Mecca. The cemetery was founded on land given to the Turkish community in the 1860s by Emperor William I (1861–1888) and includes the remains of Ottoman diplomats who died in Berlin. A more recent addition is the imposing Omar ibn Al Khattab Mosque, erected in 2008 at the junction of Wiener Strasse and Skalitzer Strasse (Kreuzberg).

The construction of mosques has inevitably caused some friction over fears that such visually arresting structures might create racial tension. It is to be hoped that the district's inhabitants, whatever their creed or colour, will fall back on their longstanding wisdom and tolerance and not only preserve but also enhance the 'Kreuzberg Mixture'.

Other places of interest nearby: 65, 66, 68, 69, 70

72 Where Einstein Lectured on Relativity

District IX (Treptow-Köpenick), the Archenhold Observatory
(Archenhold-Sternwarte) in Treptower Park at Alt-Treptow 1
S8, S9, S41, S42 Treptower Park

The theoretical physicist Albert Einstein (1879–1955), whose name is today synonymous with genius, was born into a perfectly normal German-Jewish family in Ulm, Baden-Württemberg. Aged just five his father showed him a pocket compass. Einstein realised immediately that something in 'empty' space was acting upon the needle: he would later describe this as having been a revelatory experience.

In 1889 a medical student who regularly visited the Einstein family (by this time living in Munich) introduced the young Einstein to the key scientific and philosophical texts of the day. Einstein was already a prodigous thinker, teaching himself calculus and Euclidean geometry, as well as conducting his own experiments (for example, visualising what it would be like to travel alongside a light beam). Quitting his secondary school education he followed his family to Italy and was then sent to Switzerland to complete his studies. In 1900 he presented

The astronomical telescope at the Archenhold Observatory in Treptower Park

his first published paper – on the capillary forces of a straw – in which his lifelong quest for a unified physical law is already apparent.

Einstein married a mathematician in 1903 and in 1905 he gained his doctorate. He had hoped for a teaching position but having upset too many of his professors by his brashness he ended up in the Swiss Patent Office, assessing the worth of electromagnetic devices. Despite this setback, 1905 turned out to be his *Annus Mirabilis*, during which he wrote four groundbreaking articles, one concerning the photoelectric effect (for which he would receive the Nobel Prize for Physics in 1921) and another containing his now famous mass-energy equivalence equation, $E = mc^2$. By 1911 he had become associate professor at the University of Zurich and full professor at the Charles University in Prague.

Just prior to the start of the First World War Einstein took German citizenship and became professor at Berlin's Humboldt University (Humboldt-Universität) at Unter den Linden 6. Around the same time he also became a member of the Prussian Academy of Sciences, as well as director of the new Kaiser Wilhelm Institute for Physics in Dahlem. Until his departure 20 years later Einstein would live at Haberlandstrasse 8 in Schöneberg's Jewish Bavarian Quarter (Bayerisches Viertel) (see no. 54).

On 2nd June 1915 Einstein gave the first public lecture on his new theory of gravity, known as General Relativity. The venue chosen was the large lecture hall of the Archenhold Astronomical Observatory (Archenhold-Sternwarte) in Treptower Park. Still Germany's largest public observatory it boasts the world's longest moveable refracting telescope, with a focal length of 21 metres. On 15th March 1979 the lecture hall was named Einstein Hall to mark what would have been the physicist's hundredth birthday.

The observatory itself was the brainchild of Friedrich Simon Archenhold (1861–1939), an astronomer who in 1891 had discovered a nebula that could not be confirmed because of the lack of modern telescopes in Germany. Determined to rectify the situation Archenhold had the telescope built and then paid for it by exhibiting it at the Berlin Industrial Show, held in Treptower Park in 1896. So successful was it that the observatory and its telescope remained in place and in 1909 became a permanent feature of the park.

In November 1915 Einstein lectured on relativity before the Prussian Academy of Sciences, concluding with a series of equations that effectively replaced Newton's Law of Gravity. Proved in 1919 to be scientifically correct, the so-called Einstein Field Equations (EFE) were lauded as "probably the greatest scientific discovery ever made". In order to further test Einstein's theories a special observatory was constructed on the Telegrafenberg, a hill south of Potsdam's main railway station (Potsdamer Hauptbahnhof) and reached today via Albert-Einstein-Strasse. Known as the Einstein Tower (Einsteinturm) the 20-metre-high observatory was erected in 1921 to a design by the German-Jewish Modernist architect Erich Mendelsohn (1887–1953). Its futuristic curving forms make it one of the very best examples of German Expressionist architecture, forms that were meant to demonstrate the versatility of concrete construction; in reality, prohibitive costs meant that brick and plaster was eventually used above the first floor.

Tragically for Germany by 1933 Hitler's Nazi regime passed a law forcing Jewish university professors out of their jobs, followed by a campaign denigrating so-called "Jewish Physics": needless to say, Einstein's books were amongst those burned by Nazi students in Bebelplatz in May the same year (see no. 77). At the time Einstein was a visiting professor at Princeton University: renouncing his German citizenship he remained in the United States for the rest of his life, where he concentrated his energies on generalising his theories on gravitation in order to unify and simplify the fundamental laws of physics (Unified Field Theory).

Those with an interest in astronomy will also want to visit the Zeiss Planetarium opened in 1959 at the Archenhold Observatory, as well as the large Zeiss Planetarium (Zeiss-Grossplanetarium) in Ernst Thälmann-Park at Prenzlauer Allee 80 (Pankow), the latter one of the biggest in Europe. Unveiled in 1987 it has a dome 23 metres high and an exhibition in its foyer of optical equipment produced by the renowned Carl-Zeiss-Jena company. The park itself is named after an inter-war Communist leader, who died in Buchenwald concentration camp. Another planetarium, the Planetarium am Insulaner at Munsterdamm 90 (Steglitz-Zehlendorf), is conveniently built on top of a mound of Second World War rubble (see no. 32).

Other places of interest nearby: 69, 70

73 The Sunken Garden and a Bohemian Village

District VIII (Neukölln), Körnerpark at Schierker Strasse 8
S41, S42, S45, S46 Neukölln; U7 Neukölln

Berlin is undoubtedly one of Europe's greenest capital cities, with most of its districts and suburbs boasting their own parks and gardens. One of the most unusual is the Körnerpark, which rarely makes the pages of mainstream guidebooks and can be found tucked away on Schierker Strasse in the suburb of Neukölln. What sets it apart from other gardens in Berlin is that it lies between five and seven metres below the level of the surrounding streets, on the site of an abandoned gravel pit. The land was owned originally by a Berlin entrepreneur and industrialist named Franz Körner, who agreed to donate it to the City for use as a garden on the condition that it bore his name. Thus the Körnerpark was constructed between 1912 and 1916 to a plan by the garden architect Hans Richard Küllenberg. Interestingly, during its construction the grave of a sword-wielding man and his horse dating to the 5th/6th century AD was uncovered, something unique in the Brandenburg area.

Two ornate flights of balustraded steps lead down into the west end of the garden, either side of a fine neo-Renaissance Orangery designed by city architect Reinhold Kiel; such buildings were used originally for the display and over-wintering of potted citrus trees. Beyond is a rectangular lawn flanked by narrow watercourses, or 'rills', and plantings of stately plane trees, offering shade in the summer months. The eastern end of the garden has a circular pond fed by a waterfall and fountains, either side of which are less formal lawns broken up by further trees and shrubs. Under the north wall, which like the others surrounding the park is beautifully arcaded, is a neatly clipped hedge behind which are ornamental flower beds.

Strolling through Körnerpark today it is difficult to imagine that in the 1930s it was almost destroyed as part of the construction work for the nearby Berlin-Tempelhof Airport (Flughafen Berlin-Tempelhof). Fortunately, the vociferous protests of local citizens were heeded by officials and the garden was spared. The Orangery now contains a small but lively art gallery (Galerie in Körnerpark) and café, managed by Neukölln's Department of Culture, and its terrace is used to host free concerts during the summer months.

A couple of roads away to the east, across Karl-Marx-Strasse, there lies a second unusual garden, namely the Comenius Garden (Comenius-Garten) at Richardstrasse 35. It was unveiled on 6th November 1995 to celebrate Berlin and Prague becoming twin cities. Indeed, the surrounding suburb of Rixdorf has been known as the Bohemian Village (Böhmische Dorf) since persecuted Bohemian Protestants began arriving here in 1737 (a Bohemian cemetery can be found on Kirchhofstrasse). Drawn by the religious and political freedoms offered by the Prussian King Frederick William I

A water feature in Neukölln's Körnerpark, once a quarry

(1713–1740), whose statue stands in nearby Kirchgasse, the Bohemians settled and built their own houses, imparting a rural feel that still survives today. One such building, formerly a school and church hall, stands alongside the statue and features a carved chalice on its gable end: the symbol of Hussite Protestantism (this also explains the presence of a chalice on the coat of arms of Neukölln, to which Rixdorf now belongs).

The garden itself, which is open by appointment, is named after John Amos Comenius (1592–1670), the renowned Moravian pedagogue and Protestant, whose face can be seen on an inscribed stone near the entrance. Its conceptual design is based on Comenius's "Path of Light" teachings, whereby education was to be universal, focussing less on instruction and more on active participation. The garden's many different elements represent the challenges faced by man at different stages in life and as such is especially popular with local schools. A statue of Comenius donated by the Czech government to celebrate the 400th anniversary of his birth adorns the garden.

Another unusual site in Neukölln that rarely makes the guidebooks is the local swimming pool (Stadtbad Neukölln), several roads north at Ganghofer Strasse 3. Built in 1914 to a design by the architect Reinhold Kiehl it takes the form of a classical Greek basilica, its two pools suitably adorned with Ionic columns and murals.

74 An English Park in Berlin

District IX (Treptow-Köpenick), the Späth Arboretum
(Späthsches-Arboretum) at Späthstrasse 80–81
S8, S9, S45, S46 Baumschulenweg or U7 Blaschkoallee,
then Bus 170 Späthstrasse/Ligusterweg

At Invalidenstrasse 122 in Central Berlin (Mitte) can be found the Honigmond Garden Hotel, which offers its customers the unexpected luxury of a garden residence in the heart of the city. Occupying a restored villa built in 1845 the hotel opened in October 2000. It is said that the exceptional fertility of its garden arises from it occupying the former site of a plant nursery, which until the 1960s belonged to Berlin's renowned Späth horticultural firm.

Ludwig Späth founded his family's horticultural business in 1720 and over the next six generations it gained international renown. The firm's penultimate and most successful head was Franz Späth (1839–1913), who in the early 1860s built himself a large house in Treptow, on land adjacent to the Britz Canal, which connects the River Spree with the Teltowkanal. Surrounding the house a well-stocked nursery garden and arboretum was established, the latter based on plans drafted by the Director of City Gardens, Johann Gustav Heinrich Meyer, a colleague of the famous royal landscape designer Peter Joseph Lenné (1789–1866). The arboretum was laid out in the style of traditional English landscape parks of the 18th century, typified by far-reaching vistas and punctuated by specimen trees. Covering an area of 3.5 hectares the arboretum served not only as a private garden but also as an experimental tree and shrub nursery, and an exhibition ground for potential customers. The name of the main access road to the arboretum, Baumschulenstrasse, came about at this time.

Over the next century the garden and arboretum were developed, including the addition of a rose garden in 1879, and a water garden and rockery in 1929. From 1891 onwards the dendrological department of the Späth nursery garden was responsible for the running of the arboretum, its most famous director being Gerd Krüssmann (1910–1980), a highly regarded German horticulturalist who departed at the end of the Second World War.

In 1960, after a period of lying fallow, the arboretum was taken over the Humboldt University's newly-founded Institute for Special Botany. With the Späth family no longer in residence, their former home was converted into a study centre and the entire collection of approximately 5000 plant types was catalogued and re-labelled. Since 1966 the revived Späth Arboretum (Späthsches-Arboretum) has been open to the public during the summer months, enabling those interested to explore this fascinating green corner of Berlin.

Gerd Krüssmann was also involved in the creation of an arboretum for the Botanical Garden (Botanischer Garten) at Königin-Luise-Strasse 6–8 in Dahlem (Steglitz-Zehlendorf). This tranquil garden was moved here from Potsdamer Strasse in the 1890s, during a time when the last Emperor, King William II (1888–1918) was imitating British garden design. As such it was built to rival Kew Gardens, accounting for its striking tropical palm house by the architect

Specimen trees adorn the Späth Arboretum

Alfred Koerner. One of the largest glasshouses in the world it is a fine example of glass-and-steel architecture from the late 19th and early 20th centuries. The full history of the garden is given in the Botanical Museum (Botanisches Museum) next to the entrance.

Probably the oldest English-style landscape in Berlin can be found in the park surrounding Schloss Charlottenburg (Charlottenburg-Wilmersdorf), a summer residence commenced in 1695 to a design by Johann Arnold Nering for Sophia Charlotte of Hanover, the second wife of Elector Frederick III (1688–1701), later King Frederick I in Prussia (1701–1713); it was extended by Johann Friedrich Eosander von Göthe in 1701–1707. Lying beyond a formal French-style Baroque garden and a carp lake, the informal English park was created between 1819 and 1828 under the guidance of royal gardener Peter Joseph Lenné (1789–1866).

Other places of interest nearby: 75

75   A Very Modern Crematorium

District IX (Treptow-Köpenick), the Baumschulenweg
Crematorium at Kiefholzstrasse 221
S8, S9, S45, S46 Baumschulenweg

Berlin is justifiably famous for its contemporary architecture, much of it the result of huge investments made since the city became the capital of reunified Germany in 1990. With the fall of the Wall, property developers gained access to huge swathes of prime real estate in the heart of the city, once occupied by buildings destroyed during or after the Second World War; the rebuilding of Potsdamer Platz is a case in point.

Contemporary architects have been busy leaving their mark in Berlin's suburbs too, a superb example of which is the Baumschulenweg Crematorium (Krematorium Baumschulenweg) in Treptow. Opened in May 1999, it was designed by Axel Schultes and Charlotte Frank, the architects who shortly afterwards began work on Berlin's new Federal Chancellery (Bundeskanzleramt) near the Reichstag building. Unusually for a crematorium, it has quickly established itself as a firm favourite with students of postmodern architecture, most notably because of its breathtaking Hall of Condolence (*Kondolenzhalle*), access to which is gained through automatically-operated sliding doors.

Once inside, 29 soaring

Inside the Baumschulenweg Crematorium in Treptow

concrete columns, placed at irregular intervals, rise from the floor like trees, creating the effect of an abstract sacred grove. The tops of the columns are crowned with circular capitals of daylight, which break through the ceiling allowing gentle illumination of the cavernous hall below. In the centre of the floor is a circular pool with a mirror-like surface over which is delicately suspended a single egg, a pagan symbol of regeneration. This masterly control of materials, space and light has enabled the architects to create a dignified aura of reverential mystery, which has been compared to the Great Hypostyle Hall at Karnak in Egypt, the Mezquita Mosque at Cordoba, and even Stonehenge. Such disparate cultural references offer both visitor and mourner a profound, multi-layered, and altogether unforgettable experience. The architects considered this aspect very important, taking into account the fact that there are no established rituals associated with the burning of bodies in the West, and that there is a likelihood that today's mourners may include people of different faiths, as well as those with no faith at all.

After leaving the crematorium it is only one stop further on the S-Bahn to Berlin-Schöneweide, where the National Socialist Forced Labour Documentation Centre (NS Zwangsarbeit Dokumentationszentrum) can be found at Britzer Strasse 5 (Treptow-Köpenick).

Potsdamer Platz is another location where cutting edge architects have been busy creating some of Berlin's most modern structures. The square was once Europe's busiest traffic intersection and boasted its first set of traffic lights installed in 1924. A replica of the lights stands today amongst the skyscrapers (see frontispiece). During the 1920s Potsdamer Platz was a focus for Berlin's celebrated nightlife and included institutions such as the Haus Vaterland ballroom and the glitzy Hotel Fürstenhof. Only the restaurant Haus Huth on adjoining Leipziger Platz survived the war. The Kaisersaal of the Grand Hotel Esplanade on nearby Bellevuestrasse was subsequently incorporated into the new Sony Center at Potsdamer Strasse 2, where it offers a poignant glimpse of the area's former glory.

Other places of interest nearby: 74

76 An Old Fishing Village

District IX (Treptow-Köpenick), the former fishing village
of Kietz, off Müggelheimer Strasse
S47 Spindlersfeld, then Tram 62 Schlossplatz

Across the Frauentog to Kietz

Berlin is a relatively young European city, its written history stretching back only to the early 13th century, when the two settlements of Berlin and Cölln grew up on opposite banks of the River Spree (see no. 1). Trading in fish, rye and timber they formed an alliance in 1307 to become Berlin-Cölln, a successful trading city controlled by the Margraves of Brandenburg that would eventually become the capital of Prussia – and finally of all Germany.

The small fishing settlement of Cölln occupied what is now the southern part of Museum Island (Museumsinsel). In medieval times the area was called Fishermen's Island (Fischerinsel), although little remains there today except for names and memories: during the 1960s the old, densely-packed houses were swept away by the GDR authorities and replaced by anonymous-looking apartment blocks. A few 17th century houses were left standing on Brüderstrasse (see no. 5) and a handful of buildings re-erected elsewhere (e.g. the Zum Nussbaum inn was rebuilt at Am Nussbaum 3 in the St. Nicholas Quarter (Nikolaiviertel) and the Ermeler House (Ermeler-Haus) was moved to Märkisches Ufer 10). Therefore, to gain an impression of how Cölln's Fishermen's Island might once have appeared, an excursion out to Köpenick is recommended, where parts of the former fishing village of Kietz are still extant.

Lying on the tranquil banks of the Frauentog, sleepy Kietz began life as a Slavic fishing village and was first documented in 1355; it retained its independence until its incorporation into the district of Köpenick in

Fishermen's cottages in the old village of Kietz

1898. Strung out along its main street, which is also known as Kietz and runs south from the western end of busy Müggelheimer Strasse, thirty or so single-storey houses once stood, a handful of which have been preserved. With their quaint attic windows, tranquil courtyards and tiny gardens these traditional fishermen's cottages built in the 18th and early 19th centuries are easily distinguished from the four-storey apartment buildings that sprung up when suburbanisation arrived here in the early 1900s. Typical is the cottage at number 8, with its effigy of a fish nailed above the door, opposite which is a later building carrying the Köpenick arms – one of Berlin's oldest – that again depicts fish. Farther along the street at number 22 is another cottage with a fish above its door, whilst number 21, which has been carefully restored, retains its cobblestoned passageway once used by the fishermen to gain access to the river. Across the road at number 12 is the former village bakery dating from the mid-18th century, which still keeps its traditional fishing rights; for those interested in traditional accommodation bed-and-breakfast is offered in its attic rooms.

From the riverbank at Kietz there is a good view of the Baroque Schloss Köpenick. Home to Prince Frederick, later King Frederick I (1701–1713), it contains some superb ceiling paintings and stucco ornamentation. The building is today an extension of Berlin's Museum of Applied Arts (Kunstgewerbemuseum)

77 Bookworms and Fleamarkets

District IX (Treptow-Köpenick), a tour of Berlin bookshops
including Antiquariat Brandel at Scharnweberstrasse 59
S3, RE1 Friedrichshagen, then walk

"Das war ein Vorspiel nur, dort wo man Bücher verbrennt, verbrennt man am Ende auch Menschen" ("That was only a prelude; where books are burned, in the end people will burn"). These words by the German poet Heinrich Heine (1797–1856) can be found inscribed on a plaque at the centre of Bebelplatz, just south of Unter den Linden. The words are apt for it was here on the night of 10th May 1933 that Nazi students staged their infamous burning of books written by authors they deemed "degenerate". Among the 20 000 volumes destroyed were works by Albert Einstein, Sigmund Freud, Andre Gide, Helen Keller, Jack London, Thomas and Heinrich Mann, Robert Musil, Marcel Proust, Erich Maria Remarque, H. G. Wells, Émile Zola, and Stefan Zweig. Although the square appears empty today, a glass panel inserted into the road surface alongside the plaque provides a glimpse of artist Micha Ullmann's empty-shelved *Sunken Library* (1995), reminding the onlooker of what happened here – and how impoverished the world would be without books.

Bebelplatz was originally called Opernplatz and its grand buildings, such as the neo-Classical State Opera House (Staatsoper Unter den Linden), the green-domed Cathedral of St. Hedwig (St-Hedwigs-Kathedrale), and the curving-fronted Old Library (Alte Bibliothek), were intended to be part of a forum in the style of ancient Rome. The Old Library was built in 1775 to house the royal book collection founded originally by Frederick William, the Great Elector (1640–1688), and is one of Berlin's finest Baroque buildings; it is today home to the law faculty of the Humboldt University (Humboldt-Universität) at Unter den Linden 6 (see no. 8).

Next door to the Humboldt University is the Old State Library (Alte Staatsbibliothek) at Unter den Linden 8, which replaced the library on Bebelplatz in 1914. One of the finest libraries in the world it suffered substantial damage during the Second World War and some of its holdings are thought still to be in Russia. As with most of Berlin's major cultural institutions, the remaining collection was subsequently divided between East and West Berlin, in this case between this building, which found itself in East Berlin, and a New State Library (Neue

Staatsbibliothek) in West Berlin, erected between 1967 and 1978 at Potsdamer Strasse 33; the collections remain divided to this day.

Despite such tumultuous history Berlin remains a great place for book lovers, and in common with most other capital cities it boasts a varied selection of bookshops, from the vast Dussmann at Friedrichstrasse 90 (Mitte) and Hugendubel at Tauentzienstrasse 13 (Charlottenburg-Wilmersdorf), with their tol-

Brandel's Bookshop continues a long literary tradition in Friedrichshagen

erant approach to customers' browsing, to specialist shops such as Artificium at Rosenthalerstrasse 40–41 (Mitte), with its attached art gallery, Morgenwelt at Markelstrasse 56 (Steglitz-Zehlendorf), specialising in science fiction books and board games, Camera Work at Kantstrasse 149 (Charlottenburg-Wilmersdorf) with its collection of photography books, ProQm at Almstadtstrasse 48–50 (Mitte), the urban lifestyle specialist, and Berlin Story at Unter den Linden 26 (Mitte), offering 5000 Berlin-related books, films, maps, and other souvenirs.

A singular bookshop is Antiquariat Brandel at Scharnweberstrasse 59 (Treptow-Köpenick). Although only opened in 1991, the building has been associated with publishing since 1889, when it was home to a daily newspaper. As well as books on literature, art, geography, and travel, the proprietor is especially interested in local history and the literature of the Friedrichshagen circle of writers, who were active in the area during the late 19th century.

Another unusual bookshop is the Bücherbogen am Savignyplatz (Charlottenburg-Wilmersdorf), specialising in art, architecture and design, and occupying one of the arched S-Bahn railway vaults along the south side of the square. Savignyplatz itself provided the backdrop for scenes in the 1972 film *Cabaret*, based on Christopher Isherwood's *Berlin* novels and starring Liza Minnelli (it was in venues such as the film's Kit Kat Club that *Berliner Schnauze* was perfected, the quick, sardonic wit still sometimes employed by Berliners today). The surrounding area boasts numerous other interesting bookshops including Marga Schoeller Bücherstube at Knesebackstrasse 33, a traditional

The Bücherbogen bookshop inside a railway arch on Savignyplatz

independent bookseller offering both German- and English-language titles, Gelikon Russian Books (Gelikon Russische Bücher) at Kantstrasse 84, and the Yamashina Japanese Bookshop (Japanische Buchhandlung Yamashina) at Pestalozzistrasse 67.

Probably the most dynamic environment in which to buy books is at one of Berlin's 40 or more weekend antique and flea markets. The largest and most popular is the Trödel- und Kunsthandwerkermarkt an der Strasse des 17. Juni (Charlottenburg-Wilmersdorf), with books, magazines and bric-a-brac on one side of the Charlottenburg Bridge (Charlottenburger Brücke), and arts and crafts on the other. Farther east is the Bücherhändler vor der Uni, held daily in front of the Humboldt University at Unter den Linden 6, and the Berliner Kunstmarkt am Zeughaus a little farther on, which also sells general antiques. Around the corner is the Antik- und Buchmarkt am Bodemuseum on Am Kupfergraben, which offers not only books but also records, postcards, and other ephemera.

Other noteworthy fleamarkets include the Antikmarkt Ostbahnhof on Erich-Steinfurth-Strasse (Friedrichshain-Kreuzberg), the Trödelhallen Eichenstrasse in a converted bus depot at the corner of Puschkinallee and Eichenstrasse (Treptow-Köpenick), and the Trödelmarkt auf dem Fehrbelliner Platz (Charlottenburg-Wilmersdorf).

Other places of interest nearby: 78

78 Waterworks and Water Towers

District IX (Treptow-Köpenick), the Waterworks Museum
(Museum im Wasserwerk Friedrichshagen) at Müggelsee-
damm 307
S3, RE1 Friedrichshagen, then Tram 60 Altes Wasserwerk

The suburb of Friedrichshagen, far out on the shores of the Grosser Müggelsee, was founded in 1753 by King Frederick II, 'the Great' (1740–1786) as a village of Bohemian silk and cotton spinners. This accounts for the two mulberry trees for silkworms still growing in the old market square on Bölschestrasse. The silk industry was shortlived, however, and during the second half of the 19th century Friedrichshagen turned to tourism instead, trading on the attractions of the nearby lake. It was also during this period that Friedrichshagen became home to Europe's largest and most modern municipal waterworks and wastewater treatment plant.

Until the 1850s much of Berlin's water was drawn either from stagnant wells or else taken directly from the polluted River Spree: its wastewater was poured directly back into the river, via a series of unhygienic open ditches that promoted cholera and typhoid. Evidence of one of the earliest attempts at providing the city with clean water can be found in a small park at the corner of Belforter Strasse and Kolmarerstrasse in Prenzlauer Berg (Pankow). It was here in 1856 that Berlin's first town waterworks were constructed (by the English firm Fox and Crampton) on a hill formerly occupied by windmills. Clean water was pumped from the upper Spree into a specially-constructed reservoir on the hill, the outflow regulated by means of a minaret-like brick-built standpipe, which is still

The pump room at Berlin's Waterworks Museum in Friedrichshagen

there today. In the same year the city's first wastewater treatment plant was constructed outside Stralauer Tor by the Oberbaum Bridge (Oberbaumbrücke).

In 1873, with disease still rife and Berlin's population on the increase, the municipal council took over the city's water supply and employed city planner James Hobrecht (1825–1902) to draft an ambitious wastewater system for the whole city. Comprising 12 radial networks it included numerous steam-powered pumping stations used to transfer sewage to water treatment plants beyond the city limits. The first of these stations was built in 1876 at Hallesches Ufer 78 on the Landwehrkanal, in a surprisingly ornate brick building (see no. 63). This deliberate concealment of a pumping station's function behind a decorative façade is taken to an extreme on Breite Strasse in Potsdam, where a pump built in 1843 to transfer water to the fountains of nearby Sanssouci Park was rendered by the architect Ludwig Persius (1803–1845) in the style of an Islamic mosque, complete with domed roof and minaret-shaped chimney!

Water towers were a major part of Berlin's new water system, a 30 metre-high, brick-built neo-Gothic example of which was built in 1873 alongside the old waterworks on Belforter Strasse, heralding the arrival of Germany's first pressurised running water supply. The two brick-vaulted reservoirs used to store the water prior to supply were abandoned in 1914 and used thereafter as cold stores. However, they also had a more sinister role to play in the days following the Reichstag fire on 27th February 1933, when the brownshirts of the SA (*Sturmabteilung*) used them to detain and torture Communist and Socialist opponents of the Nazi regime, thus enabling Hitler to secure a sufficient proportion of votes to assume power. (The reservoirs can be visited as part of a guided tour offered by the Under Berlin Association (unter-berlin e.V.); the tower has since been converted into an apartment complex.)

In line with Hobrecht's plan a second wastewater treatment plant was opened in Tegel in 1877, and the network was completed in 1893 with the opening of a third waterworks at Friedrichshagen. The latter comprises an extensive complex of pumping and filtration facilities spread across a 55 hectare site, which stretches far back from the lakeside on Müggelseedamm. Built to an overall design by the director of the city's water department, the Englishman Henry Gill, the machinery is contained within red-brick superstructures cleverly designed by the architect Richard Schultze to mimic traditional Brandenburg buildings.

In 1987, after the Friedrichshagen works had become redundant, a part of it was opened as the Friedrichshagen Waterworks

Museum (Museum im Wasserwerk Friedrichshagen). The museum excels in making the history of Berlin's water supply and wastewater treatment of interest to everyone, from earliest times through the dislocation of war and division, right up to the present day. The highlight of a visit is undoubtedly the machine hall with its three steam-powered pumping engines, used until 1979 to draw water from the lake as part of the purification process. One of the engines is set in motion for visitors at weekends, albeit using electricity. (The museum also offers occasional guided tours of the wastewater tunnels themselves, for example beneath the streets of Prenzlauer Berg and Schöneberg, details of which can be found on the museum's website at www.bwb.de).

Visiting Berlin's many and varied water towers makes for a thematic journey in itself, the earliest invariably built in the same sturdy crenellated neo-Gothic style seen on Belforter Strasse. They include one built in 1888 on the corner of Fidicinstrasse and Kopischstrasse (Friedrichshain-Kreuzberg) and another built in 1881 at Akazienallee 35–39 (Charlottenburg-Wilmersdorf). The latter was supplemented by a more slender tower in 1910, representative of the move away from the neo-Gothic style during the early decades of the 20th century. Examples of this new, streamlined design include the Altglienicke tower at Schirnerstrasse 17–19 (Treptow-Köpenick), another alongside the Ostkreuz S-Bahn station on Hauptstrasse (Friedrichshain-Kreuzberg), and the ribbed brick tower incorporated into the Volkspark Jungfernheide (Charlottenburg-Wilmersdorf), designed by the renowned landscape architect Erwin Barth (see no. 30). Lofty four-sided towers also became popular during this time, as witnessed on Am Wasserturm in the suburb of Heinersdorf (Pankow), as well as on Brunnenstrasse (Mitte), the latter with a public clock incorporated into its façade. Unique for this period is the elegant, neo-Classical tower in the Steglitz Cemetery (Friedhof Steglitz), just off Hühnensteig (Steglitz-Zehlendorf): erected in 1919 it has pilasters topped with capitals and an observatory-like dome on top.

Hand-in-hand with Berlin's improved sanitation went the erection of ornate cast-iron water pumps, and eight-sided, cast iron mens' urinals. The latter first appeared in 1863 and were known euphemistically as 'Café Achteck' (Café Octagon) because of their shape.

Other places of interest nearby: 77

79 Where the Second World War Ended

District XI (Lichtenberg), the German-Russian Museum
Berlin-Karlshorst (Deutsch-Russisches Museum Berlin-
Karlshorst) at Zwieseler Strasse 4
RE1, 2 Karlshorst; S3 Karlshorst

It is difficult today to appreciate the role played by the unassuming Berlin suburb of Karlshorst in the demise of the Third Reich. It was certainly a very different place on Sunday 22nd April 1945, as troops of the German SS *Nordland* division pulled back here during the Red Army's ferocious siege of the city. A little farther north German troops were trying desperately to protect the entrance to Berlin along Reichsstrasse 1, the Autobahn that led eastwards to the now devastated East Prussian capital of Königsberg. One German detachment made a stand alongside Karlshorst's trotting racetrack (*Trabrennbahn*) but soon came under heavy artillery fire and was forced to abandon Karlshorst altogether. With the suburb neutralised Marshal Georgy Zhukov (1896–1974), commander of the Red Army's 1st Belorussian Front, established his headquarters in an abandoned *Wehrmacht* engineering college at Zwieseler Strasse 4. The German military would not be seen again in Karlshorst until 8th May, when representatives of its three armed forces were brought here to sign Germany's final unconditional surrender.

Although Nazi Germany's fate had been sealed since its ill-advised invasion of the Soviet Union (Operation Barbarossa) in 1941, the immediate events leading up to the surrender at Karlshorst began with Hitler's suicide in his personal command shelter (*Führerbunker*) on 30th April 1945 (see no. 10). The next day Nazi Germany's new Chancellor Joseph Goebbels (1897–1945) sent General Hans Krebs (1898–1945), Chief of Army General Staff, to negotiate a conditional ceasefire with General Vasily Chuikov (1900–1982), commander of Soviet forces in central Berlin, whose command post was at Schulenburgring 2, near Tempelhof Airport. Not surprisingly the German proposal that the newly-formed government of Reichspräsident Karl Dönitz (1891–1980) be recognised by the Soviet Union *before* German forces downed their weapons was rejected, and Krebs returned to Goebbels empty-handed. Realising the Nazis were playing for time Zhukov demanded an unconditional surrender from Goebbels by 10.15am the same morning. When there was

Second World War artillery outside the German-Russian Museum in Karlshorst

no response Zhukov's 1st Belorussian Front unleashed a "hurricane of fire" on what was left of Hitler's capital.

Meanwhile, Goebbels and his wife Magda set about killing their six children and then themselves. Those still left in the Führer Bunker now either followed suit, attempted to escape, or else awaited the arrival of the Red Army. Faced with no choice, General Helmuth Weidling (1891–1955), the recently appointed Supreme Commander of the Defence Area Berlin, arrived at General Chuikov's command post on 2nd May and surrendered the city. As word of his order to lay down arms spread, German troops elsewhere began making fighting withdrawals in a series of frenzied attempts to surrender to the Western Allies rather than to the avenging Red Army.

Meanwhile, on 4th May the first of several instruments of surrender was signed, on this occasion by Admiral Hans-Georg von Friedeburg (1895–1945) on Lüneburg Heath (Lüneburger Heide) in Lower Saxony; it applied to all German forces in north-west Germany, Denmark and Holland. On 7th May the Western Allies summoned German commanders to the headquarters in Rheims of General Dwight Eisenhower (1890–1969), Supreme Allied Commander of the Allied Expeditionary Force, to sign a full and unconditional surrender of all German forces. This time Dönitz authorised Colonel-General Alfred Jodl (1890–1946) of the German Armed Forces High Command to sign the document, which stipulated that "All forces under German control...cease active operations at 23:01 hours Central European Time on 8th May 1945."

However, although a Soviet representative countersigned the surrender, Stalin requested that a second surrender be taken in Berlin by the Red Army, whom he claimed had borne the brunt of the fighting. So it was that during the evening of 8th May a second full surrender was signed at Marshall Zhukov's headquarters in Karlshorst. The signees again included Admiral von Friedeburg, together with Field Marshal Wilhelm Keitel (1882–1946), Chief of Staff of the Armed Forces High Command, and Colonel-General Hans-Jürgen Stumpff (1889–1968) representing the air force. The ceremony was witnessed by Arthur Tedder (1890–1967), Marshall of the Royal Air Force, who was acting as Eisenhower's representative, General Carl Spaatz (1891–1974), commander of the American Airforce in Europe, and General Jean de Lattre de Tassigny (1889–1952), commander of the First French Army. The Second World War in Europe had finally ended.

After the surrender Zhukov's headquarters in Karlshorst became the first command post of the Soviet military administration in occupied Germany. In 1949 the post was moved to Wunsdorf, south of Berlin, and in 1967 the Soviets converted the Karlshorst building into the so-called Museum of the Unconditional Surrender of Fascist Germany in the Great Patriotic War, displaying weapons, flags and uniforms from the Red Army's campaigns against Nazi Germany. When Russian troops eventually withdrew from Berlin in 1994, both Germans and Russians co-operated in handing over the museum, which was re-named the German-Russian Museum Berlin-Karlshorst (Deutsch-Russisches Museum Berlin-Karlshorst).

The museum's previous anti-Fascist bias has now been replaced by a more generalised emphasis on the suffering of civilians and soldiers on both sides. The officers' mess in which the surrender was signed has been preserved, as has Marshall Zhukov's former office. The garden contains a collection of Russian military equipment used in the Battle of Berlin, including a Katjuscha multiple rocket launcher dubbed a *Stalinorgel* ('Stalin Organ'). Visitors should be glad never to stand next to one in action!

80 The Extraordinary Life of Charlotte von Mahlsdorf

District X (Marzahn-Hellersdorf), the Mahlsdorf Manor and Gründerzeit Museum at Hultschiner Damm 333
S5 Mahlsdorf

Far out in the suburb of Mahlsdorf, where eastern Berlin gives way to Brandenburg, there stands an old house called Mahlsdorf Manor. Surrounded by tall trees, meadows and flower gardens the 200-year-old house would have been demolished were it not for the efforts of Charlotte von Mahlsdorf (1928–2002), undoubtedly one of Berlin's most colourful characters.

Charlotte von Mahlsdorf was actually born Lothar Berfelde, in Mahlsdorf on 18th March 1928. Although male, from his childhood onwards Lothar felt female inside, and according to his autobiography already enjoyed wearing girls' clothes. He also liked "old stuff" and often helped a second-hand goods dealer he knew to clear out apartments, mostly those of Jews deported under the Third Reich, retaining particular items for his own collection. Not surprisingly, one of Lothar's favourite childhood pastimes was to wear an apron and dust porcelain.

By the late 1920s Lothar's father had become an enthusiastic member of the Nazi Party and in 1942 he forced his son to join the Hitler Youth. The two often quarrelled and in 1944 Lothar's mother left the family. His father demanded that Lothar choose between his parents and even threatened him with a gun; shortly afterwards Lothar killed his father with a rolling pin while he slept. As a result, in January 1945 Lothar was sentenced to four years' detention as a juvenile delinquent, although he was released as soon as the war was over.

Now working fulltime in the second-hand goods business, and dressing publicly in

The former home of Charlotte von Mahlsdorf

women's clothing, Lothar re-invented himself as Charlotte von Mahlsdorf, taking the name from his cross-dressing, lesbian aunt's lover. He also began accumulating old-fashioned everyday household articles, saving them from the city's many bombed-out houses and taking advantage of the house clearances of people departing for West Germany. His collection gradually evolved into the Gründerzeit Museum, so-called because many of the items dated back to the late 19th century. During the 1950s Charlotte became involved in efforts to preserve the crumbling Mahlsdorf Manor, which was threatened with demolition, and she was eventually given the house to occupy rent free. In 1960 it became the permanent home of the Gründerzeit Museum, as well as a popular meeting place for those in cinematic, artistic and gay circles; during the early 1970s members of the East Berlin gay scene often held meetings here. As she commented at the time: "Nothing would have come to fruition if I had not had a feminine disposition in a masculine body. This museum is here because I played with doll's house furniture as a child, because I am still a cleaning lady today, because I enjoy this *Gründerzeit* period and because I always wanted to have a household around me".

When in 1974 the East German authorities announced their intention to bring the museum under state control Charlotte protested by giving away exhibits to visitors. With help from her supporters – and possibly due to her alleged enlistment as a Stasi collaborator – the authorities decided in 1976 that Charlotte could keep her museum. However, in 1991 neo-Nazis broke up one of her museum soirées and several participants were hurt. Despite receiving an Order of Merit in 1992 for her museum work, Charlotte announced she was leaving Germany and in 1995 guided her last visitor through Mahlsdorf Manor; in 1997 she moved to Porla Brunn in Sweden, where she opened a new museum. Fortunately for today's visitors the Gründerzeit Museum is still open, having been purchased by the City of Berlin, who now manage it as a trust.

Charlotte von Mahlsdorf died from heart failure during a return visit to Berlin on 30th April 2002 and was buried next to her mother in Mahlsdorf Cemetery (Friedhof Mahlsdorf) on Walter-Leistikow-Weg. Even in death, however, Charlotte courted controversy. An argument broke out between her family and the museum trust regarding the inscription on her memorial. The trust wanted the words "Ich bin meine eigene Frau" ("I am my own wife"), from the title of her autobiography; in the end her relatives insisted on "Lothar Berfelde, 1928–2002, known as Charlotte von Mahlsdorf".

81 In an Oriental Teahouse

District X (Marzahn-Hellersdorf), Berölin teahouses old and
new including the Chinese Teahouse – Mountain Lodge of the
Osmanthus Sap (Chinesisches Teehaus – Berghaus zum Osmanthussaft) in the Gärten der Welt/Erholungspark Marzahn
at Eisenacher Strasse 99
S7 Marzahn; U5 Cottbuser Platz

Although Berlin's historic coffeehouse tradition was all but extinguished during the Second World War, the city's Oriental teahouse culture remains vibrant. An appropriate centre for it is a park far to the east, in the suburb of Marzahn, where in 1987 a permanent display called the Gardens of the World (Gärten der Welt) was created. Clearly signposted from the main entrance can be found several delightful Asian-style gardens, including the Balinese Garden of the Three Harmonies (Garten der drei Harmonien), the Korean Seoul Garden (Seouler Garten), and the Japanese Garden of the Water Confluence (Garten des zusammen-fliessenden Wassers). Most atmospheric of all is the Chinese Garden of the Newly Won Moon (Garten des wiedergewonnen Mondes), designed by experts from the Peking Institute for Classical Gardening and fi-nanced by Volkswagen Shanghai. Its focal point is a lake on the edge of which stands the Mountain Lodge of the Osmanthus Sap (Berghaus zum Osmanthussaft), a traditional Chinese teahouse named after a fra-grant evergreen plant used in perfumes. Visitors can take tea either in the house itself, with its delicate latticework windows, or else on the terrace built out over the lake. By prior arrangement a traditional hour-long Chinese tea ceremony can be arranged during which the physical and the philosophical characteristics of tea drinking will be revealed. Indeed it should be stressed that the true art of Chinese tea drinking is found not only in a cup but also in the drinker's harmonious bond with nature, hence the traditional location of a teahouse within a garden.

For those wishing to immerse themselves further in the world of teadrinking a trip to the Berlin Teahouse (Berliner Teesalon) at Stutt-garter Platz 15 (Charlottenburg-Wilmersdorf) is highly recommended. The staff are more than happy to share their expertise with customers, which is useful to know considering that there are 300 types of tea for sale, not only from China and Japan but also Taiwan, Ceylon, India and Nepal. Pride of place goes to the rare, white Silver Needle Tea, as well as those from the secret teagardens of China, once reserved for the exclusive use of the Emperor. In the cosy tearoom itself the visitor is surrounded by a fascinating display of tea receptacles, including traditional Japanese earthenware *Raku* tea bowls, paper-thin Chinese porcelain teapots, and silver-plated Oriental teapots.

A somewhat different teadrinking experience is offered by the Tajikistan Tearoom (Tadshikische Teestube) at Oranienburger Strasse 27 (Mitte). Until recently it was located in the Palais am Festungsgraben at Am Festungsgraben 1, which for many years was home to the Prussian finance minister. However, between 1949 and 1990, when East Berlin was a part of the GDR (German Democratic Republic), the building served as the House of Soviet Culture (Haus der Kultur Sowjetunion). The tearoom, with its carved pillars, ceiling beams, cushion-covered divans, rugs, and wall murals, was once part of a Tajikistani display at a Leipzig trade fair in the 1970s and was installed in the palace after being presented as a gift to the GDR by the Soviet Union (Tajikistan being part of the USSR at the time). Visitors wishing to experience the Soviet-Central Asian tea ritual these days are asked to remove their shoes upon arrival and to then sit on the cushions laid out around the low tables. Smoking and beer-drinking are forbidden, and instead strong tea and water is mixed from a *samovar* and accompanied by sweets, dried oranges and lemons, and raisins for sweetness, sugar having always been a rarity. To neutralise the sweetness Russian soldiers drank a shot of Vodka between rounds of tea, a custom that is continued in the relocated tearoom today.

During the 18th and 19th centuries tea drinking was a fashionable pastime for Prussian royalty and several of their teahouses can still be seen in Berlin today, for example the Belvedere in the gardens at Schloss Charlottenburg. Designed in 1788 by the architect Carl Gotthard Langhans (1732–1808) for King Frederick William II (1786–1797) the green and white building, featuring a combination of curvilinear Baroque and neo-Classical elements, is three storeys high. It contains a porcelain collection from the Royal Porcelain Workshop (Königliche Porzellan Manufaktur) at Wegelystrasse 1 (Charlottenburg-Wilmersdorf), founded in 1763 by King Frederick II, 'the Great' (1740–1786) as a rival to Meissen.

Rather more modest is the Swiss-style Gasthaus Moorlake, off Nikolskoer Weg on Wannsee Island, which was built in 1841 to a design by Ludwig Persius (1803–1845) as a forester's house with a royal tearoom upstairs; today it serves as a restaurant. Farther west, along Königstrasse, is Schloss Glienicke next to which stands the so-called 'little curiosity' (Kleine Neugierde), a 1796 teahouse rebuilt by

A Chinese teahouse,
part of Marzahn's
Gardens of the World

the architect Carl Frederick Schinkel (1781–1841) as part of his brief to embellish the estate after it had been purchased in 1824 by Prince Carl of Prussia, son of King Frederick William III (1797–1840) (see no. 47). Finally, and farther west again, in Sanssouci Park in Potsdam, there stands a glittering Chinese Teahouse (Chinesisches Teehaus) on Ökonomieweg (Rehgarten), built in 1754–56 on the orders of Frederick the Great to a design by Johann Gottfried Büring. A real Orientalist fantasy, the pavilion is adorned with gilded, stereotypical Chinese figures and reflects the prevailing interest in Chinese art during the Rococo period.

Berlin's café society of the Golden Twenties (*Goldene Zwanziger*) is long gone, the legendary Café des Westens, Romanisches Café, and Café Josty consigned to history together with their intellectual habitués. But a glimpse of this vanished world can be still be had at Café Einstein at Kurfürstenstrasse 58 (Mitte), a Viennese-style coffee house in a villa used in Weimar times as a gambling den by the rich and famous.

82 Who was Rosa Luxemburg?

District XI (Lichtenberg), the Friedrichsfelde Cemetery (Zentralfriedhof Friedrichsfelde) on Gudrunstrasse
S5, S7, S75 Friedrichsfelde Ost; U5 Lichtenberg

Prior to the Second World War, Rosa-Luxemburg-Strasse was not a separate street but rather a continuation of Kaiser-Wilhelm-Strasse, which led from the old royal palace (Stadtschloss) on Museum Island (Museumsinsel), northeastwards out of the city. It was re-named in memory of Rosa Luxemburg (1870–1919) by the GDR regime, for whom she was an icon following her murder during the failed Communist revolt in Berlin in 1919; likewise, the rest of the street was named after her murdered accomplice Karl Liebknecht (1871–1919). Their story played an important part in attempts at preventing Germany's slide towards Fascism and explains why reunified Berlin decided to retain these particular street names, whilst most GDR-era names were expunged. Luxemburg's statement that "freedom must always mean freedom for those who think differently" may well have helped.

Rosa Luxemburg was born in Poland but settled in Germany in 1895, where she acquired German nationality through marriage. During the First World War she co-operated with Karl Liebknecht in anti-war propaganda and demonstrations, and together they founded the Spartacist League (Spartakusbund), which later became part of the German Communist Party. Liebknecht himself was the son of German Socialist Wilhelm Liebknecht (1826–1900), who had participated in the 1848 Revolution and was imprisoned for opposing the Franco-Prussian War. Both men entered the Reichstag as Social Democrats.

Germany's humiliation in 1919 under the terms of the Treaty of Versailles had polarised political opinions in Berlin, with the impoverished working classes favouring Communist revolution and the frustrated military favouring a more right-wing approach. Despite being imprisoned for their political beliefs in 1918, Luxemburg and Liebknecht continued to pursue their Communist dreams. On 9th November 1918, the same day that King and Emperor William II (1888–1918) was forced to abdicate, Philipp Scheidemann's Social Democrats proclaimed a Democratic Republic at the Reichstag, whilst Liebknecht proclaimed his Free Socialist Republic two hours later from the royal palace (Stadtschloss) on Schlossplatz.

A convoluted series of negotiations followed during which attempts were made to satisfy the conflicting interests of workers, soldiers, monarchists, and liberals. Little satisfied the Spartacists and in January 1919 they staged an uprising in Berlin and Munich. As the left-wing revolt threatened to transform both cities into proletarian bastions even the staunchest Social Democrats, such as Reich Chancellor Friedrich Ebert, turned to the right-wing paramilitary *Freikorps* to suppress it. It was a fatal move since the ensuing Communist defeat gave the right-wing their first taste of blood, and the Social Democrats lost all hope of future support from the Communists. The new Weimar Republic (Weimarer Republik), named after a provincial town in Thuringia, where its constitution was written on January 19th far from Berlin's troubled streets, was thus weakened before it had even taken office.

The Socialist Memorial in the Friedrichsfelde Cemetery

Meanwhile, on 15th January Luxemburg and Liebknecht had been arrested by right-wing army officers. After interrogation they were taken away and murdered: Luxemburg near the Lichtenstein Bridge (Lichtenstein Brücke) – marked today by a steel memorial rearing up out of the Landwehkanal into which her body was dumped – and Liebknecht on the bank of the Neuer See in the Tiergarten. Their funeral was held on 25th January just inside the main entrance of the Friedrichsfelde Cemetery (Zentralfriedhof Friedrichsfelde) on Gudrunstrasse, a paupers' graveyard far out in the district of Lichtenberg, the city denying the Communist Party a more prominent location. Rosa Luxemburg's coffin was actually empty since her body was not retrieved until the end of May; she was eventually buried on 13th June. The graves were marked in 1926 by a brick memorial wall designed by Mies van der Rohe, intended to evoke the walls against which historical revolutionaries had traditionally been shot.

By 1930 the Social Democrats could barely hold the republic together, especially after the Wall Street Crash had removed any chance of a long-awaited economic revival. Far from supporting democracy during such times of hardships, many Germans now blamed the republic. As unemployment soared, and Communists fought pro-Nazi SA (*Sturmabteilung*) brownshirts on the streets, Adolf Hitler bided his time. In

December 1932 Franz von Papen resigned as Chancellor and in January 1933 Hitler took his place. With the death in 1934 of Reich President Field Marshall Paul von Hindenburg Hitler declared the presidency permanently vacant and declared himself Leader *and* Chancellor (Führer und Reichskanzler). His contempt for the old regime is all too clearly demonstrated by a memorial on Scheidemannstrasse, which recalls 96 members of the Weimar-era Reichstag murdered by the Nazis.

Not surprisingly, in 1935 the graves of Luxemburg and Liebknecht were desecrated by the Nazis and the memorial wall torn down, as a result of which the bodies were lost (the original gravestones survive in the German Historical Museum (Deutsches Historisches Museum) at Unter den Linden 2). Already on 23rd January 1933 the Nazis had closed down Karl-Liebknecht-Haus, the headquarters of the German Communist Party at Weydingerstrasse 14–16. Later the same month they reopened the building as a Gestapo interrogation centre named after Horst Wessel (1907–1930), an SA member killed by Communists and transformed into a Nazi hero by Propaganda Minister Joseph Goebbels (1897–1945). Wessel was buried amidst considerable pomp in the now overgrown Cemetery of St. Nicholas (St. Nikolai-Friedhof) at the corner of Prenzlauer Allee and Moll Strasse.

The Communists got their revenge, however, when the former Karl-Liebknecht-Haus was returned to them after the war (it today serves as the headquarters the Left Party (Die Linke), which was born out of the post-communist Party of Democratic Socialism (PDS), itself the successor to the Socialist Unity Party of Germany (SED) that ruled East Germany until 1989). Additionally, an impressive Socialist Memorial (Gedenkstätte Sozialisten) was erected in the Friedrichsfelde Cemetery. Inscribed *Die Toten mahnen uns* (The dead admonish us) it became the last resting place for many of Berlin's important socialist and communist leaders, including Ernst Thälmann, the pre-1933 leader of the German Communist Party, Wilhelm Pieck, the first President of the GDR, and Walter Ulbricht, the GDR leader responsible for the construction of the Berlin Wall.

83 Evidence of a Forgotten Industry

District III (Pankow), a tour of old breweries starting with the former Königstadt Brewery (Königstadt-Brauerei) at Saarbrücker Strasse 22–24
U2 Senefelderplatz

Although wines from southern and western Germany are readily available in Berlin the city itself has very few productive vineyards because of the cold climate. Instead, beer is Berlin's most widely drunk alcoholic beverage, much of it produced in modern breweries such as Schultheiss, Berliner Kindl, Engelhardt, and Berliner Pilsner. It should not be forgotten, however, that during the 19th century Berlin also had a brewing industry, and it was bigger even than that of Munich. Unfortunately, by the end of the Second World War, those breweries that hadn't closed down through competition had been seriously damaged by Allied bombing; furthermore, those finding themselves in East Berlin would soon be asset-stripped or else mothballed indefinitely.

Berlin's 19th century brewing industry was based predominantly in the Prenzlauer Berg (Pankow) and Friedrichshain-Kreuzberg districts. Walking these streets today in search of the visually arresting, if occasionally forlorn, remains of this closed chapter of Berlin's industrial history can be enlightening. A case in point is the complex of cavernous, brick-vaulted cellars below the former Königstadt Brewery (Königstadtbrauerei) at Saarbrücker Strasse 22–24, which can be visited as part of a monthly guided tour offered by the Under Berlin Association (unter-berlin e.V.). Constructed in 1850 the sturdily constructed cellars were used until 1921 to brew and store six types of beer. During the Second World War they were reused as an air raid shelter (*Luftschutzraum*) and later still, during the Cold War era when they lay in East Berlin, their cool temperatures meant they were ideal for mushroom growing. Today the former brewery is administered by a cooperative that hires out the premises for cultural and other events.

That the surrounding area was once dominated by the brewing industry is witnessed by the existence of several other disused breweries closeby, including the Bötzow Brewery (Bötzowbrauerei) at the corner of Saarbrücker Strasse and Prenzlauer Allee, and the Pfefferberg Brewery (Pfefferburgbrauerei) at Schönhauser Allee 176, the latter with buildings and cellars dating back to the 1840s. Largest of all was the

Schultheiss Brewery (Schultheissbrauerei), occupying the entire block between Schönhauser Allee, Knaack-, Sredzki- and Danziger Strasse, which can be visited (together with the Bötzow Brewery) as part of a thematic bus tour every two months, again offered by the Under Berlin Association. It was established in 1864 and the present buildings were erected in 1889–1892 to a design by the renowned architect Franz Heinrich Schwechten (1841–1924), who was also responsible for the Anhalt Railway Station (Anhalter Bahnhof) and the Emperor William Memorial Church (Kaiser-Wilhelm-Gedächtnis-Kirche). Consisting of six courtyards and more than twenty buildings, each with mock medieval façades and towers in red and yellow brick, the brewery is considered an important example of a late 19th century industrial complex built within a predominantly residential district.

In 1987, twenty years after its closure, the Schultheiss Brewery was converted into a cultural and entertainment centre, known as the Kulturbrauerei. Many of the brewery's old buildings have been conveniently named to remind onlookers of their former use, for example 'Flaschenbier-abteilung' (beer bottling plant), where 30000 bottles were once filled daily. (Another successful brewery conversion is that of the relatively tiny Josty Brewery (Jostybrauerei) in a courtyard at Bergstrasse 22 (Mitte), its ornate red-brick building now a restaurant).

In neighbouring Friedrichshain-Kreuzberg there are further interesting brewing remains to be seen, including the former Patzenhofer Brewery (Patzenoferbrauerei) at the corner of Landsberger Allee 54 with Richard-Sorge-Strasse 51–62, and the former Bock Brewery (Bockbrauerei) at Fidicinstrasse 3, the latter founded in 1838 and now operating as a small business centre, some of its vaulted cellars providing atmospheric storage facilities for Paasburg's wine shop. Of particular interest is the former Tivoli brewery on Methfesselstrasse, founded in the 1850s and named after the Tivoli amusement park that stood on the southern slope of the nearby Kreuzberg. In 1891 the brewery was acquired by its rival, Schultheiss, which became Germany's largest brewer. Despite air raid shelters being built into its cellars in the late 1930s, and the complex being damaged during the Second World War, production continued here until 1993, with horse-drawn wagons being used until 1981. The buildings are now slowly being converted into residential and commercial units.

During the early decades of the 19th century Berliners drank weak and sour, top-fermented beers, which were supplemented in the second half of the century by the light and smooth, bottom-fermented beers of Bavaria. The construction of capacious subterranean storage cellars enabled Berlin's brewers to maintain the cool temperatures required to produce these commercially viable beers, which they still do to this day. Unique to Berlin, however, is the *Berliner Weisse*, a top-fermented, malted wheat beer first mentioned in 1642, which is slightly cloudy and low in alcohol (c. 2.8% ABV). Served in a large goblet, the sour taste is mitigated by adding red raspberry-, yellow lemon- or green Woodruff-flavoured syrup, resulting in a *Weisse mit Schuss* ('Weisse with a shot'). Served throughout Berlin it is particularly refreshing during the hot summer months.

Deserted buildings at the former Tivoli brewery on Methfesselstrasse

To understand the techniques employed by Germany's brewers a century ago, a visit to the German Technical Museum (Deutsches Technikmuseum Berlin) at Trebbiner Strasse 9 (Friedrichshain-Kreuzberg) is recommended. In a former cold storage warehouse once used by the Freiherrlich von Tucher'sche Brewery of Nuremberg there is a reconstructed brewery dating back to 1909 illustrating the complete process of traditional brewing. A traditional place to drink German beer is in an *Altberliner Kneipe* such as Zur Kneipe at Rankestrasse 9 (Charlottenburg-Wilmersdorf). Equally traditional is an outdoor beer garden *(Biergarten)* such as Schleusenkrug on Müller-Breslau-Strasse (Mitte).

Other places of interest nearby: 1, 2, 3, 5, 6, 7, 16, 17, 18, 19, 84

84 Five Jewish Cemeteries

District III (Pankow), Berlin's Jewish cemeteries including the Jewish Cemetery (Jüdischer Friedhof) at Schönhauser Allee 23–25
U2 Senefelderplatz

Although Berlin's once thriving Jewish community was all but extinguished by the Nazis during the 1930s and 40s, the streets around Grosse Hamburger Strasse, north of the River Spree, still resonate with Jewish culture both old and new. Known originally as the *Scheunenviertel*, or 'Barn Quarter', the area was established in 1671, when Frederick William, the Great Elector (1640–1688) moved his highly flammable hay barns beyond the city boundary (see no. 54). From this time onwards the area became a refuge for Jews fleeing Russia and Eastern Europe, and by the 19th century it had become a well-established centre for Berlin's Jewish community.

In 1672 the city's Old Jewish Cemetery (Alter Jüdischer Friedhof) was founded on Grosse Hamburger Strasse, just beyond where a group of bronze figures today marks the former site of the city's first Jewish old peoples' home (it was used by the Nazis as an assembly point for deportations to the death camps at Auschwitz and Theresianstadt). Containing some 12 000 burials it was systematically destroyed by the Gestapo in 1943. After the war the former cemetery became a park reserved for quiet contemplation. Only the headstone of the enlightened philosopher and social activist Moses Mendelssohn (1729–1786) has been reinstated, its flat surfaces covered in 'memory stones' left by visitors. Mendelssohn was a passionate advocate of Jewish emancipation and is generally credited with the renaissance of European Jewry during the 18th century; he is also remembered as the grandfather of the composer Felix Mendelssohn (see no. 62). All the cemetery's other Baroque-era grave markers (known as *masebas*) have either been destroyed or else incorporated into the perimeter wall.

It is an example of the tolerance for which Berlin was known at the time that the city's Old Jewish Cemetery was declared exempt from a law of 1794 prohibiting further burials in cemeteries within the city walls. Not until 1827 was it eventually declared full and a new Jewish cemetery opened *outside* the city walls at Schönhauser Allee 23–25 (Pankow). This one contains 22 000 graves offering a fascinating cross-section of the city's 19th century Jewish community. They include the composer and musical director of Berlin's State Opera Giacomo Meyerbeer (1791–1864), Prussian Chancellor Otto von Bismarck's banker Gerson Bleichröder (1822–1893), and the prominent Jewish scholars Abraham Geiger (1810–1874), Leopold Zunz (1794–1886) and David Friedländer (1750–1834), the latter responsible for one of the first translations of the Jewish prayer book into German. Few burials occurred here after 1880 due to lack of space, although a notable ex-

An abandoned Jewish cemetery on Schönhauser Allee

ception was the Berlin painter Max Liebermann (1847–1935). In 1943 his wife Martha committed suicide, after hearing that the Gestapo were about to deport her to the concentration camp at Theresianstadt, and she was buried alongside him (see no. 45). Equally tragic is a plaque recalling a group of army deserters, who hid in a water cistern here during the last months of the war only to be found by the SS and hung from the surrounding trees. The cemetery today is a melancholic place, its myriad grey stones covered with ivy.

Beyond the back wall of the cemetery is the so-called *Judengang*, or 'Jews' Walk', closed off at Knaackstrasse 43 by a gateway adorned with the Star of David. This long-abandoned path was a rear entrance to the cemetery, said to have been used by Jewish mourners so as not to disturb King Frederick William III (1797–1840) whilst on his way to and from the Niederschönhausen Palace farther north.

In 1880 Berlin's third and largest Jewish cemetery was opened at Herbert-Baum-Strasse 45 (Pankow), on land that at the time was outside the city. Called the Weissensee Jewish Cemetery (Jüdischer Friedhof Weissensee) it contains 115 000 graves making it the largest Jewish cemetery in Europe. Its most impressive tombs lie inside the perimeter wall on the right-hand side, whilst more modest ones occupy the densely wooded central section. The names and professions of those buried here remind the visitor of just how important Berlin's Jewish community was to the commercial and cultural life of the city. Amongst the industrialists, physicians, entrepreneurs, and artists are the founder of the KaDeWe department store Adolf Jandorf (1870–1932) (Plot T2), the Impressionist painter Lesser Ury (1861–1931) (Plot G1), the Hungarian-born publisher Samuel Fischer (1859–1934) (Plot I4), the co-founder of the Tietz department stores Hermann Tietz (1837–1907) (Plot O2), and the successful restaurateur Berthold Kempinski (1843–1910) (Plot T2), whose family would eventually run the legendary Haus Vaterland restaurant and ballroom on Potsdamer Platz.

The road on which the cemetery stands is named after the anti-Fascist resistance leader Herbert Baum (1912–1942), who is also buried here. Just inside the entrance to the cemetery there is a memorial to the other victims of the Holocaust, with plaques bearing the names of various concentration camps. Another memorial, farther inside the cemetery, is dedicated to those Berlin Jews who died for Germany during the First World War, on battlefields such as Verdun and the Somme.

Berlin has two other Jewish cemeteries that may also be visited. One of them was established in 1955 for the Jews of West Berlin. It can be found adjacent to the British War Cemetery at Scholzplatz, off Heerstrasse, not far from the Olympic Stadium (Olympiastadion) (Charlottenburg-Wilmersdorf). Berlin's fifth and final Jewish cemetery can be found in Potsdam, south of the Pfingstberg ('Whitsuntide Hill') near the Cecilienhof, the very last of the Prussian royal palaces (see no. 68).

Other places of interest nearby: 18, 19, 83

* * *

Standing in any one of Berlin's Jewish cemeteries is the right place to finish this odyssey, during which some of the more unusual and unsung corners of this ever-changing city have been explored. Recalling the myriad physical fragments of Berlin's tumultous past, which helped produce such highs and lows in German history, offers the city explorer the chance to reflect on the many cultures and characters that continue to shape this great metropolis at the heart of Western Europe.

Opening times

for museums and other places of interest

Correct at time of going to press but may be subject to change

Ackerhalle, District I (Mitte), Ackerstrasse 23–26/ Invalidenstrasse 158, Mon–Sat 8am–11pm

Ahmadiyya Mosque (Ahmadiyya-Moschee), District IV (Charlottenburg-Wilmersdorf), Brienner Strasse 7–8, Friday prayers 1pm

Air Force Museum (Luftwaffenmuseum), District V (Spandau), Kladower Damm 182–188, Tue–Sun 10am–6pm

Allied Museum (Alliierten-Museum), District VI (Steglitz-Zehlendorf), Clayallee 135, Tue–Sun 10am–6pm

Altes Zollhaus restaurant, District II (Friedrichshain-Kreuzberg), Carl-Herz-Ufer 30, Tue–Sat 6–11pm

Antik- und Buchmarkt am Bodemuseum, District I (Mitte), Am Kupfergraben, Sat & Sun 11am–5pm

Antikmarkt Ostbahnhof, District II (Friedrichshain-Kreuzberg), Erich-Steinfurth-Strasse, Sun 9am–5pm

Antiquariat Brandel, District IX (Treptow-Köpenick), Scharnweberstrasse 59, Wed–Fri 12am–6pm, Sat 9.30–12am

Anti-War Museum (Anti-Kriegs-Museum), District I (Mitte), Brüsseler Strasse 21, daily 4–8pm

Archenhold Observatory (Archenhold-Sternwarte), District IX (Treptow-Köpenick), Treptower Park, Alt-Treptow 1, Wed–Sun 2–4.30pm

Arminiushalle, District I (Mitte), Bremer Strasse 9/Arminiusstrasse, Mon–Thu 7.30am–6pm, Fri 7.30am–7pm, Sat 7.30am–3pm

Art Library (Kunstbibliothek), District I (Mitte), Matthäikirchplatz 6, Tue–Sun 10am–6pm

Artificium bookshop, District I (Mitte), Rosenthalerstrasse 40–41, Mon–Thu 10am–8pm, Fri & Sat 10am–9pm

Badeschiff, District II (Friedrichshain-Kreuzberg), Eichenstrasse 4, daily 8am–12pm

Barbier- und Friseursalon Kücük Istanbul, District II (Friedrichshain-Kreuzberg), Oranienstrasse 176, Mon–Sat 9am–8pm

Bauhaus Archive (Bauhaus-Archiv), District I (Mitte), Klingelhöferstrasse 14, Wed–Mon 10am–5pm

Baumschulenweg Crematorium, District IX (Treptow-Köpenick), Kiefholzstrasse 221, Mon–Fri 9am–3pm

Beate Uhse Erotik-Museum, District IV (Charlottenburg-Wilmersdorf), Joachimstaler Strasse 4, Mon–Wed 9am–10pm, Thu–Sat 9am–12pm, Sun 11am–10pm

Bell tower at the Olympic Stadium (Glockenturm am Olympiastadion), District IV (Charlottenburg-Wilmersdorf), Passenheimer Strasse, mid Mar–May, Sep & Oct daily 9am–7pm, Jun–mid Sep daily 9am–8pm, Nov–mid Mar Sat & Sun 9am–4pm

Belvedere, District IV (Charlottenburg-Wilmersdorf), Schlosspark Charlottenburg, Spandauer Damm, Apr–Oct Tue–Sun 10am–6pm

Berlin Cathedral (Berliner Dom) **and Hohenzollern Crypt** (Hohenzollerngruft), District I (Mitte), Museum Island (Museumsinsel), Am Lustgarten, Mon–Sat 9am–8pm (7pm in winter), Sun 12am–8pm

Berlin Medical History Museum (Berliner Medizinhistorisches Museum), District I (Mitte), Schumannstrasse 20–21, Tue–Sun 10am–5pm (Wed & Sat 7pm)

Berlin Story, District I (Mitte), Unter den Linden 26, Mon–Sat 10am–7pm, Sun 10am–6pm

Berlin Teahouse (Berliner Teesalon), District IV (Charlottenburg-Wilmersdorf), Stuttgarter Platz 15, Mon–Fri 10am–7pm, Sat 10am–4pm

Berlin U-Bahn Museum (Berliner U-Bahn-Museum), District IV (Charlottenburg-Wilmersdorf), U-Bahnhof Olympia-Stadion (Ost), each second Sat of the month 10.30am–4pm

Berlin Underworlds Association (Berliner Unterwelten e.V.), District I (Mitte), Brunnenstrasse 105, inside the southern entrance of the Gesundbrunnen U-Bahn station, daily 10am–4pm, for tour times and tickets, tel. 0049 (0) 30–49 91 05 17, www.berliner-unterwelten.de

Berlin Wall Memorial (Gedenkstätte Berliner Mauer), District I (Mitte), Bernauer Strasse 111, Apr–Oct Tue–Sun 9.30am–7pm, Nov–Mar Tue–Sun 9.30am–6pm

Berliner Gruselkabinett, District II (Friedrichshain-Kreuzberg), Luftschutzbunker Anhalter Bahnhof, Schöneberger Strasse 23a, Mon 10am–3pm, Tue, Thu, Fri & Sun 10am–7pm, Sat 12am–8pm

Berliner Kunstmarkt am Zeughaus, District I (Mitte), Am Zeughaus, Sat & Sun 11am–5pm

Berliner Zinnfiguren Kabinett, District IV (Charlottenburg-Wilmersdorf), Knesebeckstrasse 88, Mon–Fri 10am–6pm, Sat 10am–3pm

Biolüske, District VI (Steglitz-Zehlendorf), Drakestrasse 50, Mon–Sat 8am–8pm, Sun 8am–2pm

Blockhaus Nikolskoe restaurant, District VI (Steglitz-Zehlendorf), Wannsee island, Nikolskoer Weg 15, Mon–Sat 10.30am–8pm

Blochplatz Cold War shelter, District I (Mitte), for tour times and tickets see Berlin Underworlds Association (Berliner Unterwelten e.V.)

Bode Museum (Bode-Museum), see Museum Island (Museumsinsel)

Botanical Garden and Botanical Museum (Botanischer Garten und Botanisches Museum), District VI (Steglitz-Zehlendorf), Königin-Luise-Strasse 6–8, daily Nov–Jan 9am–4pm, Feb 9am–5pm, Mar & Oct 9am–6pm, Apr & Aug 9am–8pm, May–Jul 9am–9pm, Sep 9am–7pm; museum daily 10am–6pm

Brecht-Weigel Memorial (Brecht-Weigel-Gedenkstätte), District I (Mitte), Chausseestrasse 125, Tue 10am–3.30pm, Wed & Fri 10–11.30am, Thu 10am–6.30pm, Sat 10am–3.30pm, Sun 11am–6pm

Brücke Museum (Brücke-Museum), District VI (Steglitz-Zehlendorf), Bussardsteig 9, Wed–Mon 11am–5pm

Bücherbogen am Savignyplatz, District IV (Charlottenburg-Wilmersdorf), Savignyplatz, Mon–Fri 10am–8pm, Sat 10am–6pm

Bücherhändler vor der Uni, District I (Mitte), Humboldt University, Unter den Linden 6, daily 10am–6pm

Buddhist House (Buddhistisches Haus), District XII (Reinickendorf), Edelhofdamm 54, summer daily 8am–8pm, winter daily 9am–6pm

Burg am See beer garden, District II (Friedrichshain-Kreuzberg), Ratiborstrasse 14c, daily Apr–Sep 10am–10pm

C. Adolph, District IV (Charlottenburg-Wilmersdorf), Savignyplatz 3, Mon–Fri 9am–7pm, Sat 9am–2pm

Café Einstein, District I (Mitte), Kurfürstenstrasse 58, daily 8am–1am

Camera Work, District IV (Charlottenburg-Wilmersdorf), Kantstrasse 149, Tue–Sun 11am–6pm

Cathedral of St. Hedwig (St-Hedwigs-Kathedrale), District I (Mitte), Bebelplatz, Mon–Sat 10am–5pm, Sun 1–5pm

Central Telegraph Office Pneumatic Postal Dispatch System, District I (Mitte), for tour times (German only) see Berlin Underworlds Association (Berliner Unterwelten e.V.); collect tickets at Monbijoustrasse 1 meeting point

Centrum Judaicum (Jewish Centre), District I (Mitte), Oranienburger Strasse 28–30, Apr–Sep Sun & Mon 10am–8pm, Tue–Thu 10am–6pm, Fri 10am–5pm, Mar & Oct Sun & Mon 10am–8pm, Tue–Thu 10am–6pm, Fri 10am–2pm, Nov–Feb Sun & Mon 10am–6pm, Tue–Thu 10am–6pm, Fri 10am–2pm

Charlottenhof Palace (Schloss Charlottenhof), Potsdam, Geschwister Scholl-Strasse (Park Charlottenhof), Tue–Sat 10am–6pm

Checkpoint Charlie Museum (Museum Haus am Checkpoint Charlie), District I (Mitte), Friedrichstrasse 43–45, daily 9am–10pm

Chinese Teahouse – Mountain Lodge of the Osmanthus Sap (Chinesisches Teehaus – Berghaus zum Osmanthussaft), District X (Marzahn-Hellersdorf), Gärten der Welt, Erholungspark Marzahn, Eisenacher Strasse 99, Apr–Oct daily 10.30am–6pm, Nov–Mar Sat & Sun in fine weather only; tea ceremonies by appointment tel. 0049-(0)-179-394 55 64

Chinese Teahouse (Chinesisches Teehaus), Potsdam, Ökonomieweg (Rehgarten), Sanssouci Palace (Schloss Sanssouci), mid May–mid Oct Tue–Sun 10am–5pm

Chocolatier Erich Hamann, District IV (Charlottenburg-Wilmersdorf), Brandenburgische Strasse 17, Mon–Fri 9am–6pm, Sat 9am–1pm

Church of St. Anna (St-Annen-Kirche), District VI (Steglitz-Zehlendorf), Königin-Luise-Strasse, Sat & Sun 11am–1pm

Church of St. Elisabeth (St. Elisabeth-Kirche), District I (Mitte), Elisabethkirchstrasse, summer first Mon in month 5–6pm

Church of St. Mary (Marienkirche), District I (Mitte), Karl-Liebknecht-Strasse 8, daily 10am–6pm

Church of St. Nicholas (Nikolaikirche), District I (Mitte), Nikolaikirchplatz, daily 10am–6pm

Club der Visionäre, District II (Friedrichshain-Kreuzberg), Am Flutgraben 2, Mon–Fri from 2pm, Sat & Sun from 12am

Collection of Greek and Roman Antiquities (Antikensammlung), see Old Museum (Altes Museum)

Comenius Garden (Comenius-Garten), District VIII (Neukölln), Richardstrasse 35, for opening times telephone 0049-(0)-30-686-6106

Confiserie Melanie, District IV (Charlottenburg-Wilmersdorf), Grolmanstrasse 20, Mon–Wed, Fri 10am–7pm, Sat 10am–2pm

DDR Museum Berlin, District I (Mitte), Karl-Liebknecht-Strasse 1, daily 10am–8pm (Sat 10pm)

Defne restaurant, District II (Friedrichshain-Kreuzberg), Planufer 92c, Apr–Sep daily 4pm–1am, Oct–Mar daily 5pm–1am

Deutsche Kinemathek, District I (Mitte), Filmhaus, Potsdamer Strasse 2, Tue–Sun 10am–6pm (Thu 8pm)

Die Weltküche, District II (Friedrichshain-Kreuzberg), Graeferstrasse 18, Mon–Fri 12am–5pm

Domäne Dahlem, District VI (Steglitz-Zehlendorf), Königin-Luise-Strasse 49, Wed–Mon 10am–6pm

Dorotheenstadt Cemetery (Dorotheenstädtischer Friedhof), District I (Mitte), Chausseestrasse 126, Dec & Jan daily 8am–4pm, Feb & Nov daily 8am–5pm, Mar & Oct daily 8am–6pm, Apr & Sep daily 8am–7pm, May–Aug daily 8am–8pm

Dressler Restaurant, District I (Mitte), Unter den Linden 39, Mon–Fri 9am–12pm, Sat 9am–11.30pm

Dussmann das KulturKaufhaus, District I (Mitte), Friedrichstrasse 90, Mon–Fri 9am–12pm, Sat 9am–11.30pm

Egyptian Museum and Papyrus Collection (Ägyptisches Museum und Papyrussammlung), see New Museum (Neues Museum)

Emperor William Memorial Church (Kaiser-Wilhelm-Gedächtnis-Kirche), District IV (Charlottenburg-Wilmersdorf), Breitscheidplatz, daily 9am–7pm; Gedenkhalle Mon–Sat 10am–6pm, Sun 12am–6pm

Ethnology Museum (Ethnologisches Museum), see Museen Dahlem

Fassbender & Rausch, District I (Mitte), Charlottenstrasse 60, Mon–Sat 10am–8pm, Sun 11am–8pm

Fernsehturm, District I (Mitte), Panoramastrasse, Mar–Oct daily 9–12am, Nov–Feb daily 10am–12pm

Fire Brigade Museum (Feuerwehrmuseum Berlin), District XII (Reinickendorf), Berliner Strasse 16, Tue & Thu 9am–4pm, Wed 9am–7pm, Fri & Sat 10am–2pm

Filmmuseum Potsdam, Potsdam, Marstall, daily 10am–6pm

Filmpark Babelsberg, Potsdam, Grossbeerenstrasse, Mar–Oct daily 10am–6pm

Fleischerei Bachhuber, District IV (Charlottenburg-Wilmersdorf), Güntzelstrasse 47, Mon–Fri 8am–6pm, Sat 8am–1pm

Flutgraben e.V., District II (Friedrichshain-Kreuzberg), Am Flutgraben 3, for events www.flutgraben.org

Freischwimmer restaurant, District II (Friedrichshain-Kreuzberg), Vor dem Schlesischen Tor 2a, Mon–Fri from 4pm, Sat & Sun from 10am

French Church (Französische Kirche) and Huguenot Museum, Potsdam, Bassinplatz, Tue–Sun 12am–5pm

Funkturm Observation Terrace, District IV (Charlottenburg-Wilmersdorf), Hammarskjöldplatz, Mon 10am–8pm, Tue–Sun 10am–11pm

Gärten der Welt, District X (Marzahn-Hellersdorf), Erholungspark Marzahn, Eisenacher Strasse 99, Nov–Feb 9am–4pm, Mar & Oct 9am–6pm, Apr–Sep 9am–8pm

Galerie Mutter Fourage, District VI (Steglitz-Zehlendorf), Chausseestrasse 15a, Mon–Fri 9am–7pm, Sat & Sun 8am–7pm

Gasometerbunker, District II (Friedrichshain-Kreuzberg), Fichtestrasse 4–12, for tour times see Berlin Underworlds Association (Berliner Unterwelten e.V.)

Gelikon Russian Books (Gelikon Russische Bücher), District IV (Charlottenburg-Wilmersdorf), Kantstrasse 84, Mon–Fri 10am–6pm, Sat 11am–3pm

Georg Kolbe Museum, District IV (Charlottenburg-Wilmersdorf), Sensburger Allee 25, Tue–Sun 10am–6pm

German Cathedral (Deutscher Dom), District I (Mitte), Gendarmenmarkt 1, Tue–Sun 10am–6pm (Tue 10pm)

German Historical Museum (Deutsches Historisches Museum), District I (Mitte), Zeughaus, Unter den Linden 2, daily 10am–6pm

German-Russian Museum Berlin-Karlshorst (Deutsch-Russisches Museum Berlin-Karlshorst), District XI (Lichtenberg), Zwieseler Strasse 4, Tue–Sun 10am–6pm

German Technical Museum (Deutsches Technikmuseum Berlin), District II (Friedrichshain-Kreuzberg), Trebbiner Strasse 9, Tue–Fri 9am–5.30pm, Sat & Sun 10am–6pm

Gesundbrunnen Second World War shelter, District I (Mitte), for tour times and tickets see Berlin Underworlds Association (Berliner Unterwelten e.V.)

Grimm Zentrum, District I (Mitte), Humboldt University Library (Humboldt-Universität Berlin Universitätsbibliothek), Geschwister-Scholl-Strasse 1/3, Mon–Fri 8am–12pm, Sat & Sun 10am–6pm

Grunewald Hunting Lodge (Jagdschloss Grunewald), District VI (Steglitz-Zehlendorf), Hüttenweg 100, Apr–Oct Tue–Sun 10am–6pm, Nov–Mar Sat & Sun 10am–4pm

Hallesches Tor Cemeteries (Friedhöfe vor dem Halleschen Tor), District II (Friedrichshain-Kreuzberg), Mehringdamm 22, Jan & Dec daily 8am–4pm, Feb & Nov daily 8am–5pm, Mar & Oct daily 8am–6pm, Apr & Sep daily 8am–7pm, May–Aug 8am–8pm

Hamam, Türkisches Frauenbad, District II (Friedrichshain-Kreuzberg), Mariannenstrasse 6, Mon 3–11pm, Tue–Sun 12am–11pm

Hamburger Bahnhof, Museum for the Present (Museum für Gegenwart), District I (Mitte), Invalidenstrasse 50–51, Tue–Sun 10am–6pm (Thu 8pm)

Harry Lehmann, District IV (Charlottenburg-Wilmersdorf), Kantstrasse 106, Mon–Fri 9am–6.30pm, Sat 9am–2pm

Hase Weiss, District IV (Charlottenburg-Wilmersdorf) Windscheidstrasse 25, Tue–Fri 10am–6pm, Sat 10am–2pm

Heidi's Spielzeugladen, District IV (Charlottenburg-Wilmersdorf), Kantstrasse 61, Mon–Fri 10am–6pm, Sat 10am–4pm

Helmut Newton Foundation, District IV (Charlottenburg-Wilmersdorf), Jebensstrasse 2, Tue–Sun 10am–6pm (Thu 10pm)

Hemp Museum (Hanfmuseum), District I (Mitte), Mühlendamm 5, Tue–Fri 10am–8pm, Sat & Sun 12am–8pm

Henne Alt-Berliner Wirtshaus, District II (Friedrichshain-Kreuzberg), Leuschnerdamm 25, Tue–Sat from 6pm, Sun from 5pm

Historic Port of Berlin (Historischer Hafen Berlin), District I (Mitte), Markisches Ufer, Apr–Oct Tue–Fri 2–6pm, Sat & Sun 11am–6pm

Historic Windmill (Historische Mühle), Potsdam, Zur Historischen Mühle, just north of Schloss Sanssouci, Mon–Sat 10am–6pm

Holocaust Memorial (Holocaust Denkmal), District I (Mitte), Ebertstrasse, daily, information hall Oct–Mar Tue–Sun 10am–7pm, Apr–Sep Tue–Sun 10am–8pm

Holy Trinity Cemetery I (Friedhof der Dreifaltigkeit I), District II (Friedrichshain-Kreuzberg), Hallesches Tor Cemeteries (Friedhöfe vor dem Halleschen Tor), Zossener Strasse, daily 10am–5pm

Horenstein, District IV (Charlottenburg-Wilmersdorf), Fechner Strasse 3, Tue–Fri 1–7pm, Sat 10am–4pm

Hugendubel bookshop, District IV (Charlottenburg-Wilmersdorf), Tauentzienstrasse 13, Mon–Thu 10am–8pm, Fri 10am–9pm, Sat 9.30am–8pm

Humboldthain anti-aircraft tower, District I (Mitte), Apr–Oct only, for tour times and tickets see Berlin Underworlds Association (Berliner Unterwelten e.V.)

Jewish Cemetery (Jüdischer Friedhof), District III (Pankow), Schönhauser Allee 23–25, Mon–Thu 8am–4pm, Fri 7.30am–2.30pm (men must wear a kippah available at the gate and women must cover their heads)

Jewish Cemetery Weissensee (Jüdischer Friedhof Weissensee), District III (Pankow), Herbert-Baum-Strasse 45, Apr–Sep Mon–Thu 7.30am–5pm, Fri 7.30am–2.30pm, Sun 8am–5pm, Oct–Mar Mon–Thu 7.30am–4pm, Fri 7.30am–2.30pm, Sun 8am–4pm (men must wear a kippah available at the gate and women must cover their heads)

Jewish Museum (Jüdisches Museum Berlin), District II (Friedrichshain-Kreuzberg), Lindenstrasse 9–14, Mon 10am–10pm, Tue–Sun 10am–8pm, closed Jewish holidays

KaDeWe (Kaufhaus des Westens), District VII (Tempelhof-Schöneberg), Tauentzienstrasse 21–24, Mon–Thu 10am–8pm, Fri 10am–9pm, Sat 9.30am–8pm

Käfer im Bundestag restaurant, District I (Mitte), Reichstag, Platz der Republik, Mon–Fri 9–10am, 12am–2.30pm, 3.30–4.30pm, 6.30–12pm

Käthe Kollwitz Museum, District IV (Charlottenburg-Wilmersdorf), Fasanenstrasse 24, daily 11am–6pm

Knoblauchhaus, District I (Mitte), Poststrasse 23, Tue, Thu–Sun 10am–6pm, Wed 12am–8pm

Kohlhaas & Company/ Café im Literaturhaus, District IV (Charlottenburg-Wilmersdorf), Fasanenstrasse 23, Mon–Fri 10.30am–7.30pm, Sat 10.30am–6pm

Konditorei Buchwald, District I (Mitte), Bartningallee 29, Mon–Sat 9am–6pm, Sun 10am–6pm

Konnopke's Imbiss, District III (Pankow), Schönhauser Allee 44a, Mon–Fri 9am–8pm, Sat 11.30am–8pm

Königsberger Marzipan, District IV (Charlottenburg-Wilmersdorf), Pestalozzistrasse 54a, Mon–Fri 10am–6.30pm, Sat 10am–3.30pm

Königstadt Brewery (Königstadt-Brauerei), District III (Pankow), Saarbrücker Strasse 22–24, for tour times and tickets see Under Berlin Association (unter-berlin e.V.)

Körnerpark, District VIII (Neukölln), Schierker Strasse 8, Tue–Sun 10am–6pm

Kunstmarkt Mulackstrasse, District I (Mitte), Mulackstrasse 12, Sat & Sun 2–9pm

Liebermann Villa (Liebermann-Villa am Wannsee), District VI (Steglitz-Zehlendorf), Wannsee Island, Colomierstrasse 3, Apr–Sep Wed–Mon 10am–6pm (Thu & Sun 7pm), Oct–Mar Wed–Mon 11am–5pm

Loxx Model Railway (Loxx am Alex Miniatur Welten Berlin), District I (Mitte), Alexa-Center, Alexanderplatz, daily 10am–8pm

Luise Church (Luisenkirche), District IV (Charlottenburg-Wilmersdorf), Gierkeplatz, Mass Sun10am & 11.30am

Mahlsdorf Manor & Gründerzeit Museum, District X (Marzahn-Hellersdorf), Hultschiner Damm 333, Wed & Sun 10am–6pm

Marble Palace (Marmorpalais), Potsdam, Neuer Garten, am Ufer des Heiligen Sees, May–Oct Tue–Sun 10am–6pm, Nov–Apr Sat & Sun 10am–4pm

Marga Schoeller Bücherstube, District IV (Charlottenburg-Wilmersdorf), Knesebeckstrasse 33, Mon–Wed 9.30am–7pm, Thu & Fri 9.30am–8pm, Sat 9.30am–6pm

Märkisches Museum, District I (Mitte), Am Köllnischen Park 5, Tue–Sun 10am–6pm; presentation of mechanical musical instruments Sun 3pm

Markthalle am Marheinekeplatz, District II (Friedrichshain-Kreuzberg), Marheinekeplatz, Mon–Fri 8am–8pm, Sat 8am–6pm

Martin-Gropius-Bau, District I (Mitte), Stresemannstrasse 110, Wed–Mon 10am–7pm

Mausoleum of Queen Luise, District IV (Charlottenburg-Wilmersdorf), Schloss Charlottenburg, Schlosspark, Spandauer Damm, Tue–Sun 10am–6pm

ME (Moving Energies) Collectors Room (Stiftung Olbricht), District I (Mitte), Augustrstrasse 68, Tue–Sun 12am–6pm

Memorial to the German Resistance (Gedenkstätte Deutscher Widerstand), District I (Mitte), Stauffenbergstrasse 13–14, Mon, Wed & Fri 9am–6pm, Thu 9am–8pm, Sat & Sun 10am–6pm

Michas Bahnhof, District IV (Charlottenburg-Wilmersdorf), Nürnberger Strasse 24, Mon–Fri 10am–6.30pm, Sat 10am–3.30pm

Morgenwelt, District VI (Steglitz-Zehlendorf), Markelstrasse 56, Mon–Sat 10am–10pm

Mori Ōgai Memorial (Mori-Ogai-Gedenkstätte), District I (Mitte), Luisenstrasse 39 (First Floor), Mon–Fri 10am–2pm

Museen Dahlem, District VI (Steglitz-Zehlendorf), Lannstrasse 8, Tue–Sun 10am–6pm

Museum for Photography (Museum für Fotografie), District IV (Charlottenburg-Wilmersdorf), Jebensstrasse 2, Tue–Sun 10am–6pm (Thu 10pm)

Museum Island (Museumsinsel), District I (Mitte), Bodestrasse 1–3, Tue–Sun 10am–6pm (Thu 10pm)

Museum of Asian Art (Museum für Asiatische Kunst), see Museen Dahlem

Museum of Byzantine Art (Museum für Byzantinische Kunst), see Bode Museum

Museum of European Cultures (Museum Europäischer Kulturen), see Museen Dahlem

Museum of Islamic Art (Museum für Islamische Kunst), see Old Museum (Altes Museum)

Museum of Near Eastern Antiquities (Vorderasiatisches Museum), see Old Museum (Altes Museum)

Museum of Pre- and Early History (Museum für Vor- und Frühgeschichte), see New Museum (Neues Museum)

Museum of Telecommunications (Museum für Kommunikation), District I (Mitte), Leipziger Strasse 16, Tue 9am–8pm, Wed–Fri 9am–5pm, Sat & Sun 10am–6pm

Museum Otto Weidt's Workshop for the Blind (Museum Blindenwerkstatt Otto Weidt), District I (Mitte), Rosenthaler Strasse 39 (First Floor), daily 10am–8pm

Museumsdorf Düppel, District VI (Steglitz-Zehlendorf), Clauertstrasse 11, Apr–Oct Thu 3–7pm, Sun 10am–5pm

Musical Instrument Museum (Musikinstrumentenmuseum), District I (Mitte), Tiergartenstrasse 1, Tue–Fri 9am–5pm (Thu 8pm), Sat & Sun 10am–8pm

National Socialist Forced Labour Documentation Centre (NS Zwangsarbeit Dokumentationszentrum), District IX (Treptow-Köpenick), Britzerstrasse 5, Tue–Sun 10am–6pm

Natural History Museum (Museum für Naturkunde), District I (Mitte), Invalidenstrasse 43, Tue–Fri 9.30am–6pm, Sat & Sun 10am–6pm

Neue Wache, District I (Mitte), Unter den Linden 4, daily 10am–6pm

New Museum (Neues Museum), see Museum Island (Museumsinsel)

New National Gallery (Neue Nationalgallerie), District I (Mitte), Kulturforum, Potsdamer Strasse 50, Tue–Sun 10am–6pm (Thu 8pm)

New Palace (Neues Palais), Potsdam, Sanssouci Palace (Schloss Sanssouci), Apr–Oct Wed–Mon 10am–6pm, Nov–Mar Wed–Mon 10am–5pm

New Pavilion (Neuer-Pavillon), District IV (Charlottenburg-Wilmersdorf), Schloss Charlottenburg, Schlosspark, Apr–Oct Tue–Sun 10am–6pm, Nov–Mar Tue–Sun 10am–5pm

New State Library (Neue Staatsbibliothek), District I (Mitte), Potsdamer Strasse 33, Mon–Fri 9am–9pm, Sat 10am–7pm

New Synagogue (Neue Synagoge), District I (Mitte), Oranienburger Strasse 30, see Centrum Judaicum

Nicolaische Buchhandlung, District VII (Tempelhof-Schöneberg), Rheinstrasse 65, Mon–Fri 9am–6.30pm, Sat 10am–2pm

Numismatic Collection (Münzkabinett), see Bode Museum

Old Library (Alte Bibliothek), District I (Mitte), Bebelplatz, Mon–Fri 9am–9.30pm, Sat 9am–6pm, Sun 1–6pm

Old Museum (Altes Museum), see Museum Island (Museumsinsel)

Old National Gallery (Alte Nationalgalerie), see Museum Island (Museumsinsel)

Old State Library (Alte Staatsbibliothek), District I (Mitte), Unter den Linden 8, Mon–Fri 9am–9pm, Sat 10am–7pm

Olympic Stadium (Olympia-Stadion), District IV (Charlottenburg-Wilmersdorf), Olympischer Platz, 20th Mar–31st May 9am–7pm, 1st Jun–15th Sep 9am–8pm, 16th Sep–31st Oct 9am–7pm,

1st Nov–19th Mar 9am–4pm; guided tours (German only) 20th Mar–31st Oct daily 11am, 1pm & 3pm, 1st Jun–31st Aug daily 11am, 1pm, 3pm & 5pm, 1st Nov–19th Mar daily 11am

Paasburg's Wine Shop, District II (Friedrichshain-Kreuzberg), Fidicinstrasse 3, Mon–Wed 10am–6pm, Thu & Fri 10am–7pm, Sat 10am–2pm

Pankstrasse Cold War shelter, District I (Mitte), for tour times and tickets see Berlin Underworlds Association (Berliner Unterwelten e.V.)

Panorama Point (Panorama Punkt) observation platform, District I (Mitte), Quartier Daimler, Potsdamer Platz 1, daily 10am–8pm

Parochial Church (Parochialkirche), District I (Mitte), Klosterstrasse 67, Mon–Fri 10am–4pm

Pasternak restaurant, District III (Pankow), Knaackstrasse 22–24, 9am–1am

Peace Church (Friedenskirche), Potsdam, Allee nach Sanssouci, Sanssouci Palace (Schloss Sanssouci), Apr Mon–Sat 12am–5pm, Sun 11am–5pm, May–Sep Mon–Sat 12am–6pm, Sun 10am–6pm, Oct–Mar Sat 11am–4pm, Sun 11.30am–4pm

Pergamon Museum (Pergamonmuseum), see Museum Island (Museumsinsel)

Planetarium am Insulaner, District VI (Steglitz-Zehlendorf), Munsterdamm 90, tel. 0049-(0)-30-79 00 93 20 for current programme

Plötzensee Memorial Centre (Gedenkstätte Plötzensee), District IV (Charlottenburg-Wilmersdorf), Huttigpfad, Mar–Oct daily 9am–5pm, Nov–Feb daily 9am–4pm

Potsdamer Platz Arkaden, District I (Mitte), Alte Potsdamer Strasse 7, Mon–Sat 10am–9pm

ProQm, District I (Mitte), Almstadtstrasse 48–50, Mon–Sat 11am–8pm

Reichstag dome, District I (Mitte), Platz der Republik, daily 8am–11pm; advance booking only at www.bundestag.de

Restaurant Leibniz-Klause, District IV (Charlottenburg-Wilmersdorf), Mommsenstrasse 57 (entrance at Leibnizstrasse 46), daily from 12am

Royal Porcelain Workshop (Königliche Porzellan-Manufaktur), District IV (Charlottenburg-Wilmersdorf), Wegelystrasse 1, Mon–Sat 10am–6pm

Ruin of Arts (Ruine der Künste), District VI (Steglitz-Zehlendorf), Hittorfstrasse 5, visits by appointment only tel. 0049 (0)30-831-3708

Russian Orthodox Church of Sts. Constantine and Helen (Russische-orthodoxe Hl. Konstantin- und Helena-Kirche), District XII (Reinickendorf), Wittestrasse 37, Sat 5–7pm, Sun 9.15am–3pm

Sanssouci Palace (Schloss Sanssouci), Potsdam, Maulbeerallee, Apr–Oct Tue–Sun 10am–6pm, Nov–Mar Tue–Sun 10am–5pm

Schleusenkrug, District I (Mitte), Müller-Breslau-Strasse, daily 10am–12pm

Schloss Charlottenburg, District IV (Charlottenburg-Wilmersdorf), Spandauer Damm 10–22, Luisenplatz, Apr–Oct Tue–Sun 10am–6pm, Nov–Mar Tue–Sun 10am–5pm

Schloss Glienicke, District VI (Steglitz-Zehlendorf), Wannsee Island, Königstrasse 36, Apr–Oct Tue–Sun 10am–6pm, Nov–Mar Sat & Sun 10am–5pm

Schneidersitz, District IV (Charlottenburg-Wilmersdorf), Pestalozzistrasse 54, Tue–Fri 10am–6pm, Sat 10am–1pm

Schwules Museum, District II (Friedrichshain-Kreuzberg), Mehringdamm 61, Sun & Mon, Wed–Fri 2–6pm, Sat 2–7pm

Solar bar, District I (Mitte), Stresemannstrasse 76, Sun–Thu 6pm–2am, Fri & Sat 6pm–4am

Sophien Church (Sophienkirche), District I (Mitte), Grosse Hamburger Strasse 29, May–Oct Wed 3–6pm, Sat 3–5pm, Sun 11.30am–1pm

South Schöneberg Nature Reserve (Natur-Park Schöneberger Südgelände), District VII (Tempelhof-Schöneberg), Priesterweg, daily 9am–dusk

Späth Arboretum (Späthsches Arboretum), District IX (Treptow-Köpenick), Späthstrasse 80–81, Apr–Oct Wed, Thu, Sat & Sun 10am–6pm

Städtischer Friedhof III, District VII (Tempelhof-Schöneberg), Stubenrauchstrasse 43–45, Jan & Dec daily 8am–4pm, Feb & Dec daily 8am–5pm, Mar & Oct daily 8am–6pm, Apr & Sep daily 8am–7pm, May & Aug daily 8am–8pm

Stasi-Museum Berlin, District XI (Lichtenberg), Ruschestrasse 103 (Haus 1), Mon–Fri 10am–6pm, Sat & Sun 12am–6pm

Stasi Prison (Gedenkstätte Berlin-Hohenschönhausen), District XI (Lichtenberg), Genslerstrasse 66, English language tours daily 2.30pm

Sultan Hamam, District VII (Tempelhof-Schöneberg), Bülowstrasse 57, Mon 12am–11pm men only, Tue–Sat 9.30am–11pm women only, Sun 12am–11pm mixed

Tajikistan Tearoom (Tadschikische Teestube), District I (Mitte), Oranienburger Strasse 27, Mon–Fri from 4pm, Sat & Sun from 12am

The Story of Berlin and Atomschutzbunker, District IV (Charlottenburg-Wilmersdorf), Kurfürstendamm 207–208, daily 10am–8pm (last entry 6pm)

Tommy-Weissbecker-Haus, District I (Mitte), Wilhelmstrasse 9, office Mon–Fri 11am–2pm, Café Linie 1 daily from 6pm

Topography of Terror (Topographie des Terrors), District I (Mitte), Niederkirchnerstrasse 8, daily 10am–8pm

Trödelhallen Eichenstrasse, District IX (Treptow-Köpenick), Puschkinallee and Eichenstrasse, Sat & Sun 10am–4pm

Trödel- und Kunsthandwerkermarkt an der Strasse des 17. Juni, District I (Charlottenburg-Wilmersdorf), Strasse des 17. Juni, Sat & Sun 10am–5pm

Trödelmarkt auf dem Fehrbelliner Platz, District IV (Charlottenburg-Wilmersdorf), Fehrbelliner Platz U-Bahn station car park, Sat & Sun 10am–4pm

Turkish Market on Maybachufer (Türken Markt am Maybachufer), District II (Friedrichshain-Kreuzberg), Maybachufer, Tue & Fri 11am–6.30pm

Under Berlin Association (unter-berlin e.V.), www.unter-berlin.de

Villa Harteneck, District IV (Charlottenburg-Wilmersdorf), Douglasstrasse 9, Tue–Fri 10am–7pm, Sat 10am–6pm

Victory Column (Siegessäule) observation terrace, District I (Mitte), Grosser Stern, 17. Juni Strasse, Apr–Oct Mon–Fri 9.30am–6.30pm, Sat & Sun 9.30am–7pm, Nov–Mar Mon–Fri 10am–5pm, Sat & Sun 10am–5.30pm

Waldhaus restaurant, District VI (Steglitz-Zehlendorf), Unkel-Tom-Strasse 50, Mon–Fri from 5pm, Sat from 10am, Sun from 12am

Wannsee Conference Memorial Centre (Gedenkstätte Haus der Wannsee-Konferenz), Berlin VI (Steglitz-Zehlendorf), Am Grossen Wannsee 56–58, daily 10am–6pm

Wasserwerk Sanssouci, Potsdam, Breite Strasse, May–Oct Sat & Sun 10am–6pm

Waterworks Museum (Museum im Wasserwerk Friedrichshagen), District IX (Treptow-Köpenick), Müggelseedamm 307, Sun–Thu 10am–6pm

Winterfeldmarkt, District VII (Tempelhof-Schöneberg), Winterfeldtplatz, Wed 8am–1pm, Sat 8am–3.30pm

Wochenmarkt Wittenbergplatz, District VII (Tempelhof-Schöneberg), Wittenbergplatz, Tue 8am–2pm, Fri 8am–4pm; farmers' market (Bauernmarkt Wittenbergplatz) Thu 10am–6pm

Yamashina Japanese Bookshop (Japanische Buchhandlung Yamashina), District IV (Charlottenburg-Wilmersdorf), Mon–Fri 10am–6pm, Sat 11am–3pm

Zeiss Planetarium (Zeiss-Grossplanetarium), District III (Pankow), Ernst Thälmann-Park, Prenzlauer Allee 80, Tue–Thu 9–12am, Fri 9–12am, 1–9.30pm, Sat & Sun 2.30–9pm

Zitadelle Spandau, District V (Spandau), Am Juliusturm, daily 10am–5pm

Zoologischer Garten & Aquarium, District I (Mitte), Hardenbergplatz 8/ Budapester Strasse 32, Jan–mid Mar, mid Oct–Dec 9am–5pm, mid Mar–end Mar 9am–5.30pm, Apr–Aug 9am–7pm, Sep–mid Oct 9am–6.30pm

Zum Nussbaum Kneipe, District I (Mitte), Am Nussbaum 3, daily from 12am

Zur Kneipe, District IV (Charlottenburg-Wilmersdorf), Rankestrasse 9, daily from 6pm

Zur Letzten Instanz restaurant, District I (Mitte), Waisenstrasse 14–16, Mon–Sat 12am–1am, Sun 12am–11pm

Detail of the former Central Telegraph Office (see no. 16)

Bibliography

GUIDEBOOKS

The Companion Guide to Berlin (Brian Ladd), Boydell & Brewer Ltd., 2004

Eyewitness Travel Guide Berlin (Małgorzata Omilanowska), Dorling Kindersley, 2006

The Rough Guide to Berlin (7th ed.) (John Gawthorp), Penguin Books, 2005

Berlins Unbekannte Kulturdenkmäler (Sigrid Hoff), L & H Verlag, 2003

Das Unbekannte Berlin: Entdecken Sie die Schönheiten und Geheimnisse der Stadt (Ralph Hoppe), Ellert & Richter, 2010

Verborgene Orte in Berlin (Alex Klappoth), Yuba Edition, 2009

Geheime Orte in Berlin (Christoph Stollowsky), Nicolaische Verlagsbuchhandlung, 2007

Pastfinder – Berlin 1933–1945: Traces of German History – A Guidebook (Maik Kopleck), Christoph Links Verlag, 2007

Pastfinder – Berlin 1945–1989: Traces of German History – A Guidebook (Maik Kopleck), Christoph Links Verlag, 2007

Jewish Berlin (Bill Rebiger), Jaron Verlag, 2005

111 Orte in Berlin, die man gesehen haben muss (Lucia Jay von Seldeneck & Carolin Huder), Emons, 2011

111 Orte in Berlin die Geschichte erzählen (Lucia Jay von Seldeneck & Carolin Huder), Emons, 2012

Berlin – Hotels & More (Angelika Taschen), Taschen, 2007

ILLUSTRATED BOOKS

Berlin: A Photographic Portrait of Berlin in the 1920s (Thomas Friedrich), Tauris Parke, 1991

Berlin Then and Now (Tony Le Tissier), After the Battle, 1992

Berlin in the Twenties: Art and Culture 1918–1933 (Rainer Metzger), Thames & Hudson, 2007

Berlin (Hans Reich), Hans Reich Verlag, 1959

ARCHITECTURE AND MONUMENTS

The Berlin Wall: Division of a City (Thomas Flemming), be.bra Verlag, 2006

The Führer Bunker: Hitler's Last Refuge (Sven Felix Kellerhoff), Berlin Story Verlag, 2006

The Ghosts of Berlin – Confronting German History in the Urban Landscape (Brian Ladd), The University of Chicago Press, 1997

Die Stadt unter der Stadt – Das unterirdische Berlin (Niko Rollmann & Eberhard Elfert), Jaron Verlag, 2006

Flaktürme: Wien, Hamburg Berlin (Hans Sakkers), Fortress Books, 1998

Capital Dilemma: Germany's Search for a New Architecture of Democracy (Michael Z. Wise), Princeton Architectural Press, 1998

CHURCH, CEMETERY AND MUSEUM GUIDEBOOKS

Kirchen in Berlin (Sven Scherz-Schale), Berlin Story Verlag, 2005

Friedhöfe in Berlin (Klaus Hammer), Jaron Verlag 2006

Jewish Cemeteries in Berlin (Johanna von Koppenfels), be.bra Verlag, 2005

Berliner Museen/Museums of Berlin (Jörg Raach), L & H Verlag, 2006

Die Museen in Berlin (Arnt Cobbers), Jaron Verlag 2004

Das Pergamonmuseum (Carola Wedel), Nicolaische Verlagsbuchhandlung, 2003

Museum of Indian Art Berlin (Various), Prestel, 2000

FICTION

Berlin Alexanderplatz: The Story of Franz Biberkopf (Alfred Döblin), Continuum International Publishing Group – Academi, 2004

Mephisto (Klaus Mann), Penguin Books, 1995

HISTORY

The Fall of Berlin (Anthony Beevor), Penguin Books, 2002

Iron Kingdom: the Rise and Downfall of Prussia, 1600–1947 (Christopher Clark), Allen Lane, 2006

Before the Deluge: A Portrait of Berlin in the 1920s (Otto Friedrich), Michael Joseph, 1974

Berlin (David Clay Large), Viking, 2000

Faust's Metropolis: A History of Berlin (Alexandra Richie), Harper Collins, 1999

The Berlin Wall: 13 August 1961–9 November 1989 (Frederick Taylor), Bloomsbury, 2006

Berlin and its Culture: A Historical Portrait (Robert Taylor), Yale University Press, 1997

Wall: The Inside Story of Divided Berlin (Peter Wyden), Simon & Schuster, 1991

WEBSITES

www.berlin.de (Berlin's official website)

www.visitberlin.de (Official Berlin tourist office)

www.berlin-stadtfuehrung.de (Berlin tours and information)

www.berlin-info.de (Berlin tourist information)

www.smb.museum (Berlin city museums)

www.bvg.de (Berlin transit authority)

www.spottedbylocals.com/berlin (useful and entertaining city Blog)

www.berlin-judentum.de (Jewish Berlin)

www.unter-berlin.de (underground Berlin)

www.berliner-unterwelten.de (more underground Berlin)

www.berlin-hidden-places.de (unusual places open to the public)

www.germany.travel (German Tourist Board)

Acknowledgments

First and foremost I would like to thank my Viennese publisher, Christian Brandstätter Verlag, for realising the first edition of this book, especially Elisabeth Stein (commissioning editor), Else Rieger (editor), Ekke Wolf (design), Brigitte Hilzensauer (German translation), and Helmut Maurer (maps)

For kind permission to take photographs, as well as arranging for access and the provision of information, the following people are very gratefully acknowledged:

Ingmar Arnold, Ivona Bakovic, Silke Bieda and Florian Roeder (The Story of Berlin), Kerstin Barkmann (Filmmuseum Potsdam), Melanie Beckert and Kay Heyne (Berliner Unterwelten e.V.), Andreas Bock (Alt-Berliner Wirtshaus Henne), Katrin Brandel (Antiquariat Brandel), Arek Bojanowski, Hasan Çoban (Usta Restaurant), Checkpoint Charlie Museum, Herbert Christ (Gehörlosenverband Berlin e. V.), Europa-Center, Sepp Fiedler (Solar Lifestyle), Peter Focke (LOXX am Alex Miniatur Welten Berlin), Freischwimmer restaurant, German-Russian Museum Berlin-Karlshorst, Dr. Matthias Glaubrecht, Annette Kinitz and Stefanie Schmidt (Museum für Naturkunde), Günther Grosser (English Theatre Berlin), Eckhard Gruber and Annette Lainkenmann (Deutsches Technikmuseum Berlin), Erika Hartmann (Schneidersitz), Dirk C. Kasten (Kasten-Mann Grundstücks KG), Peter and Helge Knoche (Restaurant Leibniz-Klause), Dieter Lange (Museum im Wasserwerk Friedrichshagen), Lutz Lehmann (Harry Lehmann), Carl Loyal (Honigmond Garden Hotel), Kristine Mager and Claudia Priemer (Berliner Teesalaon), Jan Meyer-Veden (Hotel-Pension Funk), Normannenstrasse Research and Memorial Centre, Eberhard Päller (Confiserie Melanie), Niko Rollmann (unter-berlin e.V.), Jochen Schwarz, Elke Schwichtenberg and Norbert Ludwig (Bildarchiv Preußischer Kulturbesitz/Museum für Asiatische Kunst, Staatliche Museen zu Berlin), Dr. Frank D. Steinheimer, Phillip Sulke (www.shopikon.com), Theater Thikwa, The Topography of Terror, Dr. Hans V. Trotha and Julia Linke (Nicolaische Verlagsbuchhandlung), Villa Harteneck, Geoff Walden (www.thirdreichruins.com), Robert Wein (Tadshikische Teestube), Prof. Dr. Willibald Veit and Gerda Lehmann (Museum für Asiatische Kunst), and Beate Wonde and Noriko Fujimura (Mori-Ōgai-Gedenkstätte), and Jörg Wreh (LOXX am Alex – Miniatur Welten Berlin).

Also, Anong and Ralf-Peter Stephan at 123-Berlin Zimmer for the excellent accommodation, the staff of the Charité Hospital, Natalija Lacmanovic, and Stefan 'Sy' Gebharter and Richard Tinkler for website support.

For the supply of film, high-quality processing and technical advice my thanks go to Fotofachlabor (Vienna), as well as Franz and Veronika Schieder, Robert Kopetzky and Josef Slavik, formerly of Foto Wachtl (Vienna).

Thanks also to my great cousin James Dickinson for support, newspaper cuttings and bringing my work to a wider audience – his boundless enthusiasm has been both inspirational and infectious.

Finally, very special thanks to my father Trevor, not only for proof-reading and correcting my text, but for inspiring me to track down unusual locations in the first place – thanks Dad for making it all such fun!

Detail of an old Spree barge, part of the Historic Port of Berlin collection moored at Märkisches Ufer

2nd Revised Edition published by The Urban Explorer, 2014
A division of Duncan J. D. Smith
contact@duncanjdsmith.com
www.onlyinguides.com
www.duncanjdsmith.com

First published by Christian Brandstätter Verlag, 2008

Graphic design: Stefan Fuhrer
Typesetting and picture editing: Ekke Wolf
Revision typesetting and picture editing: Franz Hanns
Maps: APA, Vienna
Printed and bound by GraphyCems, Spain

ISBN 978-3-9503662-3-5